HUMAN BIOLOGY
Activities Kit

Ready-to-Use Lessons and Worksheets for General Science and Health

JOHN R. ROLAND

JOSSEY-BASS
A Wiley Imprint
www.josseybass.com

Published by Jossey-Bass
A Wiley Imprint
989 Market Street, San Francisco, CA 94103-1741   www.josseybass.com

Jossey-Bass books and products are available through most bookstores. To contact Jossey-Bass directly call our Customer Care Department within the U.S. at 800-956-7739, outside the U.S. at 317-572-3986 or fax 317-572-4002.

Jossey-Bass also publishes its books in a variety of electronic formats. Some content that appears in print may not be available in electronic books.

ISBN 0-7879-6662-2 (layflat)

FIRST EDITION
HB Printing 10 9 8 7 6 5 4

ABOUT THIS KIT

Human Biology Activities Kit: Ready-to-Use Lessons and Worksheets for General Science and Health is a collection of over 200 classroom-tested activities and worksheets for secondary science teachers who have one or more general-level science and/or health classes. This book will help you accommodate to your students' varying learning styles (including visual, auditory, and tactile) and abilities, with an emphasis on making connections between new material and concepts already familiar to students.

Human Biology Activities Kit is divided into eleven units:

Unit 1 The Microscope

Unit 2 The Cell

Unit 3 The Skeleton

Unit 4 Muscles

Unit 5 The Nervous System

Unit 6 The Circulatory System

Unit 7 The Immune System

Unit 8 The Respiratory System

Unit 9 The Digestive System

Unit 10 The Excretory System

Unit 11 Reproduction

An important feature is the inclusion of AIDS in the unit on the immune system. Included in each unit are:

- teacher instructions
- complete answer keys
- easy-to-reproduce worksheets
- structured lessons with lists of lab materials needed
- questions asked at three different cognitive levels in order to meet varying individual abilities of students and to provide increasing challenges
- easy-to-follow line illustrations and diagrams

As you'll discover for yourself, *Human Biology Activities Kit* is easy to incorporate into your present curriculum as an introduction to a course of study, reinforcement of specific principles, or a summary of material covered. The *Kit* will become an important tool in your classroom.

John R. Roland

ABOUT THE AUTHOR

JOHN R. ROLAND has taught physical science, biology, and health at the high school level for more than 16 years in League City, Texas. He received his B.S. degree in biology and education from Frostburg (Maryland) State College and is a master's degree candidate with concentration in special education and English as a second language at the University of Houston at Clear Lake.

A frequent science speaker and presentor, Mr. Roland has spoken at various organizations and presented district-level inservice workshops on modifying the science curriculum. He also has published curriculum materials for special science classes.

Mr. Roland has won recognition for the daily use of technology in the science classroom through laser disk, video camera, video microscope, and computer and for adapting the science curriculum and techniques for learning disabled and non-English speaking students. He received the Gulf Coast Science Foundation's 1983 Edward L. Hayes Memorial Award for Excellence in Teaching in the Field of Science and has been nominated for other awards including the 1992 Presidential Award for Excellence in Science Teaching.

For my wife, Fran,
and my daughters, Erin and Kristi

CONTENTS

UNIT 7   THE IMMUNE SYSTEM   187

UNIT 8   THE RESPIRATORY SYSTEM   231

UNIT 9   THE DIGESTIVE SYSTEM   247

Unit **1**

The Microscope

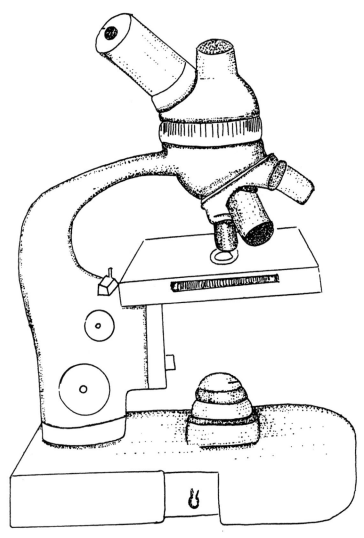

TEACHER'S GUIDE TO UNIT 1 _____

1–1 THE COMPOUND MICROSCOPE

Note: Many teachers discover that they spend a great deal of time focusing (and refocusing) their students' microscopes. Emphasize to your students that they need to become proficient in focusing their own instruments.

Teaching Suggestions:

Use a microscope to demonstrate its parts and the proper way to focus it. *Hint:* Type the steps for focusing a microscope and reproduce them on cards or small slips of paper. Laminate these and attach them to your students' microscopes.

Answers to the Questions:

Level One

1. Microscopic structures cannot be clearly observed without a microscope; macroscopic structures may be examined with the unaided eye.
2. scars on a bone where muscles were attached, holes where major blood vessels entered, and articular surfaces where bone was attached to some other part of the skeleton
3. The student's answer will reflect what he or she found on the slide.
4. A
5. H
6. J
7. D
8. E
9. F
10. I
11. C
12. to fine-tune the focus
13. to concentrate light from a high intensity bulb and direct it through the microscope's lenses
14. to make the image clearer
15. to adjust the aperture for the clearest image
17. 1, 4, 5, 2, 3

1–2 MAKING A MICROSCOPIC OBSERVATION

Note: The written assignment and discussion (see #4) that follow this investigation are important because focusing a microscope can be a frustrating experience for many students. This activity offers a valuable opportunity to share techniques, tricks, and tips.

Teaching Suggestions:

Demonstrate the steps for making a slide and focusing a microscope.

Answers to the Questions:

There are no questions as such; #3 asks for a simple discovery response, and #4 is a quality-point paragraph.

1–3 MAKING A COMPOUND MICROSCOPE

Note: This is an activity that most students enjoy doing.

Teaching Suggestions:

1. Demonstrate the procedure for making a microscope.
2. Remind your students that they must look through the lenses while they are marking on the tic-tac-toe grid.
3. Your students would probably enjoy signing their names while looking through their microscopes.
4. Maintain order during this investigation, but prepare to be tolerant if a bottle is knocked over or even broken.

Answers to the Questions:

Level One

1. The specimen assumes the shape of the lens.
2. (sketching) The sketch should give evidence that the student has observed spherical aberration; vertical and horizontal lines will be distorted.
3. The answer should be yes (one hopes).
4. The image looks upside down and backward.
5. It is difficult because the student is probably watching his or her hand; when the hand makes a downward stroke, it looks like an upward stroke through the microscope. The student is learning what it is like to work with a reversed image.

1–1. THE COMPOUND MICROSCOPE

Instructions: (1.) Read the text and the statements. (2.) Use the text and the statements to help you to label the diagram and answer the questions.

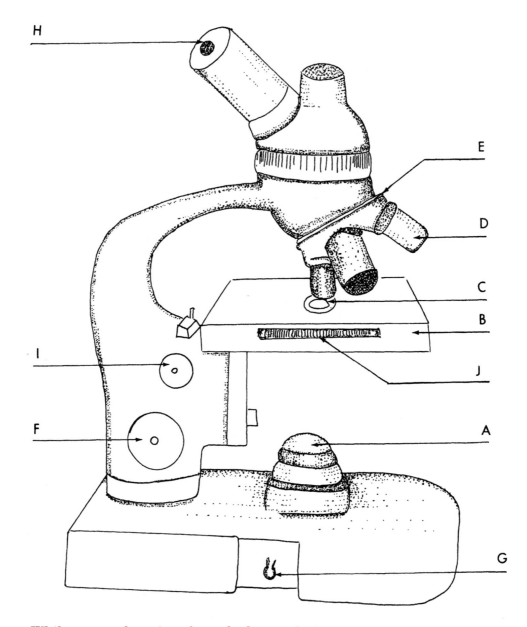

While you are learning about the human body, you will observe both macroscopic and microscopic structures.

The heart, the kidneys, and the bones have both macroscopic and microscopic structures. Macroscopic structures may be examined with the unaided eye; on a bone, for example, you can locate the scars where the muscles were attached, the holes where major blood vessels entered, and the articular surfaces—where the bone was attached to some other part of the skeleton—without using magnification. Microscopic structures, on the other hand, cannot be clearly observed without a microscope. The diagram shows a compound microscope similar to the one you will be using.

Procedure

Obtain the following materials:

☐ any prepared microscope slide with a specimen that can be located on the slide without magnification

☐ a compound microscope

1. Usually, a compound microscope uses a condenser as a light source; it concentrates light from a high-intensity bulb and directs it through the microscope's lenses. Arrow A points to the condenser. Locate this arrow on the diagram and identify the condenser.

2. To begin a microscopic observation, place a glass slide containing a specimen on the microscope's stage and clip it down. If the specimen is large enough for you to see, check to be sure it is centered over the round opening called the "aperture"; this will insure that the specimen is in line with the lenses. Arrow B points to the stage, and arrow C points to the aperture.

3. After the slide is in place, snap the low-power objective lens into place by turning the nose piece until the shortest lens (usually the one with a 5 or a 10 stamped on it) is over the specimen. You can usually tell if this lens is locked into place by listening for a click. Arrow D points to an objective lens, and arrow E points to the nose piece.

4. Lower the stage (the barrel on some microscopes) by turning the coarse adjustment knob. Arrow F points to the coarse adjustment knob.

5. After the low-power objective lens is in place, the specimen is centered, and the stage (barrel) is down, plug the microscope into an electrical outlet and turn on the light with the switch on the base of the microscope. Arrow G points to the light switch.

6. While looking through the eyepiece, slowly turn the coarse adjustment knob until the specimen comes into focus. You can fine-tune the focus by turning the fine adjustment knob. Arrow H points to the eyepiece, and arrow I points to the fine adjustment knob.

7. After your specimen is in focus, you may increase the magnification by turning the nose piece and snapping the next higher objective into place. Use the coarse and fine adjustment knobs to refocus.

8. You can make the image clearer by adjusting the aperture. While looking through the eyepiece, turn the iris adjustment wheel until you see the clearest image. Arrow J points to the iris adjustment wheel.

Level One Questions:

1. How are microscopic structures different from macroscopic structures?

_____

_____

_____

2. List three examples of macroscopic structures.

_____

_____

_____

3. Give one example of a microscopic structure.

4. On the diagram, which arrow points to the condenser? _____

5. Which arrow points to the eyepiece? _____

6. Which arrow points to the iris adjustment wheel? _____

7. Which arrow points to an objective lens? _____

8. Which arrow points to the nose piece? _____

9. Which arrow points to the coarse adjustment knob? _____

10. Which arrow points to the fine adjustment knob? _____

11. Which arrow points to the aperture? _____

12. What is the function of the fine adjustment knob?

_____

_____

13. What is the function of the condenser?

_____

_____

14. What is the purpose of adjusting the aperture?

_____

_____

15. What is the function of the iris adjustment wheel?

_____

_____

16. Label the following diagram.

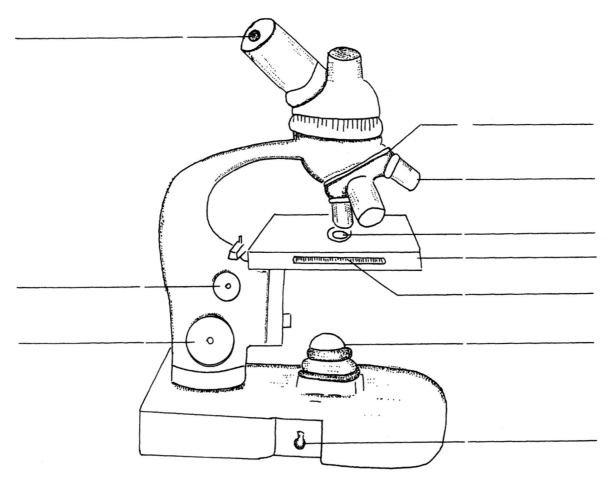

17. The steps in focusing a microscope are presented below, but not in the correct order. Rearrange these steps into the correct order by writing numbers in the spaces provided. (Reread the preceding statements if necessary.)

_____ Make sure that the low-power lens is snapped into place.

_____ Look through the microscope and slowly turn the large focusing knob until the specimen comes into focus.

_____ Move the specimen around until you see the best view.

_____ Make sure that the specimen is centered where the light shines through.

_____ Make sure that the barrel is all the way down.

1–2. MAKING A MICROSCOPIC OBSERVATION

Instructions: (1.) Read the text. (2.) Complete the investigation.

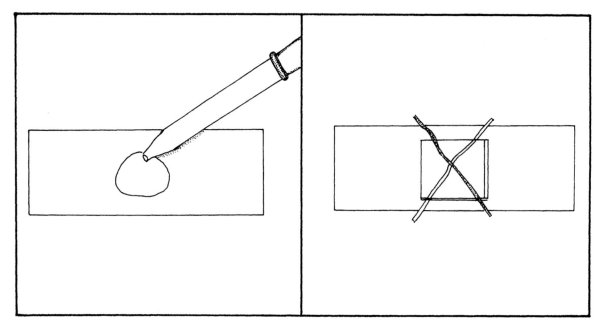

Step 2a   Step 2b

In this investigation you will prepare a microscope slide and make three observations through a compound microscope. Your experiences during this process will help you later to find different focal planes and to keep your specimens centered.

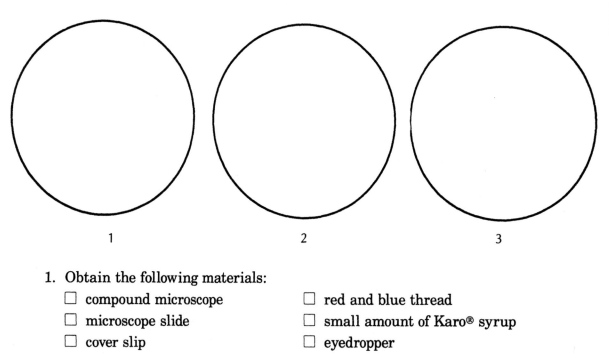

1   2   3

1. Obtain the following materials:
    - ☐ compound microscope
    - ☐ microscope slide
    - ☐ cover slip
    - ☐ red and blue thread
    - ☐ small amount of Karo® syrup
    - ☐ eyedropper

2. Follow the steps below to make a slide and to make a microscopic observation.

☐ a. Drop three drops of Karo® syrup onto the center of the slide.

☐ b. Cut two sections of thread about an inch long and place them so that they form an X on the drops of Karo® syrup.

☐ c. Place the cover slip on top of the drops and the thread.

☐ d. Follow the steps for focusing the microscope.

☐ e. Observe the thread under low power. In the first circle, sketch what you see.

   Note: At this point, read the first two statements of (3), which follows.

☐ f. Turn the nose piece so that the medium-power objective lens is securely snapped into place. Refocus. In the second circle, sketch what you see.

   Note: At this point, read the remainder of (3).

☐ g. Turn the nose piece so that the high-power objective lens is in place. Refocus. In the third circle, sketch what you see.

3. As you proceed, notice these things:

You can easily see the microscopic details of the thread, especially the twist of the smaller filaments. Could you have seen these tiny details without the help of the microscope?

In step (e), only one piece of thread is in focus; you can bring other parts of the thread into focus by using the fine adjustment knob.

As you shift from low to medium power and from medium to high, the middle of the X will seem to shift to the left or the right and must be recentered. It is difficult to distinguish color while you are looking at the thread through the microscope.

4. **Bonus points:** Write a brief paragraph describing your experiences as you performed this activity. Be sure to mention any difficulties you encountered and any parts of the observation that seemed surprising to you. Be prepared to discuss these with other class members.

1–3. MAKING A COMPOUND MICROSCOPE

Instructions: (1.) Read the text and complete the investigation. (2.) Use the text and your observations to help you answer the questions.

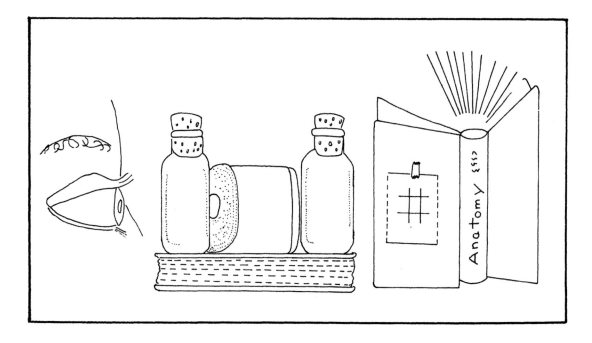

Obtain the following materials:

☐ two gas bottles filled with water and tightly sealed with cork stoppers
☐ one roll of toilet paper
☐ scissors
☐ tape
☐ two expendable textbooks (*Note:* The textbooks may get wet and may be damaged; your teacher can probably provide some out-of-adoption books.)

If the microscope you are using has high-quality lenses, you will probably not encounter very much distortion of the image. But you need to be aware of two important problems:

1. spherical aberration, in which the specimen assumes the shape of the lens
2. image reversal, in which the image appears upside down and backward

You can observe these problems by making your own compound microscope and playing a game of tic-tac-toe through it.
To complete this investigation:

☐ 1. Using the diagram as your guide, assemble a compound microscope.
☐ 2. Cut out the tic-tac-toe grid at the end of this activity and tape it to an out-of-adoption textbook. This grid will be the object to be observed; tape it so that you can see it while looking through both lenses (bottles).

□ 3. Challenge your lab partner to a game of tic-tac-toe. Take turns making X's and O's while looking through the bottles. To keep the bottles from crashing, SOMEONE MUST ALWAYS HOLD THE BOOK WITH THE GRID ATTACHED TO IT.

Level One Questions:

1. What is spherical aberration?

    _____

    _____

2. Sketch what the "tic-tac-toe" grid looks like as you see it through your microscope.

3. Did you observe spherical aberration while looking through your microscope?

    Yes   No   (circle one)

4. What is image reversal?

    _____

    _____

5. Why was it difficult to form X's and O's while looking through your microscope?

    _____

    _____

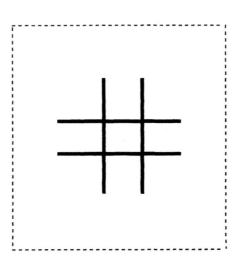

Unit 2

The Cell

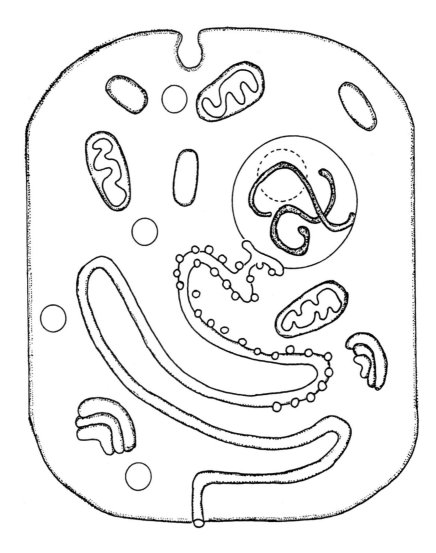

TEACHER'S GUIDE TO UNIT 2 _____

2–1 ROBERT HOOKE DISCOVERS THE CELL

Teaching Suggestions:

1. Demonstrate all of the lab procedures.
2. Illustrations of Hooke's cork drawing appear in many biology texts. If you can find one, show it to your students after they have completed this activity. They will be delighted to discover that their observations and sketches resemble Hooke's.

Answers to the Questions:

Level One

1. English scientist in 1600s; experimented with clocks, telescopes, diving bells, microscopes; famous for microscopic observations, development of compound microscope
2. two
3. *Micrographia*

Level Two

4. (composition)
5. so that light could pass through it

Level Three

6. (paragraph on derivation of title, *Micrographia*—from Greek "small" and Greek "written")

2–2 HOW THE CELL OPERATES

Note: This is a self-directed activity.

Teaching Suggestion:

Make an overhead transparency of the diagram and use it to discuss and reinforce the concepts.

Answers to the Questions:

Level One

1. analogous colors
2. yes
3. to produce power for the cell
4. chromosomes
5. ribosomes
6. the ribosomes
7. make substances (actually proteins) for the cell

8. the Golgi body
9. It gives the substance (protein) that the cell produces a covering that allows the protein to leave the cells. (Students may have difficulty in seeing this on the diagram.)
10. line, endoplasmic reticulum

Level Two

11. (diagram) Correct answers will be obvious. The checks should correspond to the functions of the organelles.

2–3 OBSERVING A HUMAN CELL

Teaching Suggestion:

Demonstrate all of the laboratory procedures.

Answers to the Questions:

Level One

1. yes or no (Answer depends on whether the student had difficulty in seeing cells without stain.)
2. Answers will vary. Essentially, the nucleus is easier to see with its brownish stain.
3. Answers will vary. The bluish stain makes the cell darker, easier to locate; the nucleus is more clearly defined.

Level Three

4. Students will surely think of AIDS; should also mention colds, flu, other communicable diseases.
5. Answers will vary; maybe "like a rounded ice cube."
6. nucleus, cell membrane (possibly cytoplasm)

2–4 THE ANATOMY OF THE CELL

Note: This is a self-directed activity.

Answers to the Questions:

Level One

1. cell
2. They make chemical substances for digestion.
3. nucleus
4. 46 (Gametes are exceptions, of course.)
5. to store instructions for the cell's activities
6. on the ribosomes
7. in the nucleolus

8. sends instructions from the chromosomes to the ribosomes
9. the endoplasmic reticulum
10. to coat protein with a molecular layer that allows protein to leave the cell
11. enzymes
12. amino acids
13. proteins
14. vacuoles
15. lysosomes (actually, enzymes released by lysosomes)
16. energy
17. energy, cell

2–5 MAKING A MODEL OF A CELL

Precaution: It is possible for a young person to have a pacemaker, and he or she may not be aware that a microwave oven constitutes a danger to him or her. Consult with your school nurse before conducting this investigation.

Note: Most of your students will have fun with this activity.

Teaching Suggestions:

1. Advance preparation is necessary.
2. Demonstrate all the steps.

2–1. ROBERT HOOKE DISCOVERS THE CELL

Instructions: (1.) Read the text. (2.) Complete the investigation. (3.) Use the text and your observations to help you answer the questions.

Procedure 1   Procedure 4

Robert Hooke, a scientist who lived in England during the 1600s, experimented with clocks, telescopes, diving bells, and microscopes. He became famous for the observations he made through a microscope he helped to develop. Unlike most of the single-lens microscopes of his time, Hooke's microscope had two lenses mounted on the ends of a tube. This compound microscope was the forerunner of the one you are using.

One of Hooke's observations led him to the discovery of the cell; he described this investigation in his book, *Micrographia*. The steps below were taken from this book. Read these steps and use them to help you to complete the investigation.

Step one: "I sharpened my knife as keen as a razor." (You will use a razor blade.)

Step two: "I, with a sharpened pen knife, cut off a thin piece of cork."

Step three: "I placed the thin piece of cork on a black object plate." (You will use a microscope slide.)

Step four: "Through the microscope, I could see that the cork was perforated and porous, much like a honeycomb." (You will record your observations by sketching them in the circle provided.)

Procedure

Obtain the following materials:

☐ microscope
☐ microscope slide
☐ cover slip
☐ cork

☐ single-edged razor blade
☐ jar of water
☐ eyedropper
☐ dissecting needle

Special Precaution: You will be using a single-edged razor blade to cut cork. Be very careful; always cut *away* from you hand and your body, and report any accidents to your teacher IMMEDIATELY.

☐ 1. Use the safety razor blade to slice a small piece of cork thinner than a piece of paper.

☐ 2. Place two drops of water on the microscope slide.

☐ 3. Use the dissecting needle to place the slice of cork on the water drops.

☐ 4. Lay a cover slip over your specimen and place it on your microscope. Focus to medium power.

☐ 5. Sketch your specimen in the circle provided.

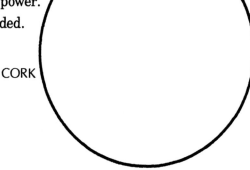

CORK

Level One Questions:

1. Who was Robert Hooke?

_____

2. Hooke's microscope had _____ lenses that he mounted on the ends of a tube.

3. Hooke wrote a book called _____.

Level Two Questions:

4. Using your own words, describe the investigation that led Robert Hooke to the discovery of the cell.

_____

_____

_____

_____

5. In the experiment, why was it important for the cork to be very thin?

_____

_____

_____

_____

Level Three Question:

6. On the back of this sheet, explain why *Micrographia* is an appropriate title for Hooke's book. (You may use a dictionary to help you to answer this question.)

2–2. HOW THE CELL OPERATES

Instructions: (1.) Read the text carefully. (2.) Complete the project. (3.) Use the text and the project to help you to answer the questions.

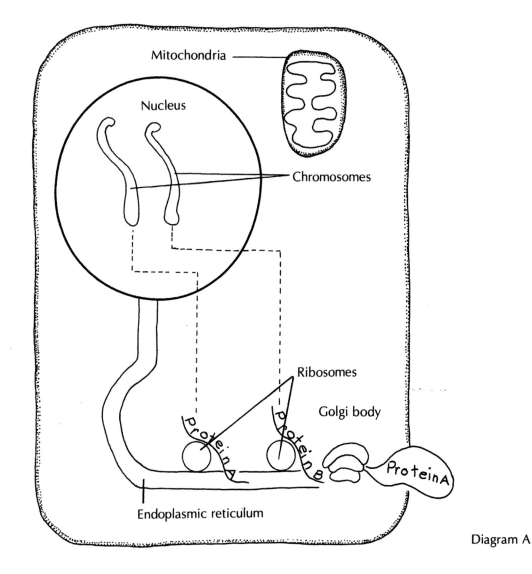

Diagram A

    Many cells in your body act like factories, assembling molecules into various beneficial secretions. The cells that line your mouth, for example, assemble molecules into the slippery mucus that prevents bacteria and other germs from entering your body.

    Diagram A shows an actual cell that produces molecules for the body. Diagram B shows a factory—a make-believe cell—in which a computer, power plant, and robots are used to represent actual structures in a real cell. By comparing Diagram A with Diagram B, you will learn how the organelles of an actual cell work together to produce molecules for the body.

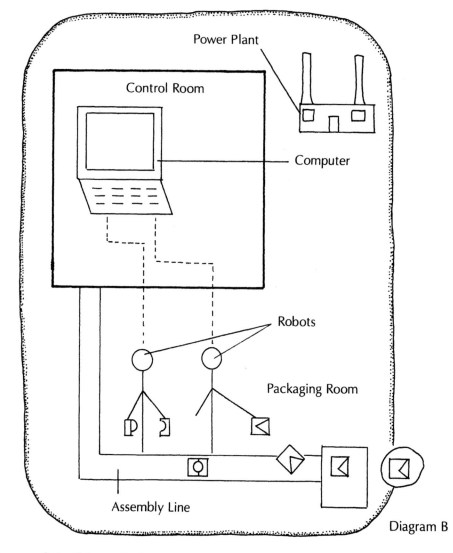

Diagram B

To complete this project—

Obtain a set of map pencils and use them to color-code Diagrams A and B as follows:

- ☐ In Diagram A, color the chromosomes orange.
- ☐ In Diagram B, color the computer orange.
- ☐ In Diagram A, color the nucleus brown.
- ☐ In Diagram B, color the control room brown.
- ☐ In Diagram A, color the mitochondria yellow.
- ☐ In Diagram B, color the power plant yellow.
- ☐ In Diagram A, color the endoplasmic reticulum blue.
- ☐ In Diagram B, color the assembly line blue.
- ☐ In Diagram A, color the ribosomes green.
- ☐ In Diagram B, color the robots green.
- ☐ In Diagram A, color the Golgi body red.
- ☐ In Diagram B, color the packaging room red.

Level One Questions:

1. How did you show that the organelles in Diagram A are similar to the structures in Diagram B?

_____

_____

2. Do the mitochondria and the power plant have similar functions? (*Hint:* match the colors.)

_____

3. The job of the power plant is to produce energy for the factory. If the mitochondrion has a similar function, what is its job?

_____

_____

4. Which structures in Diagram A are similar to the computer in Diagram B?

_____

_____

5. Which organelles in Diagram A are similar to the robots in Diagram B?

_____

_____

6. If the job of the computer is to control the robots, what do the chromosomes control?

_____

7. If the job of the robots is to make boxes, what do the ribosomes produce?

_____

8. Which organelle in Diagram A is similar to the packaging room in Diagram B?

_____

9. If the job of the packaging room is to wrap the boxes so that they can leave the factory, what is the job of the Golgi body?

_____

10. To reach the packaging room, the boxes travel on the assembly _____; to reach the Golgi body in the actual cell, the chemicals must travel through the

_____

Level Two Question:

11. Complete the chart by placing a check in the box that shows the function of the organelle.

STRUCTURE	STORES INFORMATION	RELEASES ENZYMES	CONTROL CENTER	TRANSPORTS MATERIALS	ASSEMBLES PROTEINS	PACKAGES MATERIALS
NUCLEUS						
CHROMOSOME						
ENDOPLASMIC RETICULUM						
GOLGI BODY						
LYSOSOME						
RIBOSOME						

2–3. OBSERVING A HUMAN CELL

Instructions: (1.) Read the text and complete the project. (2.) Use the text to help you to complete the investigation and answer the questions.

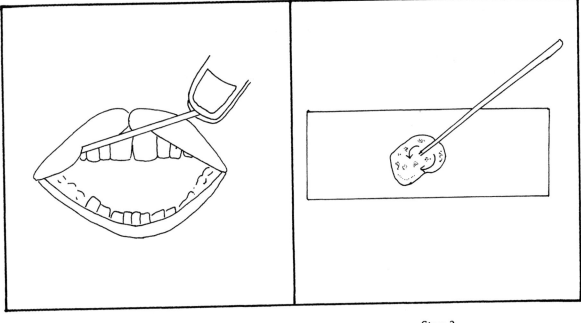

Step 1   Step 3

All living things are made of cells; scientists call cells the "building blocks of life." Your skin, muscles, skeleton, blood, internal organs, and all other parts of your body are built of trillions of cells.

Many of the cells of your body cannot be seen without the use of a microscope and special stains. While completing this investigation, you will use a microscope to observe a few of the epithelial cells that line your mouth. You will use stains to make these cells more visible.

Obtain the following materials:

☐ three toothpicks   ☐ small container of water
☐ iodine (stain)   ☐ microscope slide
☐ methylene blue (stain)   ☐ cover slip
☐ eye dropper

Special Precaution: You will use three different toothpicks to scrape (GENTLY) the lining of your mouth. After using a toothpick, IMMEDIATELY place it in the trash.

To complete this investigation—

☐ 1. Gently scrape the inside lining of your cheek with a toothpick.

☐ 2. Place two drops of water on a clean microscope slide.

☐ 3. With a toothpick, mix the cheek cells with the water on the slide.

☐ 4. THROW AWAY THE TOOTHPICK.

☐ 5. Place a cover slip over the mixture and place the slide on your microscope; focus to high power.

☐ 6. In Circle A, sketch what you see through your microscope.

☐ 7. With a new toothpick, gently scrape the lining of your cheek again.

☐ 8. Place two drops of iodine on a clean microscope slide; repeat steps 3, 4, and 5, this time with the iodine. In Circle B, sketch what you see.

☐ 9. With a new toothpick, repeat these steps—this time using methylene blue as your stain. In Circle C, sketch what you see.

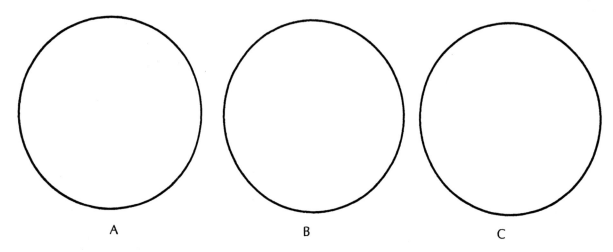

A   B   C

Level One Questions:

1. Did you have any difficulty in seeing the epithelial cells and sketching them in circle A? Explain.

   _____

   _____

   _____

   _____

2. In what way did the cells stained with iodine look different? Explain.

   _____

   _____

   _____

   _____

3. In what way did the cells stained with methylene blue look different? Explain.

_____

_____

_____

_____

Level Three Questions:

4. Why was it so essential for you to throw away the toothpick? (You are likely to think of a health risk that has been in the news in recent years. In addition to that, what other health risks might be avoided by such precautions?)

_____

_____

_____

_____

5. Describe the general shape of the epithelial cells.

_____

6. What organelle(s) within the cell did you recognize?

_____

_____

_____

2–4. THE ANATOMY OF THE CELL

Instructions: (1.) Read the text. (2.) Complete the project. (3.) Use the text and the project to help you to answer the questions.

Every cell in your body has at least one special job to do. A few examples: The cells in the outer layers of your skin are designed to protect you from your external environment, certain cells in your stomach make chemical substances to digest the food you eat, and other cells are specially designed to carry electrochemical impulses that make your muscles contract.

Even though your body cells have different jobs to do, certain aspects of their internal anatomies (structures) are similar. While doing this project, you will learn the internal anatomy of a generalized cell.

The job of the nucleus is to be the control center of the cell. The nucleus of each human cell contains 46 chromosomes, which store instructions for the cell's activities. The nucleus is the most obvious structure in the generalized cell. The following diagram shows what the nucleus and the chromosomes look like. For simplicity, the diagram contains only two chromosomes.

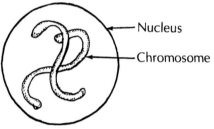

☐ 1. Color the nucleus brown.
☐ 2. Color the chromosomes blue.

One of the ways in which the nucleus directs the cell's activities is by sending instructions to the ribosomes, where proteins are assembled. The following diagram shows what a ribosome looks like.

○

☐ 3. Color this ribosome green.

Ribosomes receive instructions from the chromosomes by molecules called "messenger RNA." A round structure found within the nucleus assists in the production and storage of RNA. This structure is called the "nucleolus." The diagram below shows the nucleolus; dashed lines are used to represent molecules of RNA.

☐ 4. Color this nucleolus yellow.
☐ 5. Color the RNA molecules pink.

Once proteins are made, they are sometimes transported through the cells by a system of tubes called the "endoplasmic reticulum." The following diagram shows what the endoplasmic reticulum looks like.

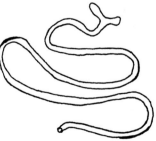

☐ 6. Color this endoplasmic reticulum blue.

The endoplasmic reticulum delivers many types of proteins to the Golgi body. The function of the Golgi body is to coat protein with a molecular layer that allows the protein to leave the cell. The diagram below shows what the Golgi body looks like.

☐ 7. Color this Golgi body yellow.

Lysosomes contain chemical substances called "enzymes." Lysosomes use these enzymes to break certain nutrients called "proteins" into their building blocks, the amino acids. As a nutrient enters the cell, it attaches to a lysosome. The amino acids that result from that breakdown are used by the ribosomes to make new proteins. The following diagram shows what a lysosome looks like.

☐ 8. Color this lysosome red.

Vacuoles are storage sacs where incoming nutrients are stored before they are broken down by lysosomes. The following diagram shows what a vacuole looks like.

☐ 9. Color this vacuole any color.

To assemble proteins and to perform other functions, the cell uses energy. The mitochondria act like power houses; that is, they produce energy in a form that the cell can use. The following diagram shows what mitochondria look like.

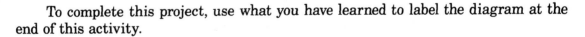

☐ 10. Color this mitochondrion orange.

To complete this project, use what you have learned to label the diagram at the end of this activity.

Level One Questions:

1. The _____ is the fundamental building block of the body.

2. How are certain cells in your stomach specialized?

   _____

   _____

   _____

3. The _____ is the control center of the cell.

4. How many chromosomes are in each human cell? _____

5. What is the function of chromosomes?

_____

_____

_____

6. Where are proteins assembled?

_____

7. Where is RNA manufactured?

_____

8. Describe the function of messenger RNA.

_____

_____

_____

9. What structure transports proteins?

_____

10. What is the function of the Golgi body?

_____

_____

_____

11. Lysosomes contain chemical substances called _____.

12. Lysosomes use their enzymes to break proteins into _____.

13. The ribosomes use these amino acids to assemble new _____.

14. _____ are storage sacs.

15. Incoming nutrients are stored in vacuoles before they are broken down by_____

_____.

16. To assemble proteins and perform other functions, the cell uses _____.

17. Mitochondria produce _____ in the form that the _____

_____ can use.

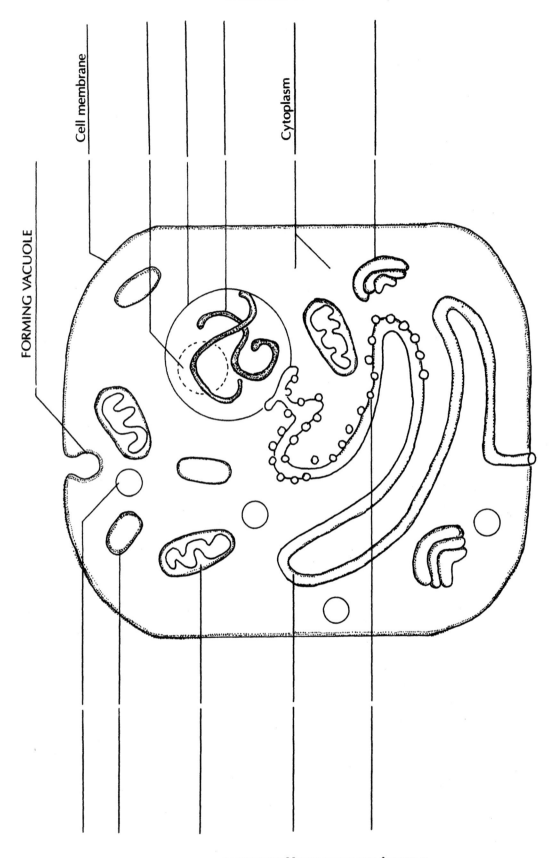

Cell membrane

Cytoplasm

FORMING VACUOLE

2–5. MAKING A MODEL OF A CELL

Instructions: Read the text and complete the project.

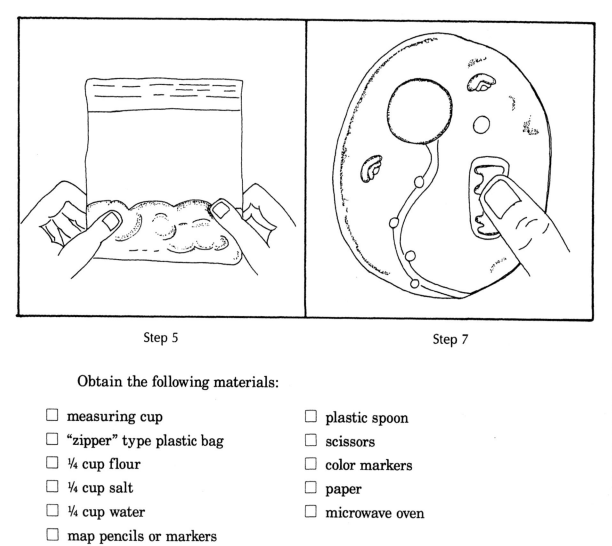

Step 5   Step 7

Obtain the following materials:

☐ measuring cup   ☐ plastic spoon

☐ "zipper" type plastic bag   ☐ scissors

☐ ¼ cup flour   ☐ color markers

☐ ¼ cup salt   ☐ paper

☐ ¼ cup water   ☐ microwave oven

☐ map pencils or markers

Special Precautions: (1.) Persons with pacemakers should not be around a microwave oven in use. (2.) After microwaving, your cell will be hot; use caution while removing it from the oven.

A diagram of a cell makes it look flat; a cell also looks flat under a microscope. But it is important to remember that a cell is not flat at all. In the next project you will make a cell model that will help you to visualize a cell as three-dimensional.

☐ 1. Locate the decal page and color the cell parts. Cut out the cell parts and labels.

☐ 2. Into the "zipper" type plastic bag, pour the flour and salt (¼ cup of each).

☐ 3. Seal the "zipper" type plastic bag and carefully shake it to mix the flour and salt.

☐ 4. Open the "zipper" type plastic bag and add the water.

☐ 5. Seal the bag again, making sure that there is no trapped air. With your fingers, gently knead the bag to mix its contents.

☐ 6. Open the bag and squeeze its contents onto a piece of paper in the shape of a large cookie. If necessary, use the spoon to smooth it.

☐ 7. Gently press the cell parts and their labels onto your model. Use the diagram for step eight as your guide.

☐ 8. Using the high setting, microwave your cell for two and a half minutes. The cell will be hot! Use caution while removing it from the oven.

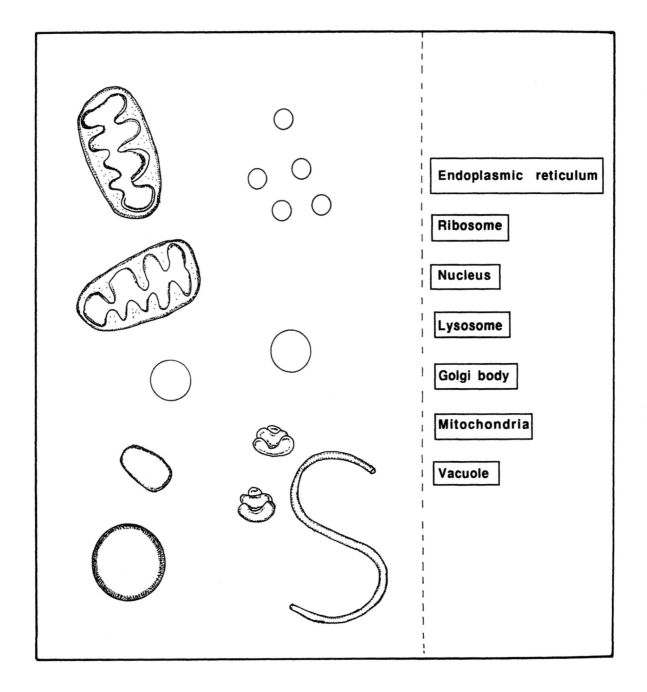

Unit 3

The Skeleton

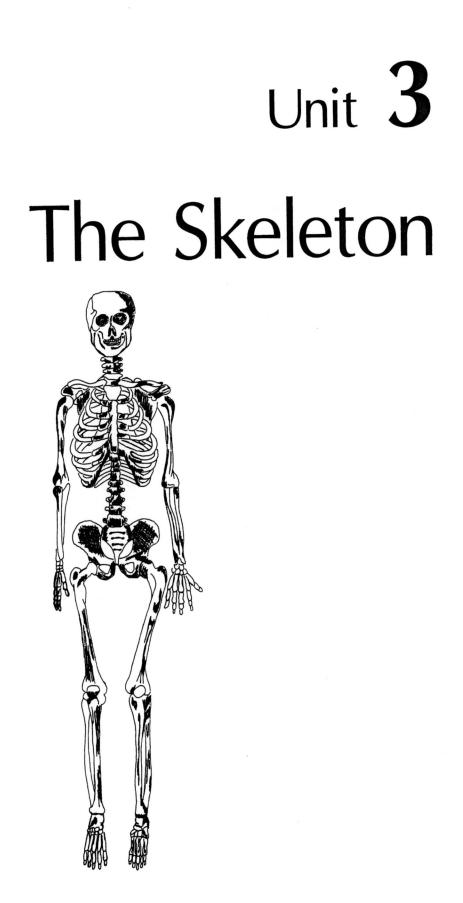

TEACHER'S GUIDE TO UNIT 3 _____

3–1 THE HUMAN SKELETON

Note: This is a self-directed activity.

Teaching Suggestions:

1. Use a human skeleton (or a model) to illustrate the concepts.
2. If available, show a mounted animal skeleton; ask your students to guess the animal it originally supported. (Use more than one skeleton if you're fortunate enough to have them.)
3. Use a bone (a dry cow bone, for example) to demonstrate its external features. If a bone is not available, use a marker to draw arrows to the tubercles, tuberosities, and nutrient foramen.

Answers to the Questions: Part I ("The Skeleton as a Structure")

Level One

1. to give support, protect people inside, give house shape
2. to provide much the same benefits—gives the body support and shape, protect the organs

Level Three

3. Answers will vary. Students may mention unnecessary time and expense, difficulty in installing wiring, plumbing, etc., and lack of later accessibility.
4. Answers will vary; essentially, excessive weight, difficulty in locomotion, lack of flexibility

Part II ("The Anatomy of the Bone")

Level One

1. the bone
2. epithesis (sing.), epitheses (pl.)
3. diaphysis
4. in the middle of the diaphysis
5. to provide a passageway through which blood vessels can enter the bone and carry nutrients to the bone marrow
6. periosteum
7. tubercles (small bumps), tuberosities (big bumps)

Level Two

8. They remove calcium from the blood and deposit it in bone tissue.

3–2 TESTING FOR CALCIUM

Notes:

1. Students enjoy this investigation.
2. Observe all safety precautions while working with acids.

3. Vinegar may be substituted for dilute hydrochloric acid, but the gas bubbles will be difficult to observe.

Answers to the Questions:

Level One

1. Answers will vary; students may know of some other substances, and your choice of samples may vary. In general, eggshells, seashells, chalk, bone, sedimentary rock (e.g., sandstone) contain calcium.
2. wood, igneous rock
3. Calcium is a strong material; it provides strength.

3–3 DOES CALCIUM REALLY MAKE BONES STRONG?

Notes:

1. Students enjoy this activity.
2. Since steak bones and other high-density bones are difficult to soften, encourage your students to use only chicken bones.

Teaching Suggestion:

Demonstrate a softened bone. Since it takes several weeks to soften a bone in vinegar, this demonstration will obviously require advance preparation. Once softened, a bone may be stored for several years in a jar of vinegar.

Answers to the Questions:

Level One

1. dissolves
2. two to three weeks

Level Two

3. Gases may be produced and may cause top to bulge or make opening difficult.
4. to insure presence of enough calcium for a strong skeleton

Level Three

5. Answers will vary; steak-bone tissue is denser, more compact.

3–4 THE INTERNAL ANATOMY OF A BONE

Note: This is a self-directed worksheet.

Answers to the Questions:

Level One

1. lifeless
2. living

3. hollow
4. marrow cavity
5. compact
6. yellow bone marrow
7. stores yellowish fat, which can be converted into useful energy if energy levels drop
8. produces red blood cells

Level Two

9. store fat, produce blood cells

Level Three

10. (Paragraph describing bone as a living organ—should include ideas that it has blood vessels, receives nutrients, grows, can be repaired by natural processes, contains yellow and red bone marrow.)
11. cancellous tissue (spongy bone), red marrow

3–5 INVESTIGATING THE INTERNAL ANATOMY OF A BONE

Notes:

1. This is a valuable investigation because it enables the students to look inside a bone.
2. Since it takes several weeks to soften chicken bones, this investigation requires advance preparation. A class collection of carefully bisected bones can be stored in vinegar for several years.

Teaching Suggestions:

1. Use a hole punch, colored construction paper, and stick-pins to make the color-coded pins.
2. Demonstrate all laboratory procedures.

Answers to the Questions:

Level One

1. cut in half from end to end

Level Two

2. because that is where red marrow is located or where red blood cells are produced
3. because that is where yellow bone marrow is located and yellowish fat is stored

Level Three

4. Cooking removes the red color.

3–6 OSTEOPOROSIS

Note: This is a self-directed worksheet.

Teaching Suggestion:

Depending on the time available and the inclinations of your students, you may wish to encourage discussion of what has happened to their grandmothers or great-grandmothers. Students may gain new insights when they think about "dowager's hump" in connection with the older women they know and when they understand that height may decrease by several inches as the vertebrae collapse. Collapsing vertebrae also produce changes in silhouette as the rib cage settles onto the pelvis and the contents of the abdomen are pushed forward.

Answers to the Questions:

Level One

1. building bones, regulating the cells, helping muscles to contract, helping to control the heart rate
2. by the circulatory system
3. may be weakened; may become brittle and easily broken or crushed
4. eat a balanced diet, including milk, cheese, yogurt, ice cream
5. early in life (actually in the thirties, but that does not seem to be "early in life" to students)
6. now

Level Two

7. Osteoclasts release chemicals that remove calcium from the bones and use it to restore the calcium level in the blood.
8. Answers will vary; basically, if intake of calcium is too low to balance the leaching of calcium into the blood. (Some students may understand that pregnancy, which involves heavy calcium requirements for forming the embryo, may result in severe calcium loss to the mother and weakening of bones, teeth, etc.)

Level Three

9. Answers will vary. Basically, what has happened is that the bone has become weak and breaks with no observable stress; after that, she falls to the floor and assumes that the fall has caused the break.

3–7 INVESTIGATING BONE USING A MICROSCOPE

Special note: If commercially prepared microscope slides are not available, bone slides can be easily made as follows:

1. Cover a dry cow bone (the sort that students sometimes bring in to show their teachers) with a cloth towel and use a hammer to break off a few small pieces.
2. Use a mortar and pestle to grind the small pieces into a powder.

3. Use two drops of white Karo® syrup and a cover slip to mount this powder on a microscope slide.

4. To make a permanent slide, sprinkle the ground bone on a dry microscope slide. Cover the bone with several drops of clear fingernail polish and allow it to dry overnight. DO NOT USE A COVER SLIP.

Answers to the Questions:

Level One

1. osteocytes
2. 1691
3. named for discoverer, Clopton Havers
4. nutrients, wastes
5. Haversian, lacunae
6. provides a space for the blood vessels to travel through the compact bone of the diaphysis
7. the fibrous covering of the bone
8. canaliculi, lacunae
9. osteocytes (bone cells)

Level Two

10. because they are embedded in bone tissue
11. Haversian canals are branches of the Volkmann's canals.

3–8 NAMING THE BONES OF THE SKELETON

Teaching Suggestions:

1. Use a human skeleton (or a skeleton model) to demonstrate and name the bones.
2. Allow your student volunteers to take turns at the skeleton to name the bones for the class.
3. Several of your students may want to make an instructional videotape of the skeleton. Record this videotape using EP (extended play) so that when it is played back for the class to watch, important segments can be paused for class discussion.

Answers to the Questions:

Level One

1. ribs
2. femur
3. cranium
4. bones (vertebrae)
5. humerus
6. shoulder blade
7. eight
8. metacarpals
9. carpals
10. in the fingers
11. humerus
12. frontal
13. fibula
14. tibia
15. foot (makes the heel)

Level Two

16. ankle
17. arch

Level Three

18. make it possible to turn the hand over (Tell students the technical terms if you want to—"supinate" for turning it palm up, "pronate" for turning it palm down.)
19. Answers will vary; basically yes; would reduce flexibility, add too much weight, interfere with breathing. Students may also include difficulty in accessing organs during surgery.
20. Answers will vary. Brain is crucial and needs serious protection; flexibility is not necessary.

3–9 THE FROG SKELETON

Note: Your students will enjoy this activity.

Teaching Suggestions:

1. Demonstrate some fossils and describe how they were formed.
2. Show a good film on paleontology or anthropology. An excellent and highly instructional film about the information that scientists obtain from bones is National Geographic's *The Shadow of Vesuvius.* This film is available at many videotape rental stores.

Answers to the Questions:

Level One

1. Spinal column, femur, humerus are noticeably similar; skulls and pelvic bones are shaped differently. (Note that there is nothing in the text to guide this answer; students can decide only by comparing the diagrams.)
2. Most likely answer: Frog's leg has fused bones called the "tibio-fibula." (If time permits, use a scalpel to cut through the tibio-fibula of a preserved frog so that students can see that it is actually two fused bones.)

Level Two

3. Its name is derived from the two bones (tibia and fibula of the human body) that are fused in the frog's leg.

Level Three

4. Answers will vary. Students will be very clever if they recognize that a human needs to be able to twist and invert his or her feet. The frog's characteristic actions—hopping, swimming—require only that the feet be able to flex strongly; a twisting action would actually be a disadvantage.

3–10 JOINTS

Note: This is a self-directed worksheet.

Answers to the Questions:

Level One

1. bones
2. three
3. Answers will vary—bend the knee, twist, turn, pivot, sit, dance, etc.
4. hinge, pivot, gliding, ball-and-socket

Level Two

5. Answers will vary—closing the hand, grasping, writing, catching things, any precise hand actions.
6. knee, fingers, toes

Level Three

7. yes; greatest flexibility required
8. at the joint between the lower arm and the hand. If the student says "wrist" he or she is in the right ball park, although the location is, technically, slightly above the wrist.
9. The "latter set"—the joints between the metacarpals and the phalanges, where the fingers connect with the hand—are modified hinge joints; they allow limited rotation as well as hinge action. Joints in the fingers themselves allow only hinge action.

3–11 IDENTIFYING THE JOINTS

Teaching Suggestions:

1. Use a human skeleton (or model) to demonstrate the joints.
2. If available, show X-rays of joints.
3. To demonstrate that a skull is really made of bones joined by sutures, try this demonstration:
   a. Obtain a skull from a medium-sized animal (my students are always bringing these in). The bones of the skull must be fairly thick.
   b. Fill the skull with dried kidney beans and soak it in a bucket of water overnight. As the beans expand, they will exert a constant pressure that will loosen the sutures so that the bones can be easily separated. (Try it; it works!)

Answers to the Questions:

Level One

1. ball-and-socket joint
2. ball-and-socket joint

3. hinge joint

4. gliding joint

Level Two

5. between scapula (shoulder blade) and humerus (upper arm bone)

Level Three

6. Answers will vary; basically, because of how it looks; the end of the long bone is spherical, and it fits into a cup-shaped socket.

7. between the ulna and the radius

8. gliding joints

3–12 EXPOSING THE SYNOVIAL SAC

Teaching Suggestion:

Demonstrate all lab procedures.

Answers to the Questions:

Level One

1. heat

2. to warm your hands (or start a fire or strike a match, etc.?)

3. damages engines, damages joints (wears out anything)

4. Surrounding tissues become swollen and painful.

5. acts like a bearing and reduces friction

6. It is a sac; it contains slippery fluid, like egg white.

7. cartilage

8. the synovial sac

Level Two

9. Both are needed; cartilage is protected by the synovial fluid.

Level Three

10. Answers will vary; generally, cartilage has worn out.

3–1. THE HUMAN SKELETON

Instructions: (1.) Read the text. (2.) Use the text and the diagram to help you to answer the questions.

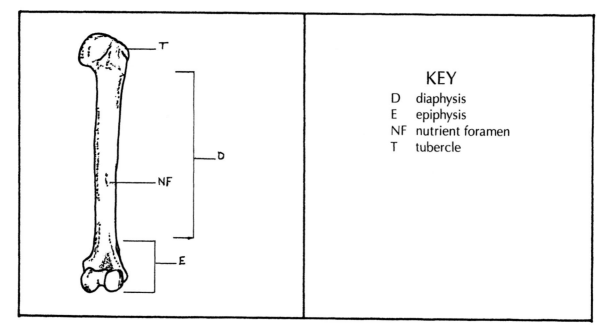

KEY
D   diaphysis
E   epiphysis
NF nutrient foramen
T   tubercle

Part I: The Skeleton as a Structure

If you have ever watched a house being built, you have noticed that the builder begins by constructing a frame; the builder uses boards to outline the walls, roof, windows, and doors. At this stage, the house looks very much like a skeleton, with boards instead of bones.

The builder has at least three good reasons for building this frame or skeleton: it gives support to the house, protects the people living inside, and gives the house shape.

The human body also needs something to support it, to give it shape, and to protect the delicate organs inside it. The human skeleton is made of bones instead of boards, but it provides the same benefits for the human body that the frame provides for the house.

Level One Questions:

1. List three reasons for beginning a house by building a frame of boards.

   _____

   _____

   _____

2. In what ways does a human body need a similar frame?

   _____

   _____

Level Three Questions:

3. A builder could also begin by constructing a solid support for a house—of boards placed edge-to-edge, for example, with no spaces between them. Why would a builder be unlikely to do this?

_____

_____

_____

4. Similarly, the support for a human body could be rigid—made of hard, solid materials without spaces between them. Why would this not be a good idea?

_____

_____

_____

The fundamental unit of the skeleton is the bone. The diagram at the beginning of this activity shows its external structure, and the lettered arrows point to its different parts. As you read the descriptions, refer to the key.

Part II: The Anatomy of the Bone

1. The end of a long bone is called an "epiphysis." At the epiphyses (plural form of epiphysis), the bone attaches to another part of the skeleton. Each epiphysis is shaped differently; each end is specially designed to fit the bone or bones it attaches to. In the diagram, notice that the shapes of the top and bottom epiphyses are different.

2. The shaft of the bone is called the "diaphysis." It is shaped like a hollow cylinder to give it strength and to make it light in weight. The hollow center also provides a place for the bone marrow.

3. Located in the middle of the diaphysis is a hole called the "nutrient foramen." Through this hole blood vessels enter the bone, bringing blood to the bone marrow.

4. The entire diaphysis (shaft of the bone) is covered by a fibrous tissue called the "periosteum." There are specialized cells called "osteoblasts" in this structure; since these cells can remove calcium from the blood and deposit it in the bone tissue, the osteoblasts help to repair broken bones.

5. The periosteum is highly vascular; this means it contains many blood vessels. To nourish the bone cells, these vessels leave the periosteum and enter the bone tissue through microscopically small openings.

6. On certain areas of the diaphysis are prominences or bumps. The smaller bumps are called "tubercles" and the larger bumps are called "tuberosities." Muscles, tendons, and ligaments attach to these structures. The tubercle on the diagram is placed where the shoulder muscle attaches.

Level One Questions:

1. What is the fundamental unit of the skeleton? _____

2. What are the ends of the bone called? _____

3. The shaft of the bone is called the _____.

4. Where on the bone is the nutrient foramen located? _____

5. What is the job of the nutrient foramen?

   _____

6. In what structure are the osteoblasts located? _____

7. To what structures do muscles, ligaments, and tendons attach?

   _____

Level Two Question:

8. How do osteoblasts help to repair bones?

   _____

   _____

   _____

3–2. TESTING FOR CALCIUM

Instructions: (1.) Read the text. (2.) Carefully watch and listen as your teacher shows you how to test for calcium. (3.) Use your observations to help you to complete the chart and answer the questions.

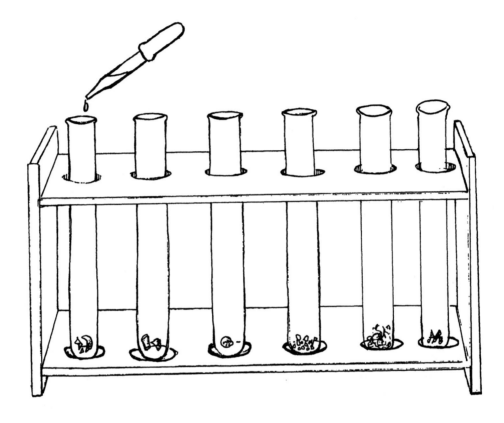

Special Caution: Dilute hydrochloric acid can irritate your eyes and skin. Be CAREFUL not to spill this acid on your skin, and use a face shield or wear protective glasses. If you or a lab partner should accidentally splash acid on your skin or in your eyes, tell your teacher IMMEDIATELY.

One job of the skeleton is to support the body. Bones are specially suited for this job because they are made of a strong material.

Bones are made of calcium. In nature, limestone contains calcium, and many animals use calcium's rocklike strength to construct their shells. Sea shells, for example, are constructed with calcium.

Scientists use weak hydrochloric acid to see if something contains calcium. This acid will react with calcium in a test sample and will produce gas bubbles. In this investigation, you will test six substances for calcium by adding a weak acid to a small sample of each substance. If bubbles are produced, then the test is positive and the sample contains calcium. If no bubbles are produced, then the test is negative and no calcium is present in the sample.

Obtain the following materials:

☐ test tube rack
☐ six test tubes
☐ dilute hydrochloric acid (or full-strength vinegar)
☐ safety goggles and apron
☐ test samples (refer to data chart)
☐ eyedropper
☐ forceps or tweezers

Procedure

1. Carefully place in a test tube one of the samples listed on the chart.
2. Fill an eyedropper with acid and add the acid to this test tube.
3. Wait a few seconds, then check to see if bubbles are released.
4. Record your results on the chart before you proceed to the next sample.

DATA CHART		
Sample	Test is positive (bubbles seen)	Test is negative (bubbles not seen)
1. Eggshell		
2. Seashell		
3. Rock		
4. Chalk		
5. Wood		
6. Bone		

Level One Questions:

1. List some substances that contain calcium.

_____

_____

2. List some substances that do not contain calcium.

_____

_____

3. Why is it important for bones to have calcium?

_____

_____

3–3. DOES CALCIUM REALLY MAKE BONES STRONG?

Instructions: (1.) Read the text. (2.) Complete the investigation. (3.) Use the text and your observations to help you to answer the questions.

Procedure 1   Procedure 3

Is calcium really important? Does it really make bones hard? What would happen if you didn't get enough calcium in your diet? To answer these questions, remove the calcium from a bone and see.

Vinegar is a weak acid that dissolves calcium. Soaking a chicken bone in a jar of vinegar will remove the calcium and make the bone soft. This experiment will take two to three weeks to complete, but after the wait is over you will be in for a surprise: The bone will appear to be made of rubber!

Procedure

1. Enjoy a chicken feast.
2. Carefully wash one of the bones.
3. Fill a jar with vinegar and place the bone in it.
4. Place the lid loosely on the jar, or punch holes in the lid.

Level One Questions:

1. Vinegar is a weak acid that _____ calcium.

2. About how long does it take for vinegar to remove all of the calcium from a chicken bone?

Level Two Questions:

3. Why do you think it is necessary to punch holes in the jar's lid?

   _____

4. Why do you think it is important to eat foods that are rich in calcium?

   _____

   _____

   _____

Level Three Question:

5. The calcium in a steak bone takes much longer to dissolve than the calcium in a chicken bone. Explain why you think this is so.

   _____

   _____

   _____

3–4. THE INTERNAL ANATOMY OF A BONE

Instructions: (1.) Read the text carefully. (2.) Use the descriptions to help you to label the diagram. (3.) Use the text and the descriptions to answer the questions.

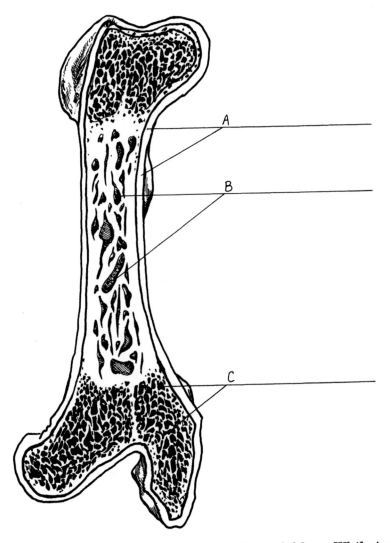

Because of its hard, stonelike texture, bone looks lifeless. While investigating its internal anatomy, however, you will quickly discover that it is very much a living part of the body.

To help you to learn about the internal anatomy of the bone, the diagram shows a bone that has been cut lengthwise.

Descriptions

1. The diaphysis or shaft of a long bone is hollow; this hollow space is called the "marrow cavity." The walls that enclose this cavity are made of compact bone. Arrow A points to the compact bone. Label arrow A "compact bone."

2. The soft tissue inside the marrow cavity is called "yellow bone marrow" because it stores yellowish fat. When the body's energy levels are low, this fat can be converted into useful energy. Arrow B points to the yellow marrow. Label arrow B "yellow marrow."

3. The epiphyses or ends of the long bone are not hollow; they are filled with spongy bone called "cancellous tissue." Red bone marrow fills the spaces of this tissue. The job of this marrow is to produce new blood cells. Arrow C points to the cancellous tissue. Label arrow C "cancellous tissue."

Level One Questions:

1. Because of its hard, stonelike appearance, bone looks as though it is _____.

2. While studying its internal anatomy, you will learn that bone is a _____ part of the human body.

3. The diaphysis of the long bone is _____.

4. What is the space in the diaphysis called? _____

5. The walls that enclose the marrow cavity are made of _____ bone.

6. What kind of marrow fills the marrow cavity of the diaphysis? _____

7. What is its function?

   _____

8. What is the function of the red marrow?

   _____

Level Two Question:

9. What are two tasks of the bone?

   a. _____

   b. _____

Level Three Questions:

10. Write a short paragraph describing bone as a living organ.

    _____

    _____

    _____

    _____

    _____

11. You learned that blood cells are produced in the ends of long bones. Blood cells are also made in the flat bones of the skull, the breast bone, and the irregularly shaped bones that form the spine. What kind of tissue would you expect to find inside these bones?

    _____

12. **Bonus points:** On the diagram, use color pencils as follows:
    a. Use yellow to color the yellow bone marrow.
    b. Use red to color the cancellous bone tissue.

Name _____ Date _____

3–5. INVESTIGATING
THE INTERNAL ANATOMY OF A BONE

Instructions: (1.) Read the text. (2.) Carefully watch and listen as your teacher shows you how to bisect a softened bone. (3.) Use the text and your observations to help you to complete the projects and answer the questions.

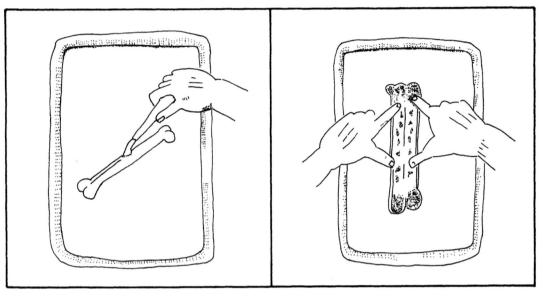

Step 2   Step 3

In this lab, you will study the internal anatomy of a softened chicken bone. This is an interesting investigation because the vinegar that was used to soften the bone also preserved its internal structures.

If your bone was cooked before it was placed in the vinegar, it will be somewhat different from a fresh bone.

Obtain the following materials:

☐ softened chicken bone
☐ scalpel (or single-edged razor blade)
☐ color-coded pins—red, yellow, brown
☐ dissecting tray

1. Place a softened chicken bone in your dissecting tray.
2. Using a scalpel, carefully bisect the bone (cut it in half from end to end).
3. Using your fingers, carefully spread the halves apart.

To complete project one—

☐ In the box titled "bisected bone," carefully sketch one of the bone halves.
☐ Label your sketch.

Bisected Bone

To complete project two—

☐ Your teacher will provide you with pins coded with construction paper. Stick these pins into your specimen as follows:
1. Stick the red pin into the cancellous tissue.
2. Stick the yellow pin into the marrow cavity.
3. Stick the brown pin into the compact bone.

Level One Question:

1. What does the term *bisect* mean? _____

Level Two Questions:

2. Why do you think the red pin was used to identify the cancellous bone?

   _____

   _____

3. Why do you think the yellow pin was used to identify the marrow cavity?

   _____

   _____

Level Three Questions:

4. Since blood cells are produced in the red marrow, the cancellous tissue of the epiphyses is bright red. Explain why this could not be observed in your specimen.

   _____

   _____

5. **Bonus points:** Ask your local butcher to bisect a long bone for your class. Wrap the bone in plastic and, if possible, freeze it before bringing it to class. Your teacher may want to show this fresh bone to the class.

3–6. OSTEOPOROSIS

Instructions: (1.) Read the text. (2.) Use the text to help you to answer the questions.

The body uses calcium for things other than building bones: for regulating the cells, helping the muscles to contract, and helping to control the heart rate. Calcium is transported through the circulatory system. If the concentration of calcium in the blood gets too low, certain cells called "osteoclasts" release chemicals that dissolve the calcium in the bones and use it to restore the blood's calcium concentration to its normal level. If calcium is removed from the bones faster than it is replaced, the bones are weakened and they can break or be crushed.

The fragile bones and the humped back that elderly persons—especially women—sometimes have are caused by a gradual loss of calcium in the bones. This condition is called "osteoporosis."

Although the signs may not appear until old age, calcium loss may actually begin early in life. To help your skeleton to remain strong as you grow older, it is important for you—now—to eat a balanced diet that includes milk, cheese, green vegetables, yogurt, and ice cream. You will be building a storehouse of calcium for the future.

Level One Questions:

1. List four things the body uses calcium for.

    a. _____

    b. _____

    c. _____

    d. _____

2. How is calcium carried through the body?

    _____

3. What can happen to your bones if they lose calcium?

    _____

4. What should you do to make sure you have enough calcium for all your body's needs?

    _____

5. When does calcium loss generally begin?

    _____

6. When should you begin to take precautions against calcium loss?

    _____

Level Two Questions:

7. How does the body restore the normal level of calcium in the blood?

   _____

8. How is it possible for the bones to lose more calcium than they gain?

   _____

   _____

Level Three Question:

9. Quite often, an elderly woman may say, "I was just standing in the middle of the floor when I fell and broke my hip!" Do you think the sequence of events may not be quite what she thinks it was? Explain your answer.

   _____

   _____

   _____

   _____

3–7. INVESTIGATING BONE USING A MICROSCOPE

Instructions: (1.) Read the text. (2.) Complete the project. (3.) Use the text and your observations to help you to answer the questions.

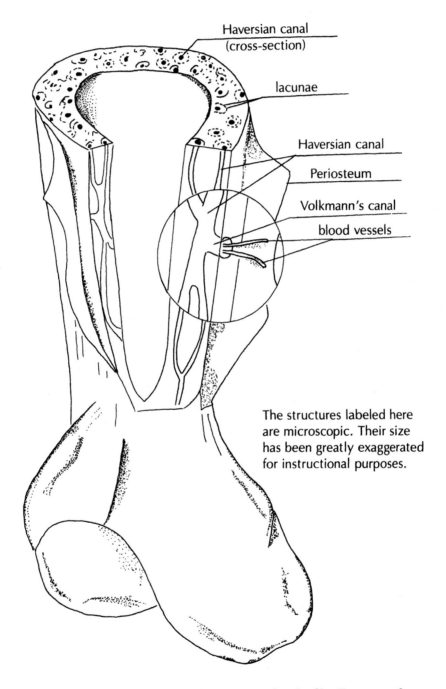

Haversian canal (cross-section)

lacunae

Haversian canal

Periosteum

Volkmann's canal

blood vessels

The structures labeled here are microscopic. Their size has been greatly exaggerated for instructional purposes.

Like all other living structures, bone is made of cells. Because they are embedded in the calcified material that makes bones hard, bone cells (called "osteocytes") have special needs; an unusual kind of circulation, for example, is needed to bring nutrients to these cells and carry away wastes.

Through the microscope, you will investigate this system. It is called the "Haversian system" after a scientist named Clopton Havers who first observed and described it in 1691.

Procedure

1. Obtain the following materials:
    ☐ prepared microscope slide of bone tissue
    ☐ microscope
2. Carefully watch and listen as your teacher shows you how to complete this investigation.
3. Lay the prepared microscope slide of bone tissue on the microscope stage and focus to 100X.

Notice the large dark dots; they are called "Haversian canals," and they are really tubes that run through the bone. Blood vessels travel through them, carrying nutrient-enriched blood plasma and carrying away wastes.

You can probably see five or six Haversian systems in a single field of vision; each one consists of a Haversian canal with small irregularly shaped spaces arranged around it in rings. These spaces are called "lacunae."

Each Haversian canal is really a branch from a network of canals that travels through the compact bone of the diaphysis. These canals are called "Volkmann's canals."

The periosteum (the fibrous covering of the bone) contains many small blood vessels. These blood vessels leave the periosteum, enter the bone, and then travel a short distance through the Volkmann's canals. As the Volkmann's canals branch to form the Haversian canals, the blood vessels traveling within the Volkmann's canals also divide, sending a branch into each of the branches of the Haversian canal.

While in the Haversian canal, blood passes out of the blood vessels and travels through small cracks in the compact bone. These cracks, called "canaliculi," direct the blood to the lacunae, where the osteocytes (bone cells) live.

To complete this project—

☐ In the circle, accurately sketch what you see in one complete field of vision.

Level One Questions:

1. Bone cells are called _____.

2. When was the Haversian system first observed?

    _____

3. How did the Haversian system get its name?

    _____

    _____

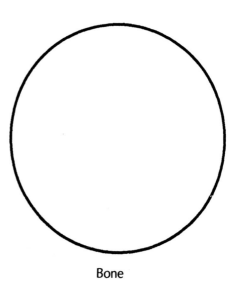

Bone

4. The Haversian system makes it possible for osteocytes to obtain _____

   and to release _____.

5. A Haversian system consists of a _____ canal with small

   irregularly shaped spaces called _____ around it.

6. What is the function of the Volkmann's canals?

   _____

7. What is the periosteum?

   _____

8. From the Haversian canal, the blood passes through small cracks called _____

   _____ on its way to the _____.

9. What lives in the lacunae?

   _____

Level Two Questions:

10. Why do osteocytes need a special kind of circulation?

    _____

    _____

11. How is a Haversian canal related to a Volkmann's canal?

    _____

    _____

3–8. NAMING THE BONES OF THE SKELETON

Instructions: (1.) Read the text. (2.) Use the text and the descriptions to help you to label the diagram and answer the questions.

The human skeleton contains 206 bones. If you ever break a bone or suffer from a bone disease, your doctor will use the bones' scientific names to describe your condition; it could be very useful for you to know the names of the most common bones.

Diagram A   Diagram B

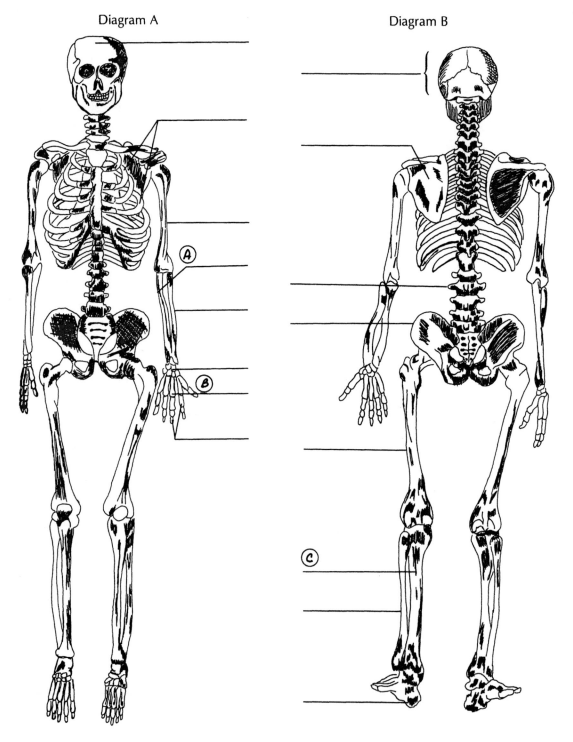

© 1993 by John Wiley & Sons, Inc.

Descriptions

1. The head is made of many tightly joined bones. The term cranium is a general name for all of the bones of the head. On Diagram B, find the arrow that points to the cranium. Label that arrow "cranium."

2. The part of the cranium above the eyes is called the "frontal bone." On Diagram A, find the arrow that points to the frontal bone. Label that arrow "frontal bone."

3. The scapula, often called the "shoulder blade," is the broad flat bone of the shoulder. On Diagram B, find the arrow that points to the scapula. Label that arrow "scapula."

4. The longest bone in the arm is the humerus. On Diagram A, find the arrow that points to the humerus. Label that arrow "humerus."

5. Below the elbow are two long bones. The long bone that points to the little finger is the ulna. On Diagram A, arrow A points to the ulna. Label arrow A "ulna."

6. The other long bone in the lower arm is called the "radius." The radius points to the thumb. Find the arrow in Diagram A that points to the radius. Label that arrow "radius."

7. There are eight small bones called the "carpal bones" in the wrist; they make it possible to rotate the hand in any direction. Find the arrow in Diagram A that points to the carpal bones. Label that arrow "carpal bones."

8. The short bones in the hand that make the palm are called the "metacarpals." Arrow B in Diagram A points to the metacarpals. Label arrow B "metacarpals."

9. Each finger is made of three bones; the thumb is made of only two. The finger and thumb bones are called "phalanges." In Diagram A, find the arrow that points to the phalanges. Label that arrow "phalanges."

10. The bones that form a cage around the chest are called the "ribs." On Diagram A, find the arrow that points to the ribs. Label that arrow "ribs."

11. The spinal column, often called the "backbone," is made of many small bones called "vertebrae" stacked one on top of another. On Diagram B, find the arrow that points to a vertebra. Label that arrow "vertebra."

12. The longest bone in the body is found in the leg; it is called the "femur." On Diagram B, find the arrow that points to the femur. Label that arrow "femur."

13. There are two bones in the lower leg; the thicker bone is called the "tibia." On Diagram B, arrow C points to the tibia. Label arrow C "tibia."

14. The thinner bone in the lower leg is called the "fibula." On Diagram B, find the arrow that points to the fibula. Label that arrow "fibula."

15. The bone in the foot that makes the heel is called the "calcaneus." On Diagram B, find the arrow that points to the calcaneus. Label that arrow "calcaneus."

16. The hips are made of three bones; together, they are called the "pelvic girdle." On Diagram B, find the arrow that points to the hip. Label that arrow "pelvic girdle."

Level One Questions:

1. The bones that form a cage around the chest are called the _____.

2. The longest bone in the body is called the _____.

3. The general term for all of the bones in the head is _____.

4. The spinal column is made of many small _____ stacked one on top of another.

5. The longest bone in the arm is the _____.

6. The common name for the scapula is _____.

7. How many bones are in the wrist? _____

8. The bones that make the palm are called _____.

9. What are the wrist bones called? _____

10. Where on the hand are the phalanges located? _____

11. The bone that attaches to the scapula is called the _____.

12. A bone found above the eyes is the _____ bone.

13. The thinner bone in the lower leg is the _____.

14. The thicker bone in the lower leg is the _____.

15. On what part of the skeleton is the calcaneus found? _____

Level Two Questions:

16. Another set of bones, similar to the carpals, are called "tarsals." What part of the foot do the tarsals make? (You can probably guess easily; if not, use a skeleton model to help you to answer this question.)

    _____

17. On the foot, the short bones that are similar to the metacarpals are called "metatarsals." What part of the foot do the metatarsals make? (Guess first; then use a skeleton model to check.)

    _____

Level Three Questions:

18. The lower arm has two long bones, the ulna and the radius. Why do you think it is necessary to have two bones in the lower arm instead of just one?

    _____

    _____

19. Many murder mysteries feature a corpse with a dagger through its ribs; obviously, the ribs do not do a perfect job of protecting the organs inside them. Better protection could be provided by a solid bony case like the skull; can you see any disadvantages in such an arrangement? Explain.

_____

_____

_____

20. Suppose your brain were protected only by a set of bones with openings between them, like the ribs. Would this be satisfactory? Explain your answer.

_____

_____

_____

3–9. THE FROG SKELETON

Instructions for Project One: (1.) Read the text. (2.) Complete the project. (3.) Use the text and the project to help you to answer the questions.

In many ways, the frog skeleton is similar to the human skeleton; most of the frog's bones have the same names as the corresponding bones on the human skeleton. One major difference between the two skeletons involves the bones in the lower leg: the frog's tibia and fibula are fused to make one bone, called the "tibio-fibula bone." The tibio-fibula bone is labeled on the diagram.

While completing this project, you will compare the frog skeleton with the human skeleton, noting both similarities and differences.

To complete this project—

☐ Observe the human skeleton you have labeled and compare it with the diagram on this page.

☐ Use the following word list to help you to label the diagram.

☐ a. cranium   ☐ c. spinal column   ☐ e. femur

☐ b. humerus   ☐ d. pelvic girdle

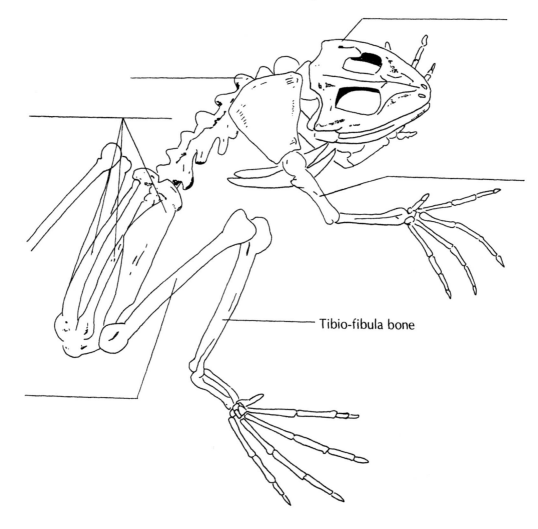

Tibio-fibula bone

Level One Questions:

1. Of the five bones you were asked to compare, which ones were similar in both skeletons?

   _____

2. Describe a major difference between the frog skeleton and the human skeleton.

   _____

   _____

Level Two Question:

3. Why is the bone in the lower leg of the frog called the "tibio-fibula bone"?

   _____

   _____

Level Three Question:

4. In the human skeleton there are two bones in the lower leg. Why do you think the frog skeleton has only one?

   _____

   _____

Instructions for Project Two: (1.) Read the text. (2.) Complete the project.

Just for fun, pretend that giant frogs ruled the Earth 400 million years ago and that you are a modern paleontologist studying them. In an Arizona canyon you stumble upon some large fossilized bones. After carefully removing them from the rock formations, you ship them to your laboratory for reconstruction. After study, you determine that the reconstructed skeleton belonged to a giant amphibian you tentatively name *Frogus bigus.*

To complete this project—

☐ Use scissors to cut out the bones.

☐ Paste the bones on a sheet of paper the way you think they go together.

☐ Sketch in any missing bones and color them to look as though they are made of clay.

☐ Use the first project in this set to help you to label your reconstructed skeleton.

   Just for fun—

☐ The International Paleontological Society will, of course, want to honor you by renaming your discovery (using some form of your last name). Do you have a suggestion for a new name for *Frogus bigus?*

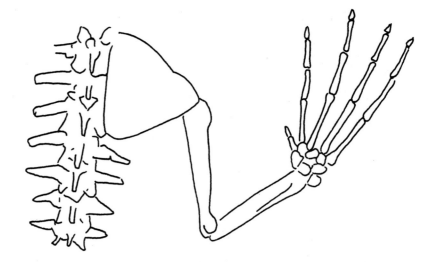

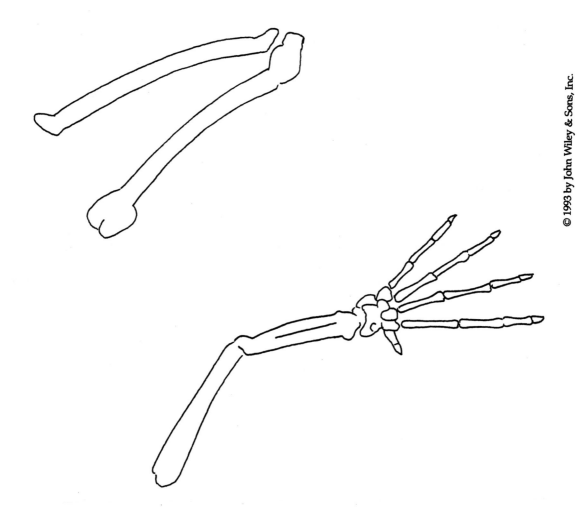

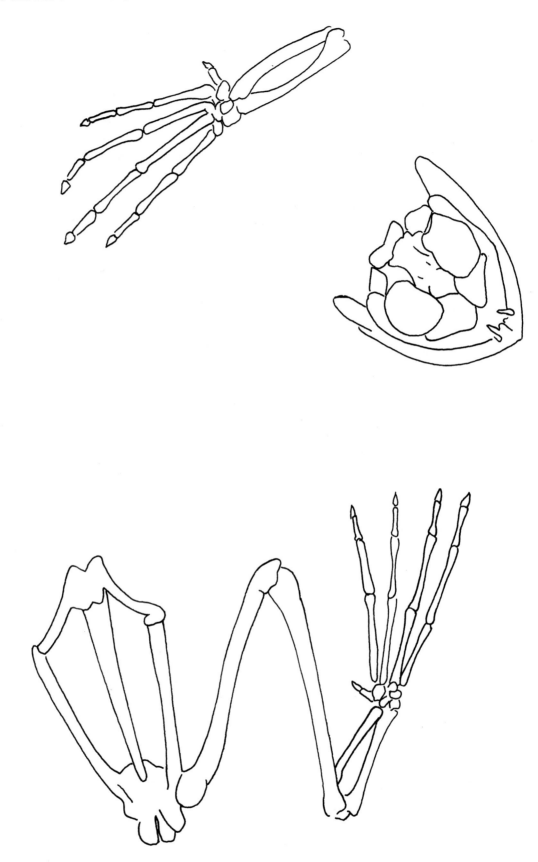

3–10. JOINTS

Instructions: (1.) Read the text. (2.) Use the text to help you to answer the questions.

It is possible for you to move because your skeleton is made of many connected bones. Your leg, for example, is marvelously flexible; at least part of the reason for its flexibility is that it is made of three main bones. Stand up, stiffen your leg, and take a few steps; can you imagine how difficult walking would be if your leg consisted of just one bone instead of three?

The skeleton can twist, turn, pivot and rotate because its bones are connected by joints. A very few joints (those in the cranium, for example) allow no movement, and some (like those in the sternum) allow flexibility but no noticeable movement. Most joints, however, allow at least one kind of movement. At the elbow, for example, the lower arm can swing back and forth like a hinged door; the elbow is classified as a hinge joint. Other types of joints include pivot joints, gliding joints, and ball-and-socket joints.

Level One Questions:

1. Movement is possible because your skeleton is made of many _____.

2. The leg is made of _____ main bones.

3. What are some of the things you would be unable to do if your leg were made of just one bone instead of three?

   _____

   _____

   _____

4. Make a list of four kinds of joints.

   a. _____

   b. _____

   c. _____

   d. _____

Level Two Questions:

5. Each finger is made of three bones. What actions would be impossible if each finger were made of just one straight bone?

   _____

   _____

   _____

6. The elbow is an example of a hinge joint. Where else on the skeleton are hinge joints located? (You may use a model skeleton to help you to answer this question.)

_____

_____

Level Three Questions:

7. More than half of the bones and joints of the skeleton are located in the hands and feet. Is this necessary? Explain your answer.

_____

_____

8. The doctor says that John injured his radio-carpal joint. Where on his skeleton was John injured?

_____

9. The joints between the phalanges are classified as hinge joints, but the joints between the metacarpals and the phalanges are different. Can you identify the latter set and explain the difference?

_____

_____

_____

_____

3–11. IDENTIFYING THE JOINTS

Instructions: (1.) Carefully read the statements. (2.) Use the statements to help you to determine which box contains a certain joint. (3.) Use the statements and the boxes to help you to answer the questions.

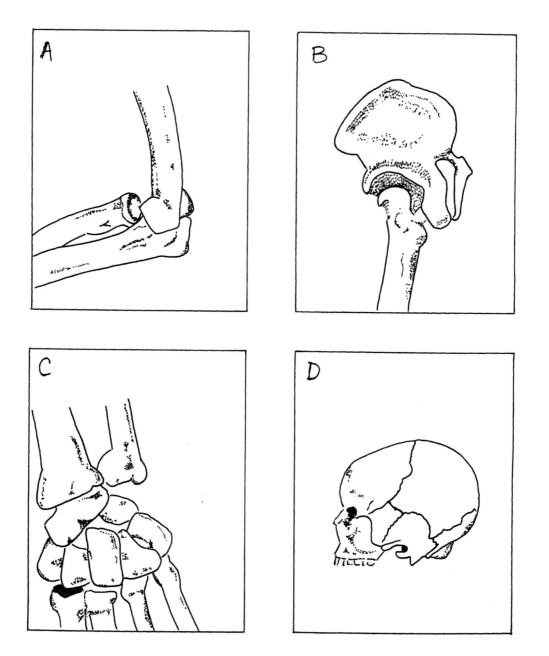

Statements

1. A highly movable joint is located between the femur and the hip; it is called a "ball-and-socket" joint, and it allows movement in all directions. Which box (A, B, C, D) shows a ball-and-socket joint?

2. Not all joints permit movement. The bones in the skull, for example, are held firmly in place by jagged joints called "sutures." This type of joint helps to make the skull a strong shell for protecting the brain. Which box shows a suture?

3. Some joints, like the hinge joint in the elbow, allow the bones to move back and forth like doors on hinges. Which box shows a hinge joint?

4. Gliding joints allow the bones to slide in all directions. Because the carpal bones in the wrist have gliding joints, the hand is very flexible. Which box shows a gliding joint?

Level One Questions:

1. The joint between the femur and the hip is called a _____ joint.

2. Which joint allows movement in all directions? _____

3. Which kind of joint allows the elbow to swing back and forth? _____

4. Which kind of joint allows bones to slide? _____

Level Two Question:

(You may use a model of a skeleton to help you answer the remaining questions.)

5. A ball-and-socket joint is located between the femur and the hip. Where else on the skeleton is there a ball-and-socket joint?

_____

Level Three Questions:

6. How do you think the ball-and-socket joint got its name?

_____

_____

7. A pivot joint allows you to turn your forearm so that the palm faces up. Between which two bones in the forearm is that pivot joint?

_____

8. The tarsal bones are similar to the carpal bones in the hand. Which type of joint would you expect to find between the carpal bones?

_____

3–12. EXPOSING THE SYNOVIAL SAC

Instructions: (1.) Read the text. (2.) Complete the investigation. (3.) Use the text and the diagrams to help you to answer the questions.

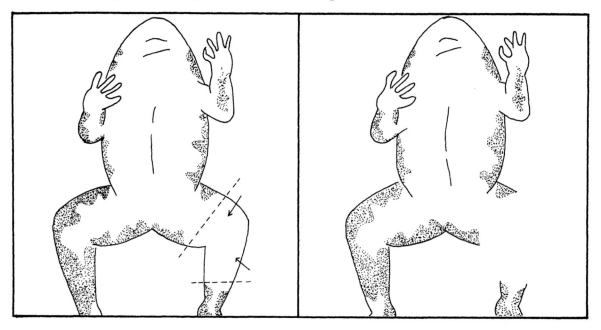

Diagram A   Diagram B

Friction between two rubbing objects produces heat; that is why you can warm your hands a little on a cold winter day by rubbing them briskly together. Most of the time, however, friction is harmful and is something to be avoided. The motor in your car, for example, would be damaged if its moving parts were not protected from friction by engine oil.

At a joint, bones rub against one another; if they are not protected from friction, surrounding tissues will become inflamed, swollen, and painful. Fortunately, the ends of bones are covered by smooth tissue that acts like a bearing and reduces friction. This strong, flexible tissue is called "cartilage."

Cartilage does not completely protect the joints from friction, and so nearly all joints are enclosed in sacs filled with a slippery liquid similar to egg white. This fluid is called "synovial fluid," and the sac that holds it is called the "synovial sac." Synovial fluid helps in much the same way that oil protects your car's motor: When the synovial sac is intact, the fluid prevents the cartilage from wearing down and reduces friction between two bones to almost zero.

By carefully removing the muscles from the knee joint on your frog, you will see what a synovial sac actually looks like. The synovial sac that you will be observing protects the knee joint (between the femur and the tibio-fibula bones).

Procedure

Obtain the following materials:

☐ preserved frog
☐ forceps or tweezers

☐ scalpel or single-edged razor blade
☐ dissecting pan

1. Place your preserved frog on its dorsal (back) side in a dissecting pan.
2. Carefully study Diagram A. The arrows and dashed lines on the left leg indicate where you are to remove its skin and muscles.
3. Using a scalpel, carefully remove the skin and muscles shown between the dashed lines on Diagram A. Be careful not to cut the white glistening tissue surrounding the knee; this is the synovial sac.

   To complete this project—

☐ Observe your dissected specimen.
☐ On Diagram B, sketch and label the femur, the tibio-fibula bone, and the synovial sac.

Level One Questions:

1. Friction between two rubbing objects produces _____.

2. In what way can friction be useful?

   _____

   _____

3. In what way can friction be harmful?

   _____

   _____

4. What happens if bones are not protected from friction?

   _____

   _____

5. How does cartilage protect bones from friction?

   _____

   _____

6. The synovial sac also protects bones from friction. Describe its structure and contents.

   _____

   _____

   _____

7. The diagram on the next sheet shows two bones being protected from friction. What structure does arrow A point to?

   _____

8. What does arrow B point to? _____

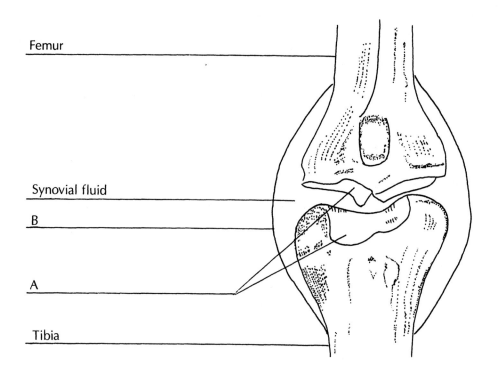

Femur

Synovial fluid

B

A

Tibia

Level Two Question:

9. The space shuttles seem to have a backup system for each of their primary systems; in case one fails, the other goes into action. Is the synovial sac merely a backup system for the cartilage in a joint or are both needed? Explain.

_____

_____

_____

_____

Level Three Question:

10. Rheumatoid arthritis is a crippling disease of the joints. Sometimes a sufferer from this disease will say that he or she can feel the ends of the bones rubbing together. What do you assume has happened?

_____

_____

_____

_____

Unit 4

Muscles

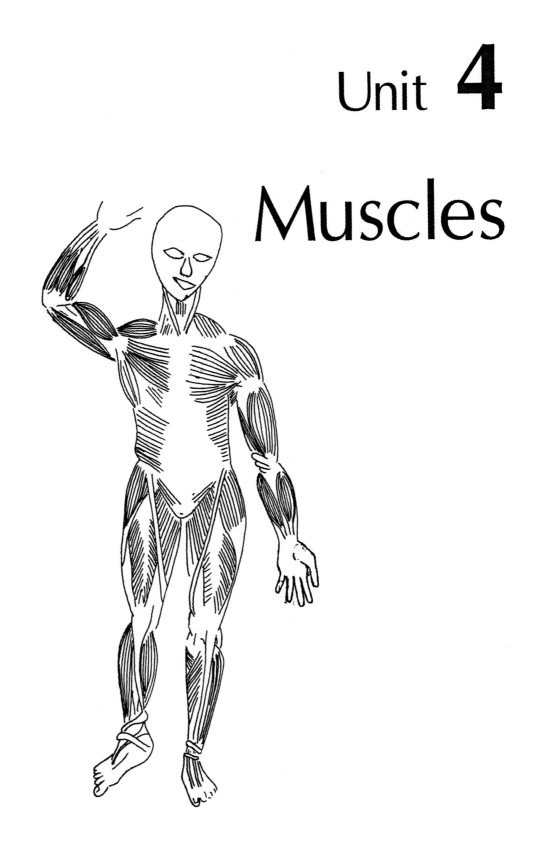

TEACHER'S GUIDE TO UNIT 4 _____

4–1 OBSERVING SKELETAL MUSCLES THROUGH THE MICROSCOPE

Teaching Suggestions:

1. Emphasize that the microscopic structure of the frog's muscles are similar to the human's.
2. Demonstrate the laboratory procedures.

Answers to the Questions:

Level One

1. connective
2. They have wavy lines that can be seen through the microscope.

4–2 IDENTIFYING THE FROG'S MUSCLES

Note: This activity gives students an opportunity to observe and identify actual muscles.

Teaching Suggestion:

Demonstrate all lab procedures.

Answers to the Questions:

Level One

1. muscle
2. 600
3. shapes

Level Two

4. Answers will vary—rotate, shrug, other things that students may notice and describe in their own ways.

Level Three

5. Answers will vary. Basically no, because muscles move in more than one way and influence the actions of other muscles.

4–3 THE MUSCLES OF THE HUMAN BODY

Note: This is a self-directed activity.

Teaching Suggestion:

Show these muscles, using a model of a human torso.

Answers to the Questions:

Level One

1. trapezius
2. deltoid
3. sartoris
4. biceps femoris
5. gastrocnemius
6. biceps femoris
7. rectus femoris
8. biceps brachii
9. triceps brachii
10. trapezius
11. latissimus dorsi
12. sartoris
13. pectoralis major

4–4 VOCABULARY: THE MUSCLES

Note: This is a self-directed activity.

Answers to Puzzle:

Across

2. bicepsbrachii
4. tricepsbrachii
7. gastrocnemius
9. trapezius
10. sartoris

Down

1. latissimusdorsi
3 pectoralismajor
5. bicepsfemoris
6. rectusfemoris
8. deltoid

4–5 NAMING MUSCLE MOVEMENTS

Note: This is a self-directed activity.

Teaching Suggestions:

1. Use a human skeleton (or a model) and a model of the human torso to help you to demonstrate the muscle movements.

2. Use a large rubber band to demonstrate muscle movement. Hold the ends of the broken rubber band against the upper end of the humerus and the lower end of the radius; it will, of course, be stretched quite a bit. Let the natural pull of the rubber band bring the lower arm toward the humerus.

Answers to Statement Questions

Level One

1. a. to turn
   b. rotators
   c. sternocleidomastoids
2. d. flexion
   e. flexors
   f. flexor digitorum profundus
3. g. flexion
   h. straighten body parts
   i. extensor digitorum communis
4. j. to move a body part away from the body
   k. deltoid
5. l. to bring a body part toward the body
   m. pectoralis major

Level Two

6. Answers will vary; essentially, for precision or to avoid confusion.
7. adductors
8. abductors

Level Three

9. Answers will vary. They may include the ideas that a single muscle may attach to more than one bone, may pull the body part in more than one direction, and may work with other muscles (here, deep muscles in the back).
10. a. region two
    b. region one
11. Answers will vary. Basically, rotation requires movement in more than one direction. (Think of a trucker's steering wheel, with one of those little handles that stick out. Imagine tying a light rope to the handle; now pull it in any *single* direction. The wheel doesn't go far, does it?)

4–6 TENDONS

Notes:

1. This investigation will fascinate many of your students. They will enjoy watching some of the more observable muscles and tendons, and you may want to suggest that they feel (between fingers and thumb) the tendons in their wrists.

2. You may want to remind them that the muscles and tendons involved in this observation are not the only ones that contribute to hand movement. The deep muscles are also important, but they are more difficult to observe and are not mentioned in this worksheet.

Teaching Suggestions:

1. Demonstrate the procedure for flexing the hand and fingers.
2. From a butcher, obtain a chicken foot and expose its tendons. Demonstrate the action of these tendons by pulling on them; this will cause the toes to close.

Answers to the Questions:

Level One

1. Most students will answer yes. (A plump student may not agree, and an occasional student will not recognize his or her tendons without assistance.)
2. Most students will answer yes.
3. Answers will vary. Students will be so busy watching the tendons that they may not pay much attention to the muscle as it tightens and relaxes. Point out the muscle— beginning two to three inches above the wrist and extending the length of the forearm—and ask each student to lay his or her other hand on it and feel it in action. Then encourage students to be creative in describing what they see and feel.
4. Most students will answer yes.
5. Most students will answer yes.

Level Three

6. Answers will vary. Students are likely to say "because there isn't room in the hand," and that's partially true; but the length of the muscle is important in giving strength to the hand, and the muscle needs to be attached to and to pull from another body part.
7. tendon C

4–7 THE FLEXORS AND EXTENSORS OF THE FROG'S LEG

Teaching Suggestions:

1. Demonstrate all laboratory procedures.
2. Use a dissected frog to demonstrate the action of the gastrocnemius. Gently pulling on this muscle will flex the frog's foot.

Answers to the Questions:

Level One

1. flexor
2. extensor

Level Two

3. extensor
4. flexor

Level Three

5. Answers will vary; essentially, by the sudden and forceful backward motion.
6. (Highly condensed version) Achilles was the son of Peleus (a mortal) and Thetis (a sea-nymph). When he was an infant, his mother dipped him in the Styx, which rendered him immortal except in the heel by which she held him. Ultimately (after he had been a hero in the Trojan War), he was fatally wounded in the heel by an arrow shot by Paris, Hector's younger brother—or perhaps by a god masquerading as Paris.

Name _____   Date _____

4–1. OBSERVING SKELETAL MUSCLE THROUGH THE MICROSCOPE

Instructions: (1.) Read the text. (2.) Carefully watch and listen as your teacher shows you how to prepare the microscope slide. (3.) Use the text and your observations to help you to complete the project and answer the questions.

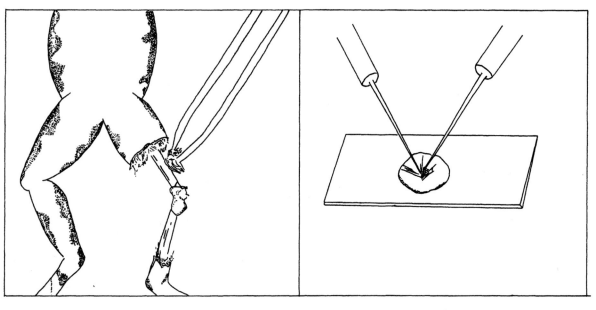

Procedure 4   Procedure 5

When you dissect the powerful leg muscles of a frog, they look like bundles of fibers. What you see are actually muscle cells held together by connective tissue, and you must tease them apart before you can see the individual cells. While doing this investigation you will use two dissecting needles to separate the muscle cells before you look at them through the microscope.

Using 100X magnification, you will see the muscle cells quite clearly. You may have to adjust the light by turning the iris adjustment on the microscope, but if you observe carefully you will see wavy lines that look as though someone had left his fingerprints on the sarcolemma (cell membrane).

Procedure

1. Obtain the following materials:
   - ☐ preserved frog
   - ☐ dissecting pan
   - ☐ dissecting kit
   - ☐ jar of water
   - ☐ microscope slide
   - ☐ cover slip
   - ☐ microscope

2. Lay your preserved frog on its dorsal (back) side in the dissecting pan.

3. Place a drop of water on the microscope slide.

4. Using forceps (tweezers) from your dissecting kit, remove a small amount of fibrous tissue from the cut muscle surrounding the exposed synovial sac.

5. Place these fibers on the drop of water and use two dissecting needles to tease the muscle fibers apart.

6. Before you place the slide on the microscope, remember to place a cover slip on top of the fibers.

7. Place the slide on the microscope and focus to 100X.

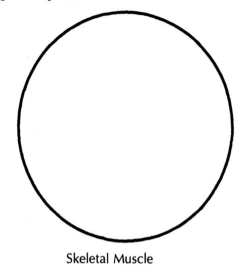

Skeletal Muscle

To complete this project—

☐ In this circle, accurately sketch what you see in one field of vision.

Level One Questions:

1. Groups of muscle cells are held together by _____ tissue.

2. Why are skeletal muscle cells called "striated muscle fibers"?

_____

_____

_____

4–2. IDENTIFYING THE FROG'S MUSCLES

Instructions: (1.) Read the text. (2.) Carefully watch as your teacher shows you how to remove the skin from the frog. (3.) Follow the steps here. (4.) Use the text and your observations to help you to answer the questions.

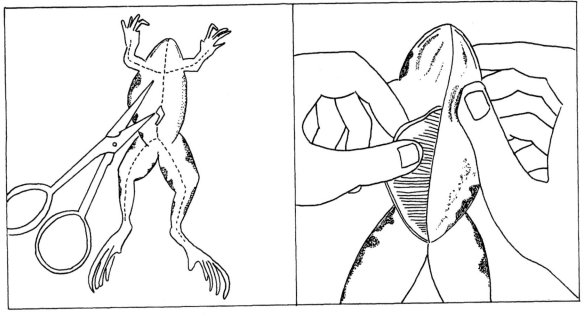

Step 3   Step 4

A single muscle fiber cannot move a heavy bone; thousands of muscle fibers must work together. When they work as a single unit, they are called simply "a muscle."

Just over 600 muscles are attached to your skeleton. By pulling the bones, they are able to make your body move in different ways. Certain muscles attached to your scapula, for example, allow you to rotate your shoulders; you can shrug your shoulders by contracting (shortening) a different set of muscles. (Try those simple, familiar motions and think about the remarkable things your muscles are doing.)

The muscles on the frog are easy to identify because most of them have well-defined shapes. While doing this investigation, you will use a muscle map to help you to identify a few of the muscles on your preserved frog.

Procedure

1. Obtain the following materials:
   - ☐ preserved frog
   - ☐ dissecting kit
   - ☐ dissecting pan
   - ☐ colored pins
2. Lay the frog on its dorsal (back) side in the dissecting pan.
3. Using scissors, carefully cut the skin. Use the dashed lines in the diagram as your guide.
4. Using your fingers and forceps (tweezers), slowly remove the skin from both sides.

To complete this project—

☐ Lay your frog on its ventral (belly) side and compare the muscles you see with the muscles on the muscle map.

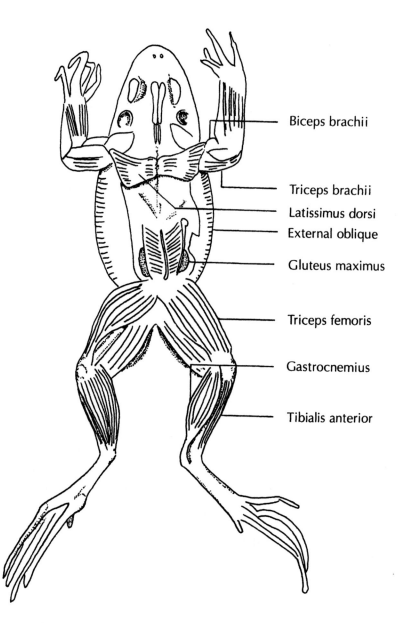

Biceps brachii

Triceps brachii

Latissimus dorsi

External oblique

Gluteus maximus

Triceps femoris

Gastrocnemius

Tibialis anterior

Stick the pins into your specimen as follows:

☐ Stick the red pin into the biceps brachii.

☐ Stick the yellow pin into the gluteus maximus.

☐ Stick the brown pin into the gastrocnemius.

☐ Stick the blue pin into the tibialis anterior.

Level One Questions:

1. It takes thousands of muscle fibers working together as a contracting unit called a

   _____ to move the bones.

2. Just over _____ muscles are attached to your skeleton.

3. The muscles on the frog are easy to identify because they have well-defined _____

   _____.

Level Two Question:

4. List at least three ways in which you can move your shoulders.

   _____

   _____

   _____

Level Three Question:

5. There are more than 600 muscles on the human skeleton; does this mean that there are only about 600 ways in which the skeleton can move? Explain your answer.

   _____

   _____

   _____

   _____

4–3. THE MUSCLES OF THE HUMAN BODY

Instructions: (1.) Read the text and the statements. (2.) Use the text and the statements to help you to label the diagram and answer the questions.

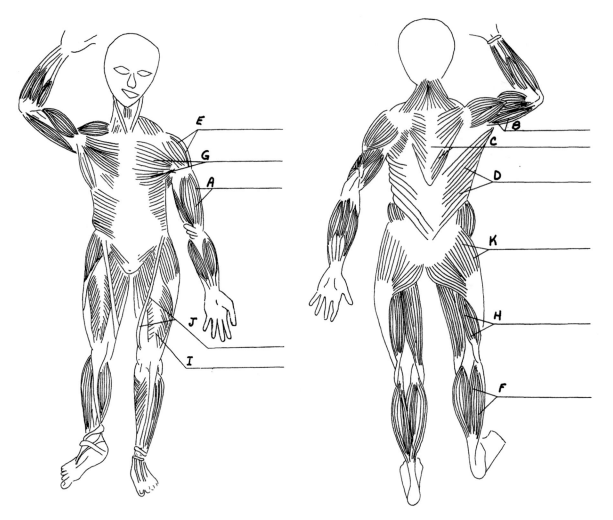

Think of the different ways in which you can move your body. While throwing a ball, for example, you grip with your fingers, raise your arm, bend your wrist, and arch your back. Suddenly your arm swings down, your wrist moves forward, your back flexes, your fingers straighten, and you release the ball. You continually shift your weight and reposition your legs; your shoulders and your other arm move to accommodate the throwing movement and to keep and maintain balance; your head moves as you watch the target or the flight of the ball.

All of these movements happen because the muscles in your arm, neck, shoulder, back, trunk, legs, hands, and feet are attached to your skeleton, and these muscles pull your bones. In this project, you will learn to name and describe some of the major muscles that move your skeleton.

Descriptions

1. One muscle that you are probably familiar with is the biceps brachii. When you bend your arm to show how strong you are, this is the muscle that pops up. (Brachii looks plural, and it is, in a way; it refers to a muscle that has two "heads.")

   The biceps brachii can move the arm in another way. By pulling the radius (one of the two bones in the lower arm), it helps to rotate the lower arm, causing the palm of the hand to turn upward. Arrow A points to the biceps brachii. Label arrow A "biceps brachii."

2. After the biceps brachii bends the arm, another muscle must straighten the arm to its original position. This muscle, called the "triceps brachii," is located just opposite the biceps brachii. Arrow B points to the triceps brachii. Label arrow B "triceps brachii."

3. The trapezius is a large, triangular muscle located on the upper back. Since this broad muscle attaches to the back of the skull and the scapulae (plural of scapula), it lets you tilt your head backward and shrug your shoulders. Arrow C points to the trapezius. Label arrow C "trapezius."

4. The large, broad muscle covering the lower back is called the "latissimus dorsi." Although this muscle helps to move the shoulders, its most important job is to move the arm by pulling on the upper end of the humerus (the upper arm bone). Arrow D points to the latissimus dorsi. Label arrow D "latissimus dorsi."

5. The deltoid muscle helps you to lift your arm above your head. This large, triangular muscle is what makes your shoulders look round. Arrow E points to the deltoid muscle. Label arrow E "deltoid."

6. The gastrocnemius is a large muscle that forms the calf of your lower leg; it also helps to bend your leg at the knee joint and to lift you onto your toes. Arrow F points to the gastrocnemius. Label arrow F "gastrocnemius."

7. The pectoralis major, which helps to move your arm toward your body, is a broad muscle that travels across your chest and attaches to the humerus. Arrow G points to the pectoralis major. Label arrow G "pectoralis major."

8. When you prepare to kick a ball, your knee joint bends and your lower leg is pulled back by the muscles that belong to the hamstring group. The biceps femoris—one of the hamstring muscles—can easily be seen on the back of your leg. Arrow H points to the biceps femoris. Label arrow H "biceps femoris."

9. After your leg is pulled back, it must swing quickly forward to kick the ball. A muscle on the front of your leg, called the "rectus femoris," pulls your lower leg rapidly forward, bringing the foot into contact with the ball. Arrow I points to the rectus femoris. Label arrow I "rectus femoris."

10. At some time you have surely sat on the floor "Indian style" or cross-legged; you may be interested to know that the muscle that brings your leg outward and over (making this position possible) is the sartoris. It is a thin band that crosses over the thigh. Arrow J points to the sartoris. Label arrow J "sartoris."

11. The gluteus maximus is the large muscle that forms the buttocks. The fibers of this muscle shorten when you stand and then lengthen slowly to let you sit down gently. Arrow K points to the gluteus maximus. Label arrow K "gluteus maximus."

Level One Questions:

1. The muscle that tilts your head backward is the _____.

2. The triangular muscle that helps you to lift your arm above your head is the

    _____.

3. The _____ is a thin band of muscle that crosses over the thigh.

4. A muscle that is part of the hamstring group is the _____.

5. The muscle that helps to lift you onto your toes is the _____.

6. The muscle that pulls your leg back as you prepare to kick a ball is the _____

    _____.

7. The muscle that pulls your leg rapidly forward so that you can kick the ball is the

    _____.

8. The muscle that pops up when you bend your arm to show your muscles is the

    _____.

9. The muscle that straightens your arm is the _____.

10. The muscle that shrugs your shoulders is the _____.

11. The broad muscle that covers your lower back is the _____.

12. The muscle that helps you to sit "Indian style" is the _____.

13. The muscle that helps you to move your arm toward your body is the _____

    _____.

4–4. VOCABULARY: THE MUSCLES

Part I: Crossword Puzzle

Instructions: Use the last project, "The Muscles of the Human Body," to help you to find the answers to this puzzle. (*Note:* If the answer has two or more words, *do not* leave spaces between the words.)

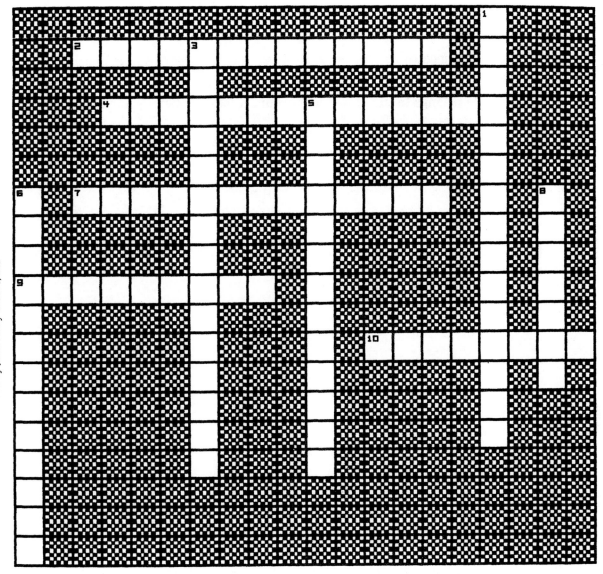

Across

2. This pops up when you show off your muscles.

4. This muscle helps to straighten your arm.

7. This muscle helps to lift you onto your toes. It also forms the calf of your leg.

9. This muscle of the upper back helps you to shrug your shoulders.

10. This muscle lets you bring your leg outward and over, so that you can sit "Indian style."

Down

1. This muscle is located in your back. It moves your shoulders and humerus.

3. This muscle crosses your chest and helps to move your arm toward your body.

5. This muscle belongs to the hamstring group. It lets you bend your leg at the knee joint.

6. This muscle is on the front of your leg. It rapidly swings the leg forward so that you can kick a ball.

8. This large, triangular muscle helps you to raise your hand above your head.

Part II: Flash Cards

Instructions: (1.) Cut out these cards. (2.) Use the clues from the crossword puzzle to help you to write the definitions on the backs of these cards. (3.) Study these cards until you have learned the terms on them.

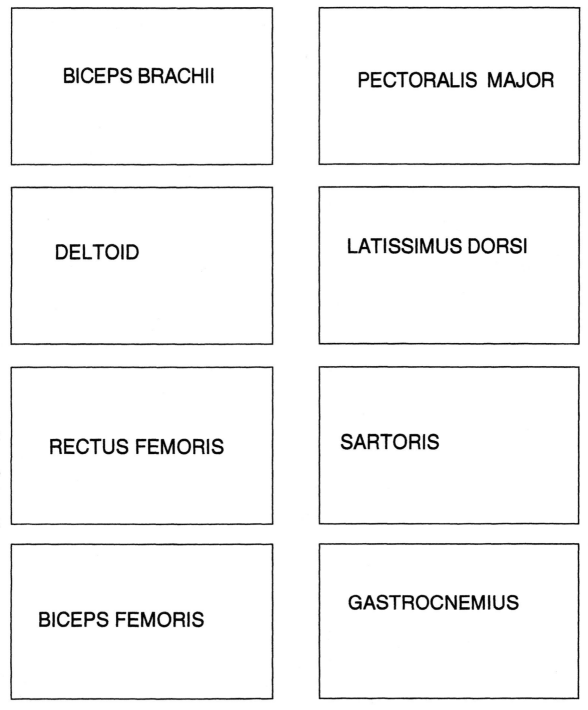

BICEPS BRACHII

PECTORALIS MAJOR

DELTOID

LATISSIMUS DORSI

RECTUS FEMORIS

SARTORIS

BICEPS FEMORIS

GASTROCNEMIUS

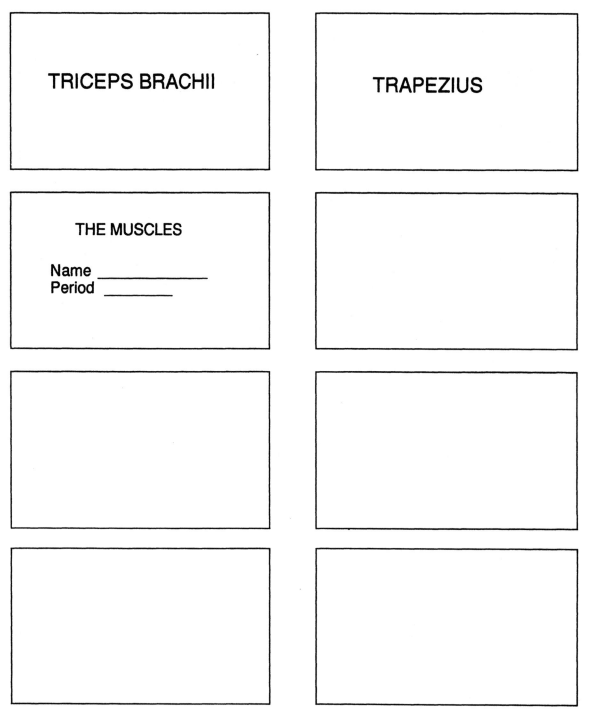

TRICEPS BRACHII

TRAPEZIUS

THE MUSCLES

Name _____
Period _____

4–5. NAMING MUSCLE MOVEMENTS

Instructions: (1.) Read the text and the statements. (2.) Use the text, the statements, and the diagrams to help you to answer the questions that follow each statement. (3.) Use what you have learned to help you to answer the questions.

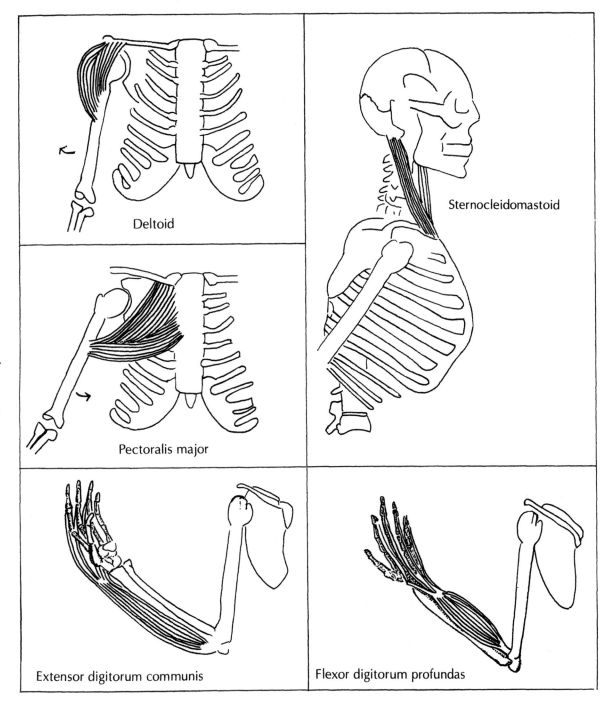

Deltoid

Sternocleidomastoid

Pectoralis major

Extensor digitorum communis

Flexor digitorum profundas

Because phrases like "the leg bends backward" or "the arm moves swiftly forward" are not very precise, scientists and doctors use special terms that accurately describe how a muscle does its job. The diagrams with this project will help you to learn how to use these terms.

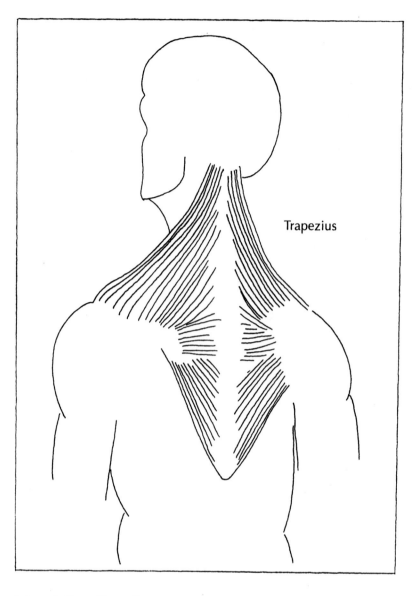

Trapezius

Statements and Level One Questions:

1. The term *rotate* means "to turn." Muscles that turn the parts of the body are called "rotators." On the neck, for example, there are two muscles, the sternoclei-domastoids, that rotate the head.

   a. What does the term *rotate* mean? _____

   b. Muscles that turn the parts of the body are called _____.

   c. Name two muscles on the neck that allow you to rotate your head.

   _____

2. Muscles that bend body parts at a joint are called "flexors," and their bending action is called "flexion." Certain muscles in your forearm allow you to bend or flex your hand at the wrist joint.

   d. Bending action at a joint is called _____

e. Muscles that bend body parts are called _____.

f. Use the diagrams to help you to determine which muscle flexes the hand. Write the name of this muscle.

_____

3. Extension is the opposite of flexion. Body parts that are bent by flexors are straightened by extensors. An extensor, therefore, is a muscle that straightens a body part at a joint.

g. Extension is the opposite of _____.

h. Describe what extensors do. _____

_____

i. Use the diagrams to help you to determine which muscle extends the hand.

Write the name of this muscle. _____

4. The term *abduct* means to move a body part away from the body. If you move your arm away from your side, you are abducting your arm.

j. What does the term *abduct* mean?

_____

k. Use the diagrams to help you to determine which muscle abducts the arm.

Write the name of this muscle. _____

5. Bringing a body part toward the body is adduction. If you move your arm to your side, you have adducted your arm.

l. What does the term *adduct* mean?

_____

m. Use the diagram to help you to determine which muscle adducts the arm.

Write the name of this muscle. _____

To complete this project—

Because not all of its muscle fibers travel in the same direction, the trapezius is divided into regions. Study the diagram carefully; then identify and color the three regions as follows:

a. The fibers in region one sweep upward from the shoulder to the base of the skull. Locate the fibers in region one and color them yellow.

b. The fibers in region two run horizontally (straight across). Locate the fibers in region two and color them red.

c. The fibers in region three travel downward and end in a point. Locate the fibers in region three and color them green.

Level Two Questions:

6. Why do scientists and doctors use special terms to describe the different ways in which the muscles can move the bones of the skeleton?

   _____

   _____

7. The muscles that rotate the head are called "rotators," and the muscles that allow a joint to bend are called "flexors." What are the muscles called that bring a body part toward the body?

   _____

8. What are the muscles called that move a body part away from the body?

   _____

Level Three Questions:

9. It is possible for a single muscle to move a body part in more than one way. Explain how this is possible. (Use the diagram of the trapezius to help you to answer this question.)

   _____

   _____

   _____

10. While completing this worksheet, you learned to use the terms *flexion, extension, rotation, abduction,* and *adduction.* Following are more terms used to describe how the muscles can move the skeleton. Use the diagram that you colored to help you to identify the regions responsible for these movements.

   a. The term *retract* means "to draw back." Which region of the trapezius is responsible for drawing back the shoulders?

      _____

   b. The term *elevate* means "to raise." Which region of the trapezius muscle is responsible for elevating the shoulders?

      _____

11. Regions one and two assist each other in rotating the shoulders. Explain why it takes both of these regions to accomplish this movement.

   _____

   _____

   _____

4–6. TENDONS

Instructions: (1.) Carefully read the text and complete the investigation. (2.) Use the text and your observations to help you to answer the questions.

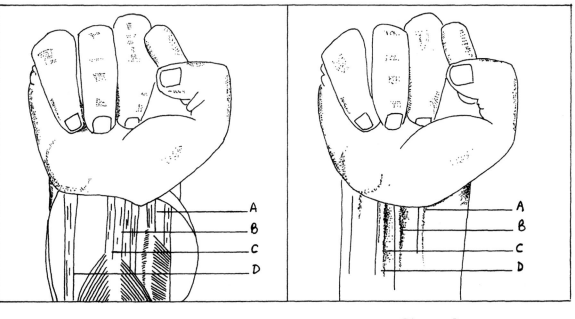

Diagram A   Diagram B

To move the skeleton, the muscles must be firmly attached to the bones by strong, inelastic tissues called "tendons."

The muscles that operate the hand and fingers are located on the forearm. These muscles have long, cordlike tendons attached to the bones in the hand. Flex and extend your hand and fingers and watch these tendons at work.

Special note: The muscles and tendons you observe are not the only ones that move your hand and fingers.

To complete this investigation—

☐ 1. Lay your right forearm, hand, and fingers firmly against the lab table with your palm up.

☐ 2. Close your hand, making a tight fist. Slowly, with as much tension as possible, flex your wrist by moving your hand upward. Watch the tendons in your wrist pull your hand.

☐ 3. With the back of your hand firmly against the lab table, flex your fingers—one at a time—while you watch the tendons in your wrist and the muscles in your forearm. (Remember to do this with as much tension as possible.)

Level One Questions:

1. While flexing your hand, were you able to see the four tendons illustrated in Diagram B? (Flex your hand again if you are not sure.)

    Yes   No   (Circle one.)

2. While flexing your hand, were you able to see the muscles in your forearm move? (Flex your hand again if you are not sure.)

    Yes   No   (Circle one.)

3. The muscles in your forearm and the tendons in your wrist work together. Using the terms *flexing* and *extending,* describe what you observed.

    _____

    _____

4. While flexing your fingers, did you see the tendons in your forearm move? (Flex them again if you need to.)

    Yes   No   (Circle one.)

5. While flexing your fingers, did you see the muscles in your forearm move?

    Yes   No   (Circle one.)

Level Three Questions:

6. Why are the muscles that flex the hand located in the forearm instead of in the hand?

    _____

    _____

7. Only one of the tendons you observed is responsible for moving the fingers. Which tendon flexes the fingers?

    _____

4–7. THE FLEXORS AND EXTENSORS OF THE FROG'S LEG

Instructions: (1.) Read the text and complete the investigation. (2.) Use the text and your observations to help you to answer the questions.

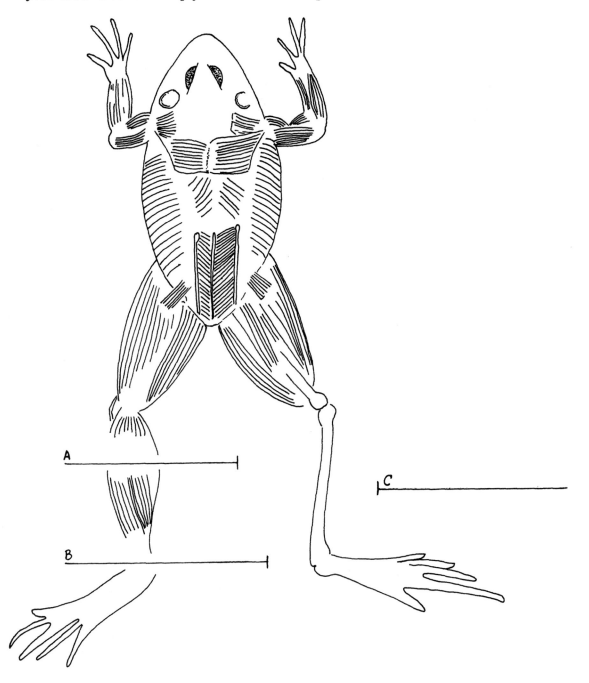

If you have ever watched a frog hop, you have probably noticed that it can make its legs act like springs. First it folds them tightly under its body; then it suddenly straightens its legs and feet and shoots itself into the air.

The frog uses flexor muscles to bend its legs and to position its body; it uses strong extensor muscles to straighten its legs and feet. While doing this investigation, you will identify and sketch the frog's powerful leg muscles.

Step one: Obtain the following materials:

☐ preserved frog

☐ dissecting pan

☐ dissecting kit

Step two: Lay the preserved frog on its ventral (belly) side in the dissecting pan.

Step three: Compare the preserved frog with the diagram on the previous page and carefully sketch the missing muscles on the diagram.

Step four: Arrow A points to the gastrocnemius muscle, which forms the calf of the leg. Notice that a white fibrous tendon attaches this muscle to the foot. Using your fingers, gently pull this muscle and watch the action of the foot.

Step five: Label the diagram.

Label arrow A "gastrocnemius."

Label arrow B "Achilles tendon."

Label arrow C "tibialis anterior."

Level One Questions:

1. The frog uses _____ muscles to bend its legs.

2. It uses _____ muscles to straighten its legs.

Level Two Questions:

3. Is the gastrocnemius a flexor or an extensor muscle? _____

4. Is the tibialis anterior a flexor or an extensor muscle? _____

Level Three Questions:

5. How does the action of the gastrocnemius help to lift the frog into the air?

   _____

   _____

   _____

6. **Bonus points:** The tendon that attaches the gastrocnemius to the foot was named for the Greek god Achilles. Go to the library; look for Greek mythology and read the story about Achilles and how his mother protected him (or nearly all of him) from injury. Write a one-page summary of the story of Achilles and give your explanation of why this tendon was named for him.

Unit 5

The Nervous System

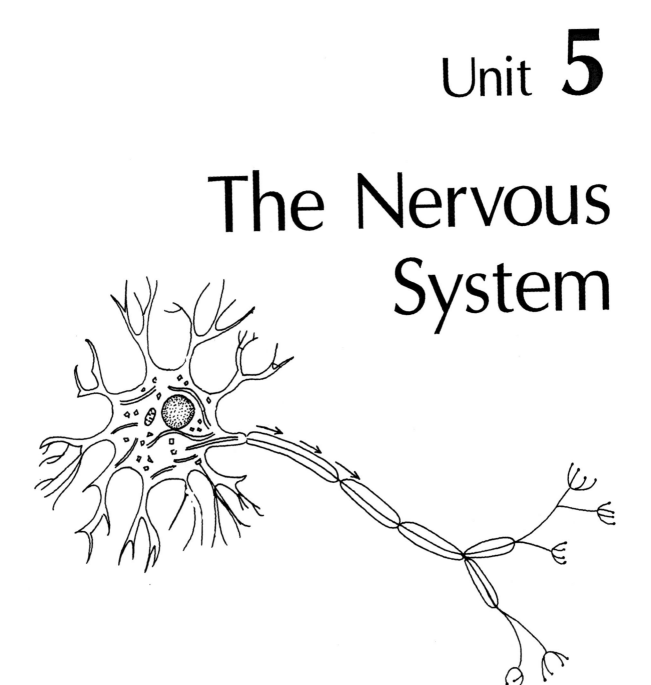

5-1 ELECTRICITY FROM THE BRAIN

Note: This is a self-directed worksheet.

Answers to the Questions:

Level One

1. voluntary
2. under conscious control
3. sends electrochemical signals to your muscles
4. spinal
5. to carry electrochemical messages
6. the muscles contract
7. medial pectoralis
8. no

Level Two

9. pectoralis
10. adducts the arm (brings the arm toward the body)

Level Three

11. Answers will vary. It is to be hoped that students will say that the intention to move is seldom the result of conscious thought; and even when movement is deliberate, the attention tends to be on the result of the movement, not on specific actions of the muscles. Athletes may have somewhat different responses.

5-2 THE STRUCTURE OF THE BRAIN

Note: This is a self-directed activity.

Teaching Suggestion:

Use a model of the brain to show your students its structural features.

Answers to the Questions:

Level One

1. thinking, direction of motor functions, registering sensory perceptions, speech, hearing, vision
2. cerebrum
3. cerebral cortex
4. gyri (plural of gyrus)

5. sulci (plural of sulcus)
6. areas of the brain, defined by sulci (grooves) on the cerebral cortex
7. medulla oblongata
8. cerebellum
9. muscle coordination, helping body to maintain balance

Level Two

10. These folds provide more area while enabling the brain to fit inside the skull. (Students may be interested to know that the surface of the brain, if unfolded, would cover an area approximately equal to the area covered by an average-sized adult's skin.)

Level Three

11. Answers will vary. Students will probably describe the automatic pilot that controls a boat or plane without the direct intervention of a pilot or helmsman and will make the parallel with the brain.
12. cerebrum

5–3 THE PARTS AND FUNCTIONS OF THE FROG'S BRAIN

Note: This investigation gives your students an opportunity to study the structure and function of an actual brain.

Teaching Suggestions:

1. Demonstrate all laboratory procedures.
2. Because the frog's skull is very hard, you will probably want to crack it yourself; your students can then remove the bone fragments. To crack the skull, gently insert the tips of a pair of needle-nosed pliers under the eyes and into the optic orbits. Squeezing the handles gently will crack the skull without damaging the brain. The procedure for doing this is illustrated in step five.

Answers to the Questions:

Level One

1. information
2. olfactory nerve
3. at the front of the brain
4. odors are detected
5. optic lobe
6. optic lobe
7. medulla oblongata
8. receives impulses from different areas of the brain and makes decisions about its environment (or responds to the environment)
9. cerebellum

5–4 THE ANATOMY OF THE NEURON

Note: This is a self-directed activity.

Answers to the Questions:

Level One

1. electrochemical signals
2. muscle will contract
3. soma
4. irregularly shaped particles
5. assembling proteins
6. in the cytoplasm
7. carry proteins and other substances to the cells
8. on the soma
9. directs incoming electrochemical signals toward the soma
10. directs electrochemical signals away from the neuron

Level Two

11. Answers will vary. The students will probably mention something about the distances the electrochemical impulses must travel. Long neurons are especially important in the spinal cord.
12. Answers will vary. They are both long and thin (shaped like a wire). They both carry signals.

Level Three

13. that the neuron uses energy
14. the direction in which electrochemical impulses flow through the neuron

5–5 VOCABULARY: THE NEURON

Note: This is a self-directed activity.

Answers to the Puzzle:

Across

4. microtubules
5. nucleus
6. dendrite

Down

1. axon
2. nisslbody
3. soma

5–6 NERVES

Note: This is a self-directed worksheet.

Answers to the Questions:

Level One

1. trillions
2. in the central nervous system (the brain and spinal cord)
3. large cablelike structure or a bundle of neurons
4. carries both motor and sensory neurons
5. carry stimuli to the central nervous system (brain and spinal cord)
6. carry electrochemical signals from the brain to the muscles (and the organs and glands)

Level Two

7. Nerves are like cables; neurons are like wires.
8. from its location (travels through the middle of the arm)
9. the directions in which electrochemical impulses are traveling

Level Three

10. an axon

5–7 THE SPINAL CORD

Note: This is a self-directed activity.

Answers to the Questions:

Level One

1. an elongated extension of the brain
2. 18 inches
3. large nerves that attach to the spinal cord
4. impulses carrying sensory information
5. impulses carrying motor information
6. a collection of neuron fibers that travel to the same general place
7. sensory
8. motor
9. #2
10. #1
11. dendrites and cell bodies
12. sends sensory impulses for pressure to the sensory area of the brain

Level Two

13. It splits, forming a "Y."
14. Sensory information (pain, touch, pressure, etc.) is sent from the nerve endings to the central nervous system; motor information is sent from the central nervous system to the body.

5-8 OBSERVING THE SPINAL CORD THROUGH THE MICROSCOPE

Note: The light from the microscope's condenser will not pass through much of the teased specimen. Instruct your students to look around the edges of their specimens to locate the torn nerve tracts and fibers.

Teaching Suggestion:

Demonstrate all laboratory procedures.

Answers to the Questions:

Level One

1. how the brain thinks, makes decisions, perceives its environment
2. because it is so complex

5-9 INVESTIGATING THE NERVE RECEPTORS ON YOUR SKIN

Note: Most of your students will enjoy this activity.

Teaching Suggestions:

1. Demonstrate all laboratory procedures.
2. Many of your students may have difficulty understanding the difference between pain and pressure. Because this is a difficult concept to describe using words, ask them to make the test mentioned in #8 (Procedure). Ask them to pinch (gently) the tender skin on the inside surface of their forearms; the sensation is obviously pain. Then ask them to pinch the skin covering their elbows. No matter how hard they pinch (within limits, of course) they will experience only pressure.
3. For question #7, it will probably be necessary to work a few sample calculations on the chalkboard. Use student data for this.

Answers to the Questions:

Level One

1. modified ends of sensory neurons
2. stimulus
3. warmth
4. cold

5. Answers will vary, depending on the number found.
6. Answers will vary, depending on the number found.

Level Three

7. Answers will vary. Remind them to multiply by 100, or move the decimal point two places to the right.

5–10 THE FOUR SENSES

Note: This is a self-directed activity.

Teaching Suggestion:

If models of the human eye and ear are available, show your students both the external and internal structures of these sensory organs.

Answers to the Questions:

Level One

1. Answers will include sensory cells for smell (which are stimulated by the olfactory hairs), olfactory hairs, rods, cones, sensory cells for taste (in the taste buds).
2. stimuli
3. structures on the tongue that contain sensory cells for taste
4. sugar and salt molecules (or just sweet and salty)
5. alkaline substances
6. hair cells
7. stimulate the sensory cells for smell
8. rods, cones

Level Two

9. taste bud
10. cochlea
11. auditory nerve
12. olfactory hairs
13. olfactory nerve
14. optic nerve

Level Three

15. Answers will vary. Basically, solar cells change light into electricity, and the sensory cells on the retina change light into electrochemical impulses.

5–11 SPECIALIZED AREAS OF THE BRAIN

Note: This is a self-directed activity.

Teaching Suggestions:

1. Use a model of the human brain to show your students the approximate locations of the controlling areas on the brain.
2. Show your students a good film that illustrates the functions of the brain. Carl Sagan's *Cosmos* series is excellent and may be found in many video rental stores.

Answers to the Questions:

Level One

1. Gustav Fritsch, Eduard Hitzig
2. Specific parts of the dog's body would move.
3. by studying persons suffering from brain damage
4. 1
5. 4
6. 3

5–12 PERCEPTION AND INK BLOTS

Note: In most cases, this activity is as much fun for the teacher as it is for the students.

Teaching Suggestions:

1. Make overhead transparencies of these ink blots and use them for the class discussion.
2. It often puts the students at ease if you tell them what you see in the ink blots before they share their perceptions.
3. Students enjoy bringing their favorite optical illusions to show the class. Encourage them to do so.

No Questions

5–1. ELECTRICITY FROM THE BRAIN

Instructions: (1.) Carefully read the text and study the diagram. (2.) Use the diagram and what you have read to help you to answer the questions.

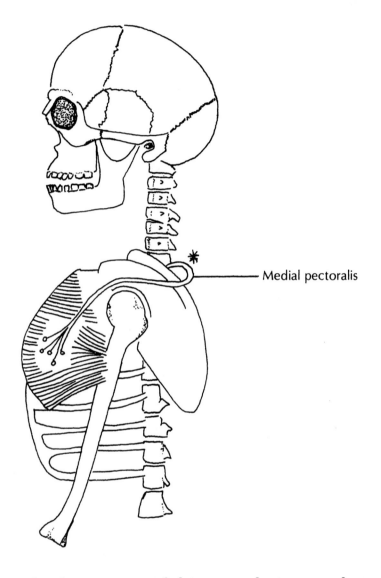

— Medial pectoralis

The muscles that move your skeleton are voluntary muscles, or muscles that are under your conscious control. You can stand up or sit down or swing your foot or wave your hand or do thousands of other things with your voluntary muscles.

Most of the time, of course, you don't think about it; you just wave, for example, without thinking, "I believe I'll use my muscles and tendons to move my hand and arm." But you *can* do it consciously.

In either case, your brain sends electrochemical signals to your muscles. These signals, which are similar to electricity, leave your brain through a large cablelike structure called the "spinal cord"; they travel a short distance through it before leaving through branches called "nerves." The nerves direct the signals to the muscles that move your arm, hand, and shoulder. When these signals arrive, the appropriate muscles contract and your hand and arm move as you want them to.

You are undoubtedly aware that some muscles in your body are not under your voluntary control; these are the involuntary muscles. Here are a few examples of what your involuntary muscles do: They cause your stomach to contract, control movements in your intestines, make your heart pump, constrict your arteries to increase blood pressure, and cause the hair on your arm to stand up when you get goose bumps. Because the structure and function of your involuntary muscles are different from those of your skeletal muscles, your teacher will mention them in other units.

Level One Questions:

1. The muscles that move your skeleton are _____ muscles.

2. What does the term **voluntary** mean?

   _____

3. What does your brain do when you want to wave your hand?

   _____

4. Electricity leaves the brain through a cable-like structure called the _____ cord.

5. What is the job of the nerves?

   _____

6. What happens after the electricity reaches the muscles?

   _____

7. The diagram shows a nerve leaving the spinal cord. What is the name of this nerve?

   _____

8. The star on the nerve (in the diagram) represents an electrochemical impulse traveling to a muscle. Has this electrochemical impulse reached the muscle?

   _____

Level Two Questions:

9. What is the name of the muscle in the diagram? (Use your completed worksheets to help you to answer this question.)

   _____

10. Describe the motion of the arm when the muscle in the diagram contracts.

    _____

    _____

Level Three Question:

11. Since the muscles that move your skeleton are voluntary, you can decide when and how you want them to perform. However, to what extent do you actually make conscious decisions about the movement of your muscles and tendons when you move your body parts? Think about this and, on the back of this sheet, write a short paragraph explaining your conclusions.

5–2. THE STRUCTURE OF THE BRAIN

Instructions: (1.) Read the text. (2.) Use the text and the diagrams to help you to answer the questions.

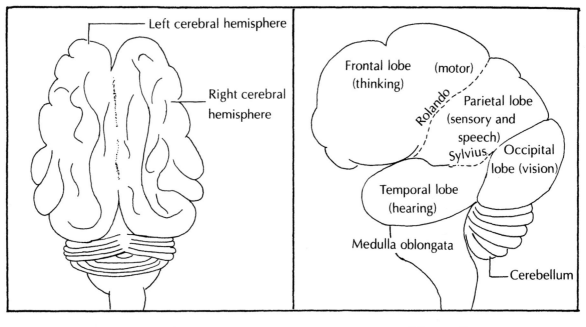

Diagram A   Diagram B

The brain is the control center of the body, in charge of all your mental activities and physical functions. Because of the brain's importance, the bones of the skull form a shell around it, giving it the best possible protection.

The largest part of the brain is the cerebrum. Diagram A shows that this structure is divided into two halves, the right and left cerebral hemispheres. On the surface of these hemispheres, most of the brain's work takes place.

The surface of the cerebrum is called the "cerebral cortex." Since it is only about four millimeters (¼ inch) thick, it needs a large surface area to accomplish its task; this large area is provided by folds. If you were somehow able to pump water or air into the cerebral cortex and make it expand enough to smooth out all the folds, the inflated brain would be far too large to fit inside the skull. The folds of the brain are called "gyri" (plural of "gyrus"), and the grooves or furrows between the gyri are called "sulci" (plural of "sulcus").

Note: While you read the following statements, look at Diagram B and observe the locations of the lobes of the brain.

Scientists use the sulci or the grooves on the cerebral cortex (called "fissures") as lines of demarcation that naturally divide the brain into lobes. The area in front of the sulcus of Rolando is called the "frontal lobe," and the region behind this sulcus is called the "parietal lobe." The line where the parietal lobe ends and the occipital lobe begins is called the "parieto-occipital sulcus." A deep fissure called the "fissure of Sylvius" separates the temporal lobe from the rest of the cerebrum.

As you can also see on the diagram, the primary functions that the different lobes control are as follows:

1. frontal lobe:
   a. thinking
   b. in front of the line of Rolando, motor—which means moving the parts of the body
2. parietal lobe:
   a. behind the line of Rolando, sensory—such as perception of heat, cold, pressure, pain
   b. mainly in the left hemisphere, speech
3. temporal lobe: hearing
4. occipital lobe: vision

Diagram B also shows two more parts of the brain. The tubelike structure directly below the cerebrum is called the "medulla oblongata." This part of the brain does certain automatic tasks: it regulates the respiration and heart rate, for example. At the base of your skull, where your head joins the back of your neck, the medulla oblongata extends downward and becomes the spinal cord.

The second-largest part of the brain lies under the optic lobes. This part of the brain is called the "cerebellum"; it is responsible for muscle coordination. The cerebellum also helps the body to maintain its balance.

To complete this project—

☐ Locate the indicated structures on Diagram B and color them as follows:
   a. Color the frontal lobe red.
   b. Color the parietal lobe yellow.
   c. Color the occipital lobe blue.
   d. Color the medulla oblongata green.
   e. Color the cerebellum orange.
   f. Color the temporal lobe brown.

Level One Questions:

1. List six jobs of the brain.

   _____

   _____

   _____

2. The largest part of the brain is the _____.

3. Where does most of the brain's work take place? _____

4. What are the folds of the brain called? _____

5. What are the grooves of the brain called? _____

6. What are lobes? _____

7. Which part of the brain controls certain automatic functions such as the regulation of breathing and heart rate?

_____

8. The second-largest part of the brain is the _____.

9. Name two jobs of the cerebellum.

_____

_____

Level Two Question:

10. Why does the brain have gyri?

_____

Level Three Questions:

11. The medulla oblongata can be thought of as the "automatic pilot" of the brain. Explain the reason for this designation.

_____

_____

12. Many people think that the brain distinguishes human beings from the lower animals. If this is so, which part of the brain is responsible for this distinction?

_____

5–3. THE PARTS AND FUNCTIONS OF THE FROG'S BRAIN

Instructions: (1.) Read the text. (2.) Use the text and the descriptions to help you to label the diagram and answer the questions.

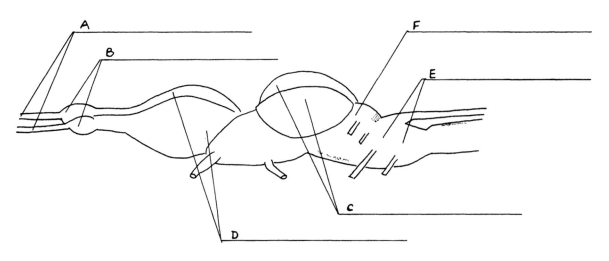

A frog's reactions to its environment are based on the information that reaches its brain. Most of the areas of the frog's brain are used for receiving information (stimuli), while other areas, such as the cerebrum, are used for processing information and for formulating responses.

Although the structure of the frog's brain is different from that of the human brain, many of its functions are the same. The optic lobes on both brains are responsible for receiving and processing visual information; the functions of the olfactory and temporal lobes, the medulla oblongata, the cerebrum, and the cerebellum are also similar.

While completing part one, you will name and describe the different parts of the frog's brain. It is probably not possible for you to dissect a human brain, but while you are doing the dissection in part two, you will be able to make some valid comparisons between the frog brain and a human brain.

© 1993 by John Wiley & Sons, Inc.

Part I: Parts and Function

Statements

1. The olfactory nerve acts like an electric cable: it directs electrochemical impulses from two external nares (openings that correspond to the human nostrils) to the area of the brain that detects odors. Arrow A points to the olfactory nerve. Label arrow A "olfactory nerve."

2. The olfactory lobe is located at the front of the brain. When electrochemical impulses from the olfactory nerve reach this area of the brain, the frog detects odors. Arrow B points to the olfactory lobe. Label arrow B "olfactory lobe."

3. The largest area of the frog's brain is the optic lobe, which is responsible for vision. When electrochemical impulses from the eyes reach this region of the brain, the frog sees its environment. Arrow C points to the optic lobe. Label arrow C "optic lobe."

4. Between the olfactory lobe and the optic lobe is the cerebrum; it receives impulses from the olfactory lobe, the optic lobe, and other parts of the brain. These impulses

enable the cerebrum to respond to the environment. Arrow D points to the cerebrum. Label arrow D "cerebrum."

5. The medulla oblongata, located at the back of the brain, looks like a thick white cord; it becomes thinner as it leaves the skull and forms the spinal cord. Arrow E points to the medulla oblongata. Label arrow E "medulla oblongata."

6. Between the optic lobe and the medulla oblongata is the cerebellum, which coordinates muscle movements. Arrow F points to the cerebellum. Label arrow F "cerebellum."

Level One Questions:

1. The frog's reactions to its environment are based on the _____ that reaches its brain.

2. The _____ acts like an electric cable.

3. Where on the frog's brain is the olfactory lobe located?

   _____

4. What happens when electrochemical impulses reach the olfactory lobe?

   _____

5. What is the largest area of the frog's brain? _____

6. Which part of the brain is responsible for vision? _____

7. Which part of the brain becomes the spinal cord? _____

8. What is the job of the cerebrum?

   _____

9. Which part of the brain coordinates muscle movements?

   _____

Part II: Dissecting a Frog's Brain

Instructions: (1.) Carefully listen and watch as your teacher shows you how to complete this lab. (2.) Follow the steps below.

Special note to the student: Brain tissue is soft, and the dissection that you are about to do is delicate. It is important that you follow the directions exactly. While removing parts of the skull, *be careful not to damage the underlying tissues.*

Special note to the teacher: Because the frog's skull is very hard, you will probably want to crack it yourself; your students can then remove the bone fragments. To crack the skull, gently insert the tips of a pair of needle-nosed pliers under the eyes and into the optic orbits. Squeezing the handles gently will crack the skull without damaging the brain. The procedure for doing this is illustrated in step five.

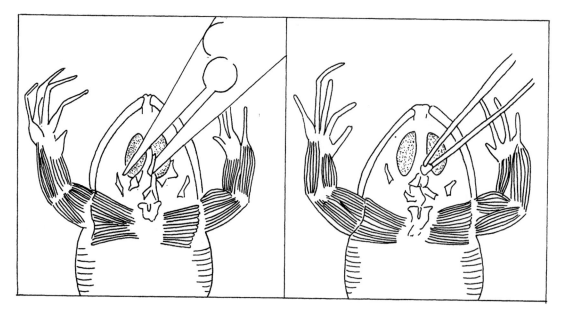

Procedure 5   Procedure 6

Procedure

1. Obtain the following materials:
   - ☐ preserved frog
   - ☐ dissecting pan
   - ☐ scalpel
   - ☐ dissecting kit
   - ☐ needle-nosed pliers
   - ☐ forceps

2. Lay the frog on its ventral (belly) side in the dissecting pan.

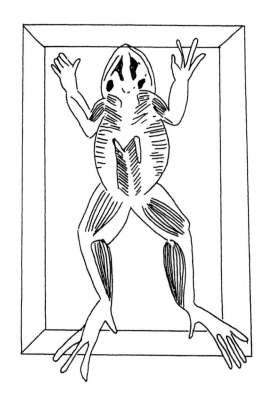

3. Use a scalpel and forceps (tweezers) to remove the muscles from the neck; start at the base of the skull and proceed to about the level of the "shoulders."

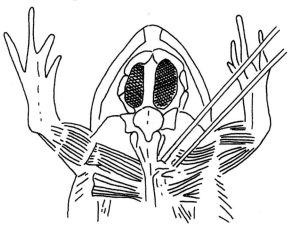

4. Use the scalpel carefully to scrape the muscles from the top of the skull.

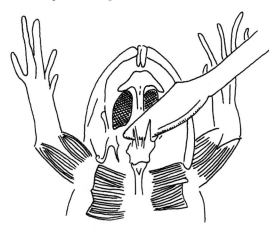

5. Wait for your teacher to crack the skull before you begin step six.

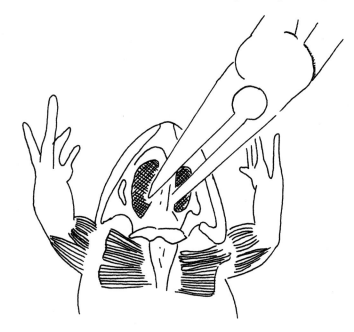

6. Using forceps, carefully remove the pieces of the skull to expose the brain and the medulla oblongata (the beginning of the spinal cord).

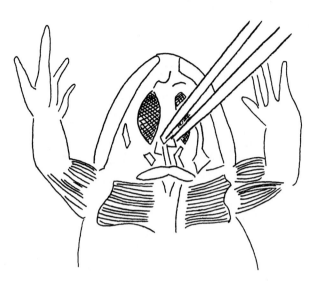

7. Carefully study the structure of the brain; in the blank area in the following diagram, sketch what you have observed.

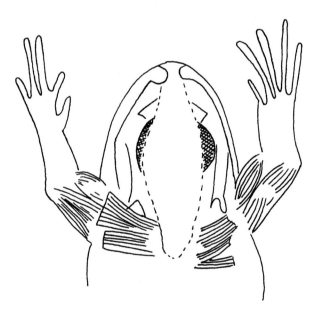

8. Use what you learned in Part I to help you to label your lab drawing.

Name _____ Date _____

5-4. THE ANATOMY OF THE NEURON

Instructions: (1.) Carefully read the text. (2.) Use the descriptions to help you to label the diagram. (3.) Use the text and the descriptions to help you to answer the questions.

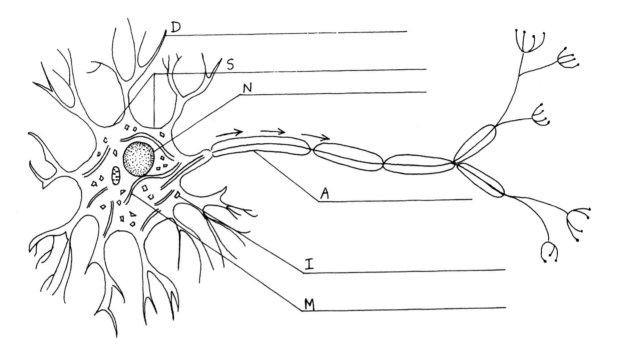

Neurons are long, threadlike cells that carry electrochemical signals. Signals from the sensory organs may be perceived by the brain as sound, sight, smell, taste, touch, or pain; signals sent by the brain to the body may cause the skeletal muscles to contract, the internal organs to operate, or the glands to release their chemicals.

In many ways, a neuron is like an electric wire. Although electric wires and neurons carry signals in different ways, their basic jobs are the same; to carry electricity. An electric wire in a radio, for example, may carry signals from a transistor to a speaker, where the signals are changed into sound. Similarly, the neurons leaving your ears send electrochemical signals to a specific area of your brain so that you can hear the sound.

While completing this project, you will learn how to name the parts of a typical neuron.

Descriptions

1. The main part of the neuron is the cell body or soma. Like other cells, the soma contains cytoplasm, mitochondria, a nucleus, and other organelles. Arrow S points to the soma, and arrow N points to the nucleus. Locate these arrows on the diagram and label them.

2. Floating in the cytoplasm are irregularly shaped particles called "Nissl bodies"; scientists think that they are responsible for assembling proteins. Arrow I points to a Nissl body. Label arrow I "Nissl body."

© 1993 by John Wiley & Sons, Inc.

3. The cytoplasm is filled with small tubes called "microtubules." Scientists think that these tubes carry proteins and other substances through the cell. Arrow M points to a microtubule. Label arrow M "microtubule."

4. The treelike structures on the soma are called "dendrites"; the term comes from a Greek word meaning "tree." Dendrites direct incoming electrochemical signals toward the soma. Arrow D points to a dendrite. Label arrow D "dendrite."

5. Incoming electrochemical impulses pass through the soma and leave the neuron through a long threadlike structure called the "axon." Although axons are microscopically thin, many can reach lengths of up to three feet or more. Arrow A points to the axon. Label arrow A "axon."

Level One Questions:

1. Neurons are long threadlike cells that carry _____ signals.

2. When electrochemical signals are sent from the brain to a muscle, what might be the response?

   _____

3. The cell body of the neuron is also called the _____.

4. What do the Nissl bodies look like?

   _____

5. Scientists think that Nissl bodies are responsible for _____.

6. In what part of the soma are the microtubules located?

   _____

7. What do scientists think the microtubules do?

   _____

8. Where on the neurons are the dendrites located?

   _____

9. What is the job of the dendrite?

   _____

10. What is the job of the axon?

    _____

Level Two Questions:

11. The axon can reach lengths of three feet or more. In what way might this be important?

    _____

    _____

12. How is a neuron similar to an electric wire?

_____

_____

Level Three Questions:

13. If you look carefully, you will notice that the soma has a mitochondrion in it. What does the presence of mitochondria indicate?

_____

_____

14. There are three arrows on the diagram. What do you think these arrow show?

_____

_____

5–5. VOCABULARY: THE NEURON

Part I: Crossword Puzzle

Instructions: Use the last project, "The Anatomy of the Neuron," to help you to find the answers to this puzzle.

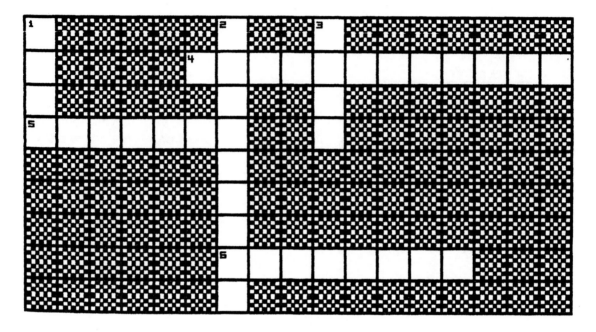

Across

4. small tubes in the cytoplasm; scientists think they carry substances through the cell
5. an organelle found in the soma
6. treelike structures that direct electro-chemical signals toward the soma

Down

1. Electrochemical impulses leave the neuron through this long threadlike structure.
2. irregularly shaped particles that float in the cytoplasm
3. on neurons, another way of saying "cell body"

Part II: Flash Cards

Instructions: (1.) Cut out these cards. (2.) Use the clues from the crossword puzzle to help you to write definitions on the backs of these cards. (3.) Study these definitions until you know them.

AXON

MICROTUBULES

DENDRITE

NUCLEUS

NISSL BODY

SOMA

THE NEURON

Name _____
Period _____

5–6. NERVES

Instructions: (1.) Read the text. (2.) Use the text and the diagram to help you to answer the questions.

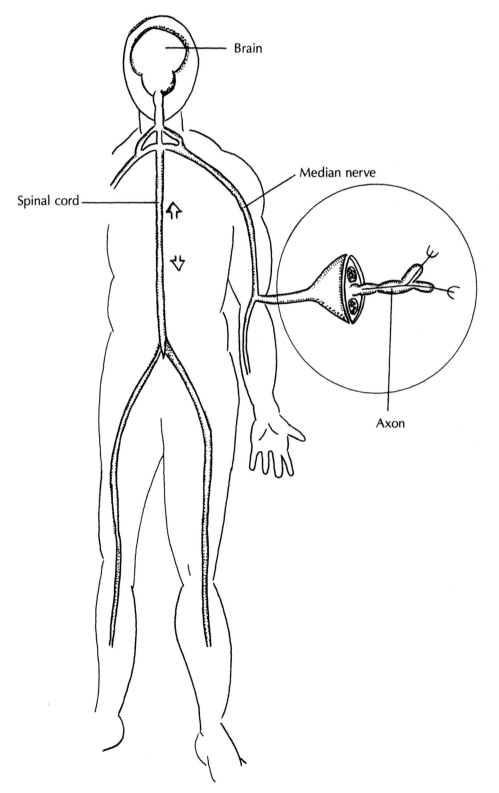

Brain

Median nerve

Spinal cord

Axon

The human nervous system is composed of trillions of neurons, most of which are located in the central nervous system (the brain and spinal cord). Other neurons are part of the peripheral nervous system, which carries impulses to various parts of the body. Neurons that lie outside the central nervous system travel through the body through large cablelike structures called "nerves"; each nerve is a bundle of neurons. Through a microscope, a cut nerve looks like a tightly wrapped bundle of wires.

The diagram shows several large nerves as they branch from the spinal cord. Notice that one nerve branches from the spinal cord and travels through the middle of the arm; it is called the "median nerve." The left median nerve has been cut and expanded to show the neurons inside.

The median nerve is "mixed" because it contains both motor and sensory neurons. When you touch something, or when some part of your body experiences pressure or pain, sensory neurons carry stimuli—in the form of electrochemical impulses—to the spinal cord and brain. Once the central nervous system receives these incoming signals, motor neurons send signals from the brain and spinal cord to the muscles; the body then moves in response. A mixed nerve, therefore, sends electrochemical signals in two directions—into and away from the central nervous system.

Level One Questions:

1. How many neurons are in the human nervous system? _____

2. Where are most of the neurons located?

_____

3. What is a nerve?

_____

_____

4. What is a "mixed" nerve?

_____

_____

5. What do sensory neurons do?

_____

_____

6. What do motor neurons do?

_____

_____

Level Two Questions:

7. How is a nerve different from a neuron?

    _____

    _____

8. How did the median nerve get its name?

    _____

    _____

9. There are two arrowheads on the diagram. What do you think these arrowheads show?

    _____

    _____

Level Three Question:

10. On the diagram, the expanded nerve shows part of a neuron sticking out. Which anatomical part of the neuron do you see?

    _____

5–7. THE SPINAL CORD

Instructions: (1.) Read the text. (2.) Use the text and the diagram to help you to answer the questions.

The spinal cord is an elongated extension of the brain. It is less than an inch in diameter, and in a person of average height it is about eighteen inches long. The spinal cord leaves the brain through a large hole in the base of the skull and travels downward through the vertebrae.

As the spinal cord travels through the vertebrae, 31 pairs of nerves, called "spinal nerves," attach to it. These large nerves enter the spinal cord through the spaces between the vertebrae. But before a nerve actually joins the spinal cord, it splits to make a Y. The branch of the Y that enters through the front of the spinal cord (belly side) is called the "ventral root." The branch of the Y that enters through the back of the spinal cord is called the "dorsal root."

Each spinal nerve carries thousands of neurons. Some of these neurons carry sensory information (impulses from the nerve endings such as pain, touch, and pressure), while other neurons carry motor signals (impulses that are sent to the muscles to make them contract). The neurons that carry sensory information enter the spinal cord through the dorsal root, and the neurons that carry motor signals leave the spinal cord through the ventral root.

The diagram shows a spinal cord that has been cut. If you look at this cross section closely, you will notice a shaded area shaped like a butterfly. This area is called the "gray matter"; it appears gray because it contains mostly dendrites and cell bodies. Many neurons cross to the opposite side of the spinal cord through the gray matter.

The portion of the spinal cord that surrounds the gray matter is called the "white matter." The circles on the diagram show that the white matter is divided into tracts. A tract is a collection of neuron fibers (axons) that travel to the same general place. Some tracts, called "ascending tracts," have fibers that direct impulses toward the brain, while other tracts, called "descending tracts," direct impulses away from the brain. The tracts on the diagram and their functions are identified below.

#1—ascending; sends sensory impulses for touch from the upper body to the sensory area of the brain

#2—ascending; sends sensory impulses for touch from the lower body to the sensory area of the brain

#3—descending; sends impulses from the motor region of the brain to the muscles of the arms and legs

#4—ascending; sends impulses from the spinal cord to the cerebellum

#5—ascending; sends sensory signals for pain and temperature to the sensory area of the brain

#6—ascending; sends sensory impulses for pressure to the sensory area of the brain

To complete this project—

☐ Use the text and the labels to help you to locate and identify the structures on the diagram. Color the structures as follows:

   a. Color the dorsal root red.

   b. Color the ventral root yellow.

   c. Color the ascending nerve tracts blue.

   d. Color the descending nerve tracts green.

Level One Questions:

1. What is the spinal cord?

   _____

   _____

2. About how long is the spinal cord of a person of average height? _____

3. What is a spinal nerve?

   _____

   _____

4. What kind of impulses enter through the dorsal root?

   _____

5. What kind of impulses leave through the ventral root?

   _____

6. What is a tract?

   _____

7. What kinds of impulses are sent through an ascending tract? _____

8. What kinds of impulses are sent through a descending tract? _____

9. If a part of the lower body is touched, which tract (on the chart) carries that sensory information to the brain? _____

10. If a part of the upper body is touched, which tract carries that sensory information to the brain? _____

11. What makes the butterflylike structure in the center of the spinal cord look gray?

_____

12. Describe what tract 6 does.

_____

_____

Level Two Questions:

13. How does a spinal nerve join the spinal cord?

_____

_____

14. How is sensory information different from motor signals?

_____

_____

_____

5–8. OBSERVING THE SPINAL CORD THROUGH THE MICROSCOPE

Instructions: (1.) Read the text. (2.) Carefully watch and listen as your teacher shows you how to prepare the microscope slide. (3.) Use the text and your observations to help you to do the project and answer the questions.

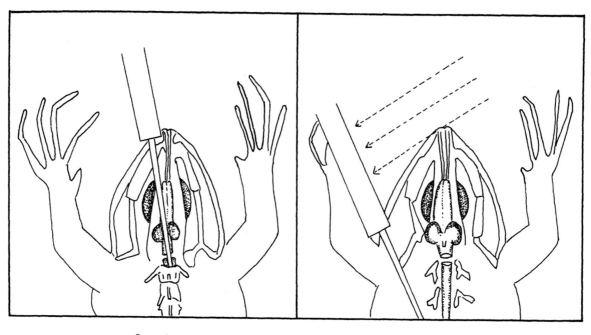

Step 4   Step 5

Scientists know about electrochemical impulses and neurons; they have even made maps showing which part of the brain controls what. But even with all of this knowledge, no one can explain exactly how the central nervous system works. No one can explain how the brain thinks, makes decisions, or perceives its environment.

One reason why the central nervous system is so difficult to understand is its complexity. As you know, the brain and spinal cord are made of trillions of microscopically thin neurons. While observing a few of these neurons through the microscope, you will begin to realize how complex the central nervous system actually is.

In this lab, you will remove the frog's spinal cord, cut off a small section, and look at the section through the microscope.

Since the spinal cord is dense, most of what you will see will look like dark clumps. Search carefully on the edges of these clumps to see the nerves and neurons. You will have to move the slide on the microscope stage as you look.

Procedure

1. Obtain the following materials:
   - ☐ preserved frog
   - ☐ dissecting pan
   - ☐ dissecting kit
   - ☐ beaker of water
   - ☐ microscope slide
   - ☐ cover slip
   - ☐ microscope

2. Lay your preserved frog on its ventral (belly) side in the dissecting pan.
3. Locate the beginning of the spinal cord and cut it with a pair of scissors.
4. Insert the dissecting needle into the first vertebra so that the point of the needle lies on top of the spinal cord. Carefully push the needle through the entire length of the spinal column.
5. Using a sudden upward motion, lift the dissecting needle to break the vertebrae.
6. Using forceps (tweezers), lift out the spinal cord.
7. Use a scalpel to cut off a small section of the spinal cord; use your forceps to place the section on the microscope slide.
8. Put two drops of water on the section and use two dissecting needles to tease the tissue apart.
9. Place a cover slip on top of the teased tissue.
10. Place the slide on the microscope and focus to 100X.

To complete this project—

☐ While looking through the microscope, use your thumbs to move the slide around until you see some axons and nerve fibers.

☐ In this circle, sketch what you see in one field of vision.

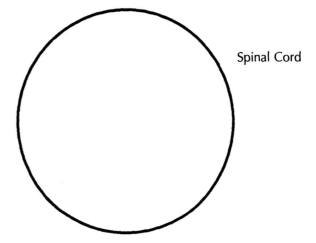

Spinal Cord

Level One Questions:

1. List three things that scientists do not understand about the central nervous system.

_____

_____

_____

2. Why is the central nervous system difficult to understand?

_____

_____

_____

5–9. INVESTIGATING THE NERVE RECEPTORS ON YOUR SKIN

SPECIAL PRECAUTION: While locating the nerve receptors for pain, use only a round toothpick. DO NOT press the toothpick with enough force to break through your skin. Throw your toothpick away after you have finished with it.

Instructions: (1.) Read the text. (2.) Carefully watch as your teacher shows you how to complete this investigation. (3.) Use the text and your observations to help you to answer the questions.

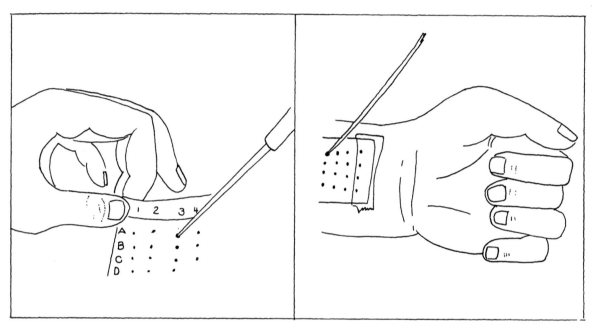

Procedure 3   Procedure 5

Your skin plays an important role in providing your central nervous system with information about your environment. To detect stimuli, sensory neurons in your skin have specially designed ends. These modified ends are called "nerve receptors."

Each type of nerve receptor can detect only one type of stimulus. The nerve receptor for pressure, for example, will change only the force of deep pressure—from a hand shake, for example—into an electrochemical signal. The prick from a sharp needle will cause a pain receptor to fire, but not a receptor for pressure.

Most nerve receptors were named for the scientists who discovered them. On the list below are five types of stimuli and the names of the nerve receptors that detect them.

Type of stimulus	Name of the nerve receptor
cold	Krause's end bulbs
warmth	Ruffini's end organ
touch	Meissner's corpuscle
deep pressure	Pacinian corpuscle
pain (free nerve ending)	(no special name)

Procedure

1. Obtain the following materials:
    - ☐ scissors
    - ☐ one round toothpick
    - ☐ two pieces of tape, 1" long
    - ☐ dissecting needle
    - ☐ one piece of straw from a broom

2. Carefully cut out the test grid at the end of this activity.

3. Use the dissecting needle to punch holes through the dots.

4. Tape the grid to the inside of your forearm.

5. To locate the nerve receptors for touch, carefully push the straw through each of the holes on the grid so that it *lightly* touches the skin.

6. When you feel the touch of the straw through a hole, carefully *circle* the corresponding dot on the data grid.

7. To locate the nerve receptors for pressure, carefully push the toothpick through the holes on the grid a tiny bit harder than you pushed the straw when you were testing for touch.

8. For each hole through which you feel pressure, *draw a small triangle* around the corresponding hole on the data grid. *Note:* To determine the difference between pressure and pain, pinch the skin on your elbow. Since there are no pain receptors on your elbow, you will not feel pain as you would if you pinched the skin on your forearm.

9. To locate the nerve receptors for pain, carefully push the toothpick through the holes on the grid and apply still a little more pressure. **CAUTION:** DO NOT PUSH THE TOOTHPICK WITH ENOUGH FORCE TO BREAK THE SKIN.

10. When you feel a slight pain as the toothpick comes through the hole, *draw a small square* around the corresponding dot on the data grid. (Some dots on the data grid will have more than one symbol.)

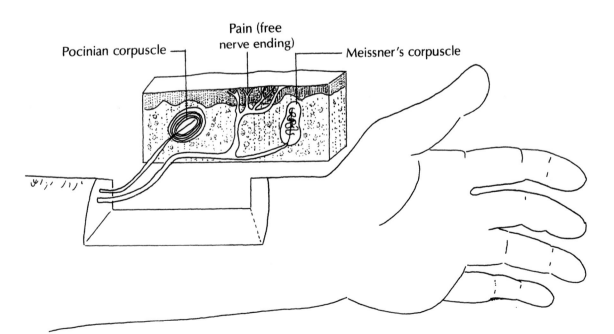

To complete this project—

☐ Use the chart to help you to determine which nerve receptor is responsible for the appropriate stimulus. Color the nerve receptors on the diagram as follows:

  a. Use red to color the nerve receptor for pain.
  b. Use yellow to color the nerve receptor for touch.
  c. Use green to color the nerve receptor for pressure.

Level One Questions:

1. What are nerve receptors?

  _____

  _____

2. Each type of nerve receptor can detect only one type of _____.

3. What kind of stimulus can a Ruffini's end organ detect? _____

4. What kind of stimulus can Krause's end bulbs detect? _____

5. How many nerve receptors for touch did you locate on your skin? _____

6. How many nerve receptors for pain did you locate on your skin? _____

Level Three Question:

7. The test grid that you taped to your skin had fifty-four locations (dots). Use the following space to calculate the percent of occurrence for the types of nerve receptors. Show your work and circle your answers.

Note:—for easy percentage calculation, use this method: Let x = the number of receptors found; x divided by 54 = percentage. (Multiply your answer by 100 or move the decimal point two places to the right.) If you found 25 receptors for pain, you would divide 25 by 54; your answer will be 0.4629, or (rounded off and with the decimal point moved) 46%.

Data Grid

Skin Test

5–10. THE FOUR SENSES

Instructions: (1.) Read the text and the descriptions. (2.) Use the descriptions to help you to label the diagrams. (3.) Use the text, diagrams, and descriptions to help you to answer the questions.

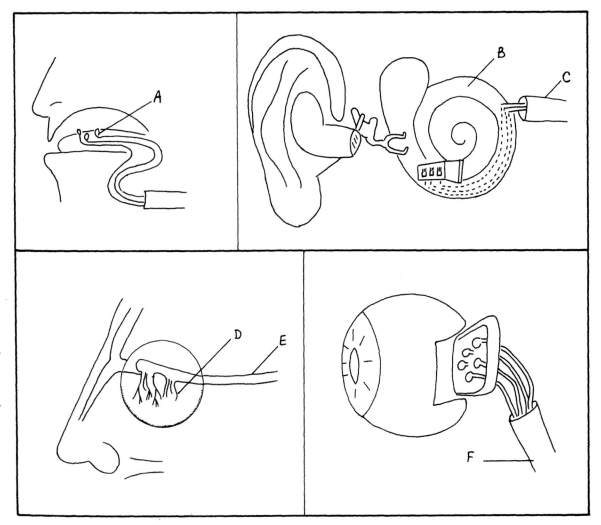

Pretend for a moment that you are walking to your neighborhood store. To get there, you cut across the park where some boys are playing baseball; you cautiously pass behind the outfielders. Suddenly, you hear one of the boys yell, "Look out!" At that instant you turn your head and look over your shoulder to see a ball coming straight toward you. Without stopping to think, you duck out of the way and the ball barely misses you.

Obviously, you could easily have had a concussion and a quick trip to the hospital. But your eyes and ears picked up stimuli from your environment and sent impulses to your brain; your brain interpreted the impulses and sent messages to your muscles, which moved you out of harm's way in less time than it takes to tell about it.

Your eyes and ears are not the only structures that work constantly to protect you; your tongue and nose (as well as your skin) are also on watch, monitoring your environment for changes. All of these structures, called "sensory organs," have specialized sensory cells that can change specific types of stimuli into electrochemical signals.

While reading the statements that follow, you will learn more about your eye and your other sensory organs and how they convert specific stimuli into electrochemical signals that your brain interprets and uses for making decisions about your changing environment.

Statements

1. On your tongue there are small structures that look like tiny onions. These structures, called "taste buds," contain sensory cells that can change certain kinds of molecules into electrochemical signals. The taste buds on the tip of your tongue are stimulated by sugar and salt molecules. If you eat something sweet or salty, these sensory cells fire, sending an electrochemical signal to your brain. As your brain interprets this signal, you experience a sweet or salty taste in your mouth. The taste buds on the sides of your tongue are stimulated by acids and those on the back of your tongue by alkaline substances; when those taste buds fire your brain tells you that you are tasting something sour or bitter.

2. In your inner ear is a snail-shaped structure called the "cochlea." Inside this structure are rows of sensory cells called "hair cells." When sound waves—which are really rapidly vibrating air molecules—enter your inner ear, they are directed into the cochlea, where they cause the hair cells to wave back and forth. Acting like "on and off" switches, these hair cells cause electrochemical signals to flow to the brain through the auditory nerve.

3. The nasal cavity is a large opening in your skull, just behind your nose. The roof of the nasal cavity is lined with sensory cells with small hairlike bristles called "olfactory hairs." These olfactory hairs are believed to react with certain molecules in the air; they stimulate the sensory cells, which produce electrochemical signals that the brain perceives as odor.

4. On the back wall of each of your eyes is a structure about the size and thickness of a small postage stamp. This structure, called the "retina," has two kinds of sensory cells called "rods" and "cones." The cones are chiefly responsible for vision in bright light and for recognizing color; the rods are more sensitive to dim light. The electric signals produced by both of these sensory cells are sent to the brain through the optic nerve.

Level One Questions:

1. List four kinds of sensory cells.

   _____

   _____

   _____

   _____

2. Sensory cells change specific types of _____ into electrochemical signals.

3. What are taste buds?

   _____

4. What kinds of stimuli are detected by the tip of your tongue? _____

5. What kinds of stimuli are detected by the back of your tongue? _____

6. What are the sensory cells in the cochlea called? _____

7. What do olfactory hairs do?

_____

8. Name two sensory cells on the retina.

_____

_____

Level Two Questions:

9. What structure does arrow A point to? _____

10. What structure does arrow B point to? _____

11. What structure does arrow C point to? _____

12. What structure does arrow D point to? _____

13. What structure does arrow E point to? _____

14. What structure does arrow F point to? _____

Level Three Question:

15. In what way(s) is a solar cell similar to the sensory cells on the retina?

_____

_____

_____

_____

5–11. SPECIALIZED AREAS OF THE BRAIN

Instructions: (1.) Read the text. (2.) Use the text and the diagram to help you to answer the questions.

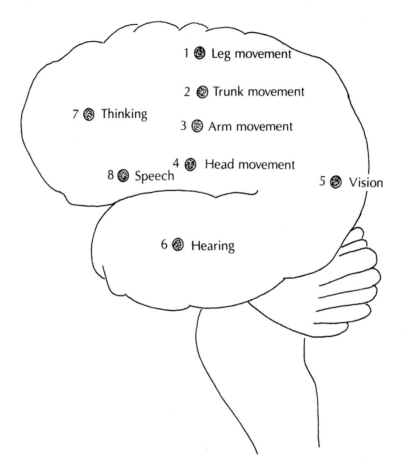

In the early 1870s two German scientists, Gustav Fritsch and Eduard Hitzig, learned about the brain by experimenting on dogs. They removed a part of the skull of a living dog and gave the exposed brain mild shocks of electricity. They discovered that when certain areas of the brain were stimulated, specific parts of the dog's body would move. A shock of electricity to one area of the brain, for example, would cause a paw to twitch. From these experiments, Fritsch and Hitzig were able to construct a brain map showing locations on the dog's cerebral cortex that are responsible for operating specific muscles.

Scientists were, of course, unable to experiment on living people. But over a long period of time, studies of persons suffering from brain damage finally led to the construction of a human brain map. If a person had lost his vision from a head injury, for example, and the doctors were able to determine which area of his brain had been damaged, then that area could be shown on a map of the human brain as the area that controls vision.

The dots on the diagram show the general locations on the human brain that are responsible for detecting certain stimuli and initiating certain responses. All areas except one are located on both sides of the brain; the area that controls speech is the exception. This area (dot 8) is located only on the left side of the brain.

Level One Questions:

1. Name the two scientists who studied the dog's brain.

   _____

   _____

2. What did the scientists discover after giving the dog's brain mild shocks of electricity?

   _____

   _____

3. How were scientists able to construct a human brain map?

   _____

   _____

4. On the brain map (diagram), which number points to the area that controls leg movement?

   _____

5. On the brain map, which number points to the area that controls the movement of the head?

   _____

6. On the brain map, which number points to the area that controls arm movement?

   _____

5–12. PERCEPTION AND INK BLOTS

Instructions: (1.) Read the text. (2.) Complete the project.

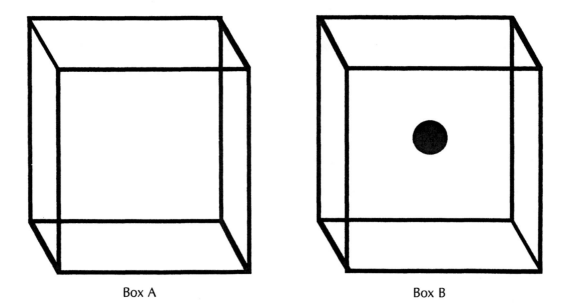

Box A   Box B

The word *perceive* means "to become aware of one's environment through the senses." Certain nerve receptors, for example, allow you to perceive certain environmental stimuli through your skin. Your eyes allow you to perceive light (which also allows the perception of color and movement), and your ears allow you to perceive sound.

"Perception" is more than just the reception of stimuli; it includes your brain's interpretation of what you perceive. For example, when you look at Box A, you actually see only twelve connected lines—some horizontal, some vertical, some at an angle. The taking in of this raw data is the job of the primary visual cortex. If your brain had never had any experience with three-dimensional figures, you would continue to see *only* those twelve lines, on a flat surface. But your brain *has* had experience with such lines and what they normally represent, and so it interprets these lines as a box. Your perception, or how you interpret these lines, is the job of the secondary visual cortex.

Perception is obviously a complex function. The secondary visual cortex interprets size, detail, and geometric shape, and it utilizes input from other areas of the brain. Total perception of an object may be based on past experiences, visual memories, or what you expect to see.

Now look at Box B—the one with the dot. Is the front of the box angled toward your left or your right? Now stare fixedly at the dot and then blink your eyes; the orientation of the box (the direction toward which it faces) will change. Sometimes the box is oriented toward the left, and the side toward you is higher than the back; sometimes the reverse is true. The box and its dot have been drawn so that your brain can make more than one interpretation. (If you look back at Box A, you can probably see it move in the same way.)

When you look at shapes in a cloud, what you see may remind you of something that you have seen in the past—a flower, a bird, or maybe a castle. Another person may see a dragon, a face, or a tree.

Looking at ink blots is similar to looking at clouds. While doing this project you will look at six different ink blots. Your brain will make some interpretation of each one—based on your past experiences, your visual memories, and what you expect to see.

To complete this project—

☐ 1. Examine each ink blot. Turn it upside down and sideways and hold it at an angle.

☐ 2. On the lines provided, respond to each ink blot by writing what you see. You may write more than one response to each blot.

☐ 3. During the class discussion that follows, compare your responses with the responses made by the other members of your class.

Responses

1. _____

2. _____

3. _____

Responses

1. _____

2. _____

3. _____

Responses

1. _____

2. _____

3. _____

Responses

1. _____
2. _____
3. _____

Responses

1. _____
2. _____
3. _____

Responses

1. _____
2. _____
3. _____

Unit **6**

The Circulatory System

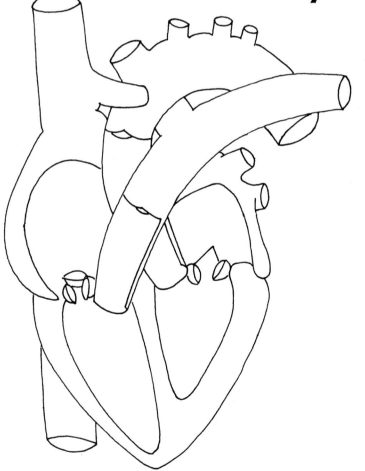

6-1 THE CIRCULATORY SYSTEM

Note: This is a self-directed activity.

Answers to the Questions:

Level One

1. Answers will vary. One assumes students will say things like run the engine, operate the radio, lights, windshield wipers, maybe operate onboard computers, etc.
2. primarily from gasoline
3. through a pump and a system of tubes
4. primarily from certain sugars
5. Answers will vary. They may include making proteins, building and repairing cells, providing for the overall operation of tissues and organs, gross motor activities, removing wastes, sending messages to other cells, even thinking.
6. urea, carbon dioxide
7. heart
8. blood
9. circulatory system
10. heart, veins, arteries, capillaries, blood

Level Two

11. Answers will vary. Let us hope that students will mention that energy must be brought in from an external source (gasoline, food), and must be transformed to some extent into useful forms in order to perform necessary functions. There is a waste-removal function in both cases.

Note: The English Department will love you and the students will benefit if you pay some attention to the form of the occasional paragraphs that students will be directed to write—topic sentences, one idea per paragraph, examples and details used in support, complete sentences, reasonable spelling, etc.

6-2 INVESTIGATING A DROP OF BLOOD

Teaching Suggestion:

Before your students begin this observation, use a chart or a textbook illustration to show them what the solid components of blood look like.

Answers to the Questions:

Level One

1. plasma
2. red blood cells
3. five

4. tiny pink dots

5. larger dots with purple spots (nuclei)

Level Two

6. looking at their nuclei and cytoplasm

6–3 RED BLOOD CELLS

Note: This is a self-directed activity.

Answers to the Questions:

Level One

1. about 2.5 million
2. erythrocytes
3. the red marrow of the bones
4. B
5. a cell that produces and stores hemoglobin molecules
6. Its nucleus begins to shrink and eventually disappears.
7. F
8. acts as a gas-carrier—transports oxygen and carbon dioxide
9. E
10. Molecules of oxygen attach loosely to the iron atoms.
11. C
12. It passes into the cell.
13. D
14. carbon dioxide
15. Its hemoglobin picks up carbon dioxide and carries it to the lungs. (Note: This is, of course, not the only way in which carbon dioxide is carried in the blood.)
16. A
17. releases the carbon dioxide, and picks up more oxygen
18. They become old and brittle and finally break apart.

Level Two

19. A cell called the hemocytoblast makes new blood cells in the bone marrow. The students should mention something about the nucleus of the forming erythrocyte—it shrinks and disappears.

20. (Paragraph) Answers will vary. Students should mention that hemoglobin molecules containing four iron atoms are found in the erythrocyte; that the oxygen combines with the iron atoms in the lungs; that the heart pumps the blood from the lungs throughout the body. Since oxygen is held loosely by the iron molecules, it leaves the hemoglobin molecules at the cell level.

Level Three

21. Red blood cells cannot reproduce by mitosis because they do not have nuclei and chromosomes.

6–4 THE EXTERNAL ANATOMY OF THE HEART

Teaching Suggestion:

Use a model to show your students the external structures of the heart.

Answers to the Questions:

Level One (statement questions)

a. 5

b. 3

c. 2

d. pulmonary artery

e. aorta

f. vein

g. inferior vena cava

h. A

i. the contracting heart muscle

j. right coronary artery, left coronary artery

k. aorta

l. B

m. because it travels along the margin of the heart

n. D

6–5 THE INTERNAL ANATOMY OF THE HEART

Teaching Suggestions:

1. Use a model of the heart to show your students its inside structure. Use this demonstration as an opportunity to describe the heartbeat and the flow of blood through the heart.

2. If possible, use a sectioned sheep heart or a sectioned beef heart to help you to describe the internal anatomy of the human heart. Butcher shops can sometimes supply them; sheep hearts can be ordered from biological supply houses.

Notes:

1. On the diagram, as you may have noticed, the heart valves look more like small cups than they actually would. This exaggeration should help you in explaining how the valves derived their names—tricuspid, meaning "three-cupped," and bicuspid, meaning "two-cupped." This modification should also help you to explain how the downward flow of blood fills the cups (valves), causing them to become heavy and to close. It is probably important that you tell your students that heart valves do not really look like this.

2. Many students become confused when they read that a structure (the heart, for example) is on the left side of the body, although that structure appears on the right side of the page in the accompanying diagram. Tell your students that this is simply

a problem of orientation. A heart diagram is generally drawn from the perspective of the possessor of that heart. Demonstrate this by holding a heart diagram to your chest.

Teaching Suggestion:

If a sheep or a cow heart (which may be purchased from a butcher) is available, dissect and demonstrate its internal structures.

Answers to the Questions:

Level One

1. four
2. atria
3. ventricles
4. superior vena cava, inferior vena cava
5. sends deoxygenated blood from the right ventricle to the lungs
6. to bring oxygen-rich blood from the lungs to the left atrium
7. between the right atrium and the right ventricle
8. between the left atrium and the left ventricle
9. deoxygenated
10. oxygenated
11. sends oxygen-rich blood from the left ventricle to the body

6–6 VOCABULARY: THE INTERNAL ANATOMY OF THE HEART

Note: This is a self-directed activity.

Answers to Puzzle:

Across

1. superiorvenacava
6. veins
7. tricuspidvalve
8. ventricles

Down

2. pulmonaryartery
3. atria
4. aorta
5. bicuspidvalve

6–7 THE HEART CYCLE

Note: This is a self-directed activity. Its purpose is to help students to visualize the flow of blood through both sides of the heart.

Answers to the Questions:

Level One

1. superior and inferior venae cavae
2. tricuspid valve
3. through the pulmonary artery and to the lungs
4. to return blood from the lungs to the left atrium
5. Blood next travels into the left ventricle.
6. The bicuspid valve slams shut and oxygen-enriched blood is pumped out of the left ventricle. The blood passes through the aorta on its way to the body's cells.

6–8 INVESTIGATING CARDIAC MUSCLE

Note: This is a self-directed activity.

Answers to the Questions:

Level One

1. cardiac muscle
2. striated
3. pull
4. tightening, squeezing

Level Two

5. Answers will vary. Essentially, both have striated cells, and the cells of the skeletal muscles are long and slender, whereas the cells that make cardiac muscle are short and branched.
6. Answers will vary. The cells of the skeletal muscles are long and slender so that they can travel longer distances. The cells that make cardiac muscle are short and branched so that they can pull on other muscle cells and create a squeezing action like the tightening of a net.

6–9 THE PARTS AND FUNCTION OF THE FROG'S HEART

Note: This investigation gives the student an opportunity to study the external and internal anatomy of an actual heart.

Teaching Suggestions:

1. Demonstrate all lab procedures.
2. Make sure that the students are careful to cut *above* the superior end of the frog's heart so that they will not slice into the ventricles. You may want to show students how to clear away muscle tissue that might be obstructing their view of the heart.

Answers to the Questions:

Level One

1. three
2. four
3. two
4. two
5. one
6. two
7. anterior venae cavae
8. pulmonary veins
9. It directs blood from the frog's heart to its body.

6–10 THE POWER STATION OF THE HUMAN HEART

Note: This is a self-directed worksheet.

Answers to the Questions:

Level One

1. no
2. sinoatrial node
3. on the back wall of the right atrium
4. sodium ions
5. 72
6. electrochemical impulses
7. The atria contract.
8. above the ventricles
9. directs impulses through a special bundle of fibers called the "bundle of His"
10. Its fibers direct electrochemical impulses through the muscular walls of the ventricles.
11. The ventricles contract at the same time.

Level Two

12. A
13. B
14. B
15. A

Level Three

16. Answers will vary. The sinoatrial node sets the pace of the heartbeat by firing about 72 times a minute. (*Note:* This is not the only regulating mechanism of the heart.)

6–11 HOW MUCH BLOOD DOES YOUR HEART PUMP IN A MINUTE?

Note: A few students will have difficulty in finding their pulse spots. Demonstrate the locations of these spots; help some students to locate theirs.

General Instructions:

"Hold both of your hands out in front of your body, palms up, about a foot apart. With your right hand, reach under your left wrist and wrap your fingers around the wrist. *Your left wrist will be lying in the palm of your right hand.* Now press all four fingers into the soft spot at the base of your thumb. Your pulse will be under one or two of your fingers." (Some students may insist that it's easier to find a pulse with their thumbs. Remind them that this is not the way to do it, because the thumb has a pulse of its own.)

Teaching Suggestion:

To show how much blood leaves the heart through the aorta with each heartbeat, fill a small beaker with 80 ml of water and add a drop of red food coloring.

Answers to the Questions:

Level One

1. heart rate
2. the amount of oxygen your cells need
3. 72
4. stroke volume

Level Two

5. The cells of the body are working harder and use more oxygen.
6. a shock wave of blood pressure passing through the arteries

Level Three

7. Answers will vary. Exercise strengthens the heart's muscle. A stronger heart is more efficient and does not need to contract as many times to supply the cells with oxygen.
8. Answers will vary. Essentially, the answer is "no," because many factors such as age, sex, and physical condition influence the heart rate.
9. Answers will vary. Most students will say "in less than a minute."

6–12 THE BLOOD VESSELS

Note: This is a self-directed worksheet.

Answers to the Questions:

Level One

1. arteries
2. veins

3. aorta

4. distributing arteries

5. arterioles

6. capillaries

7. in the capillaries

8. a net made of extremely small tubes

9. venule

10. left and right common carotid artery

11. right and left external jugular veins, right and left internal jugular veins

12. left subclavian artery

13. left subclavian vein

14. left femoral artery

15. great saphenous vein

16. A

17. B

18. C

Level Two

19. contains oxygen and nutrients

20. contains carbon dioxide and other cellular wastes

21. A venule is smaller than a vein.

Level Three

22. Answers will vary. As the name implies, these arteries branch so that they can distribute or transport blood to different areas of the body.

23. It is called the "femoral artery" because it passes alongside the femur.

24. Answers will vary. Since capillaries are extremely thin, high pressure would cause them to burst.

25. A. capillary net   I. capillary net

     B. arteriole   J. venule

     C. carotid artery   K. jugular

     D. aorta   L. superior vena cava

     E. heart   M. inferior vena cava

     F. descending aorta   N. great saphenous vein

     G. femoral artery   O. venule

     H. arteriole

6–13 MICROSCOPIC OBSERVATION OF A VEIN AND AN ARTERY

Note: This is a self-directed activity.

Answers to the Questions:

Level One

1. three
2. tunica intima
3. tunica media
4. tunica adventitia
5. elastic fibers, endothelium
6. smooth muscle cells
7. nonelastic fibers, tunica adventitia
8. pressure
9. elastic
10. shrink
11. pressure
12. around your stomach and intestines
13. arterioles
14. reduced
15. skeletal
16. valves, backward (or away from the heart)
17. blood cells
18. D
19. C

Level Two

20. Answers will vary. The tunica media has three layers of circularly arranged smooth muscle cells. When these muscles contract, they narrow the diameter of the artery. When the diameter decreases, the pressure of the blood inside increases.
21. Answers will vary. Arterioles act like on-and-off valves; each one has a band of smooth muscle that can completely shut off the flow of blood to the capillary and redirect blood to other areas of the body.
22. Answers will vary. While a skeletal muscle is doing its work, it compresses nearby veins. This places the blood under pressure and pushes it toward the heart.
23. Answers will vary. The valves inside the vein have cup-shaped flaps; as blood begins to flow backward and fill these cups, the weight of the blood causes them to slam shut.

Level Three

24. Answers will vary. The veins above the heart do not need valves because the blood flowing through them is under low pressure and gravity prevents the blood from flowing backward.

6–1. THE CIRCULATORY SYSTEM

Instructions: (1.) Read the text. (2.) Use the text to help you to answer the questions.

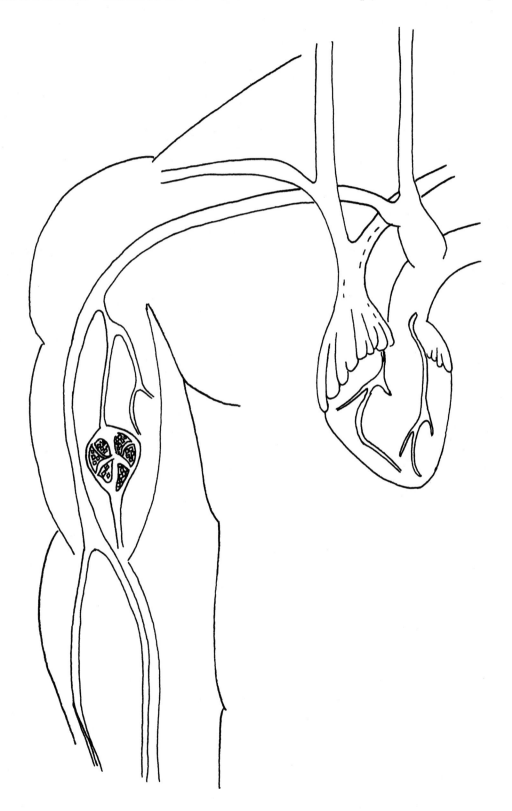

In many ways, the human body can be compared to a machine. Like a car, it uses energy to do work. The car uses energy to move forward and backward and to operate its systems and accessories; the body also uses energy to move and to operate all its systems and "accessories."

The car gets its energy primarily from gasoline; a pump and a system of tubes transport gasoline from the gas tank to the engine. Your body gets its energy primarily from certain kinds of sugars that your digestive system produces from the foods that you eat; these sugars are pumped to every cell of your body, where oxygen molecules (removed by your lungs from the air you breathe and then transported to your cells) help to convert it into energy. As the car uses gasoline for energy, carbon monoxide and other wastes are produced; they are removed from the car through the exhaust system. Similarly, when energy is used by body cells, wastes such as urea and carbon dioxide are produced. These waste products would be harmful if they were not quickly carried away from the cells and removed from the body; your body has specialized organs and tissues to accomplish this.

Your heart is the center of your body's transportation system. It pumps blood through tubes called "veins," "arteries," and "capillaries." Sugars, oxygen, waste, and other substances are carried by the blood through these tubes.

The heart, veins, arteries, capillaries, and blood make up the body's transportation system, which is called the "circulatory system." The preceding diagram will help you to understand how the circulatory system does its job. Notice that the artery leaving the heart is quite large; on its way to other parts of your body, its branches get continually smaller—so small, in fact, that they can pass between the cells. These small branches (which, at their tiniest, form oval nets called "capillary nets") make it possible for blood to reach every cell of your body.

Level One Questions:

1. List three ways in which a car uses energy.

   _____

   _____

   _____

2. Where does a car get its energy?

   _____

3. How does energy get from a car's gasoline tank to its engine?

   _____

   _____

   _____

4. What does your body use for energy? _____

5. List three ways in which the cells of your body use energy.

    _____

    _____

    _____

6. When energy is used by the cells, waste products are produced. Name two waste products produced by your cells.

    _____

    _____

7. What is the name of the pump located in the center of your chest? _____

8. What does it pump through the veins and arteries? _____

9. What is the body's transportation system called? _____

10. List five parts of the human circulatory system.

    _____

    _____

    _____

    _____

    _____

Level Two Question:

11. On the back of this sheet, write a paragraph that compares (a) how energy is transported and used by the car with (b) how energy is transported and used by the human body.

Bonus Points

Use the library to find information on some of the waste products produced by a car. Write a two-page report on these waste products and explain the ways in which they are harmful.

6–2. INVESTIGATING A DROP OF BLOOD

Instructions: (1.) Read the text. (2.) Complete the investigation. (3.) Use the text and your observations to help you to answer the questions.

The liquid part of your blood is a straw-colored fluid called "plasma"; floating in it are three kinds of microscopic solids. Most of these solid particles are the red blood cells, which give your blood its characteristic color. Through your microscope, red blood cells will look like tiny pink dots; or, if you have a higher-powered microscope, like pinkish Life-savers™ without the center hole.

Through your microscope you will also see some slightly larger dots with purple spots or nuclei; they are the white blood cells. There are five different types of white blood cells. You will notice that the nuclei of the five types are different in shape and that some white blood cells are clear while others are granular (grainy).

A third kind of solid in blood, the platelets, can be difficult to see through the microscope. Platelets are colorless and extremely small. If they are properly stained, however, they look like small purple specks at 500X magnification.

Procedure

1. Obtain the following materials:
   - ☐ prepared microscope slide of human blood
   - ☐ microscope

2. Place the slide on the microscope and focus to 500X magnification.

3. Look through the microscope as you slowly move the slide on the stage. Try to find examples of the three types of solids found in blood.

4. In the circle, sketch blood as it looks through the microscope.

Blood
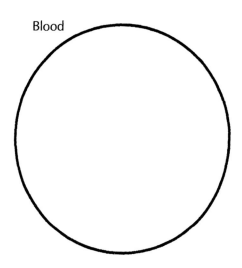

Level One Questions:

1. What is the liquid part of blood called? _____

2. What makes your blood look red? _____

3. How many different types of white blood cells are known? _____

4. What do red blood cells look like through the microscope? _____

5. What do white blood cells look like through the microscope? _____

Level Two Question:

6. How can you identify the five types of white blood cells?

_____

_____

_____

6–3. RED BLOOD CELLS

Instructions: (1.) Read the text. (2.) Use the text and the diagrams to help you to answer the questions.

Count three seconds (one one thousand, two one thousand, three one thousand). Your body has just destroyed about 7.5 million red blood cells! Every second, your body destroys about 2.5 million "old" blood cells and replaces them with new ones.

Red blood cells, also called "erythrocytes," are made in the red marrow of your bones, where specialized cells begin producing an erythrocyte by first making a hemocytoblast. A hemocytoblast is a cell that produces and stores hemoglobin molecules. As the hemocytoblast begins to fill with hemoglobin, its nucleus begins to shrink. Eventually the nucleus disappears, leaving a cell filled with hundreds of thousands of hemoglobin molecules. This cell, now an erythrocyte or red blood cell, enters the circulatory system. It is ready to begin work.

The job of the erythrocyte is to carry the gases **oxygen** and **carbon dioxide**. Hemoglobin, a gas carrier, makes this job possible because each molecule of hemoglobin contains atoms of iron. When the heart pumps the blood to the lungs, molecules of oxygen—a gas mixed in the air that you breathe—attach loosely to these iron atoms. After the erythrocytes become oxygen-enriched, the heart pumps these oxygen-filled erythrocytes through the capillary nets (roughly oval networks of microscopic blood vessels) to reach the body's cells.

Since iron holds oxygen loosely, the oxygen easily leaves the hemoglobin and passes into the cell where it is used to convert sugars into energy.

When oxygen is used by the cell, a waste product called "carbon dioxide" is produced. Carbon dioxide, like oxygen, is a gas; it must be sent to the lungs to be breathed out and thus removed from the body. Again, hemoglobin makes this possible. A part of each hemoglobin molecule can pick up carbon dioxide from the cells and carry it to the lungs. In the lungs, the carbon dioxide is released as the other parts of the hemoglobin molecule pick up more oxygen for a return trip to the cells.

The erythrocyte continues to carry oxygen and carbon dioxide back and forth from the cells for about 120 days. After this period, the red blood cell becomes old and brittle and finally breaks apart. It is quickly replaced by a new erythrocyte formed in the red bone marrow.

Level One Questions:

1. About how many red blood cells are destroyed and replaced by your body every second? _____

2. Red blood cells are also called _____.

3. Where in the body are the red blood cells (erythrocytes) produced? _____

4. Study the diagrams and write the letter of the box that shows where erythrocytes are made. _____

5. What is a hemocytoblast? _____

6. What happens to the hemocytoblast as it begins to produce and fill up with hemoglobin molecules? _____

7. Study the diagrams and write the letter of the box that shows a hemocytoblast making erythrocytes. _____

8. What is the job of hemoglobin? _____

9. Study the diagrams and write the letter of the box that shows a hemoglobin molecule. _____

10. When the heart pumps blood to the lungs, what attaches to the iron atoms in the hemoglobin molecules? _____

11. Study the diagrams and write the letter of the box that shows the heart pumping blood to the lungs. _____

12. What happens to the oxygen after the erythrocytes are pumped into the cells?

_____

13. Study the diagrams and write the letter of the box that shows oxygen (O_2) leaving the blood and entering a cell. _____

14. When oxygen is used by the cell, a waste product called _____ is produced.

15. What happens after the hemoglobin gives up oxygen? _____

_____

16. Study the diagrams and write the letter of the box that shows carbon dioxide (CO_2) leaving a cell and entering the blood. _____

17. What does the hemoglobin do after it leaves the cells and returns to the lungs?

_____

18. What happens to the erythrocytes after they are about 120 days old? _____

_____

Level Two Questions:

19. How are new erythrocytes made in the bone marrow?

_____

_____

20. Write a short paragraph on the back of this sheet describing the process by which blood transports oxygen throughout the body.

Level Three Question:

21. Most cells of the body reproduce by mitosis (a form of cellular division). Why don't erythrocytes reproduce by mitosis?

_____

_____

_____

_____

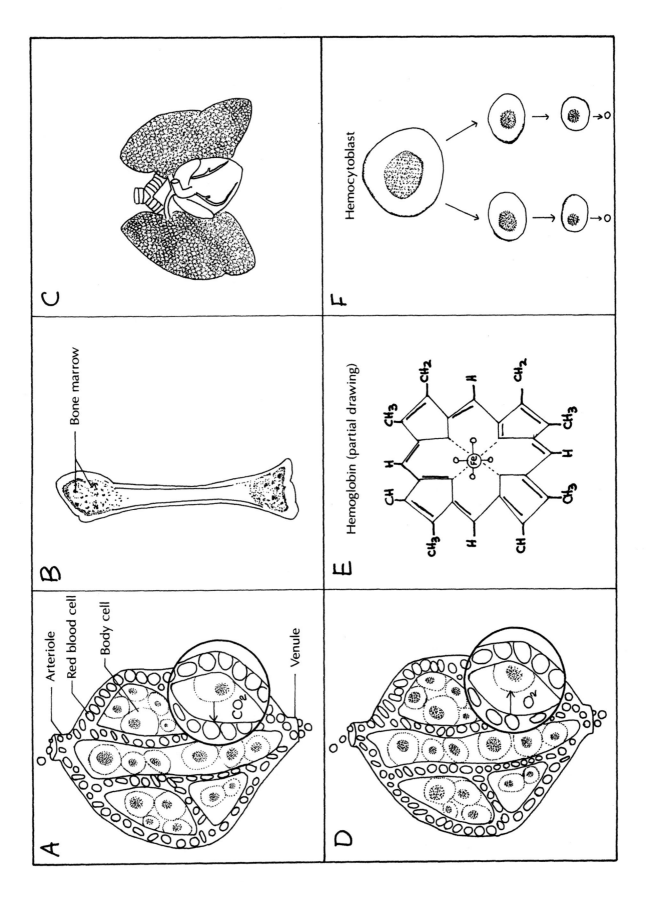

A

Arteriole
Red blood cell
Body cell
CO_2
Venule

B

Bone marrow

C

D

CO_2
O_2

E

Hemoglobin (partial drawing)

CH_2
CH_3
H
CH_2
CH_3
H
Fe
H
CH_3
CH
CH_3
H
CH

F

Hemocytoblast

6–4. THE EXTERNAL ANATOMY OF THE HEART

Instructions: (1.) Examine the diagram carefully. (2.) Read the text and the statements. (3.) Use the text, the statements, and the diagram to help you to answer the questions.

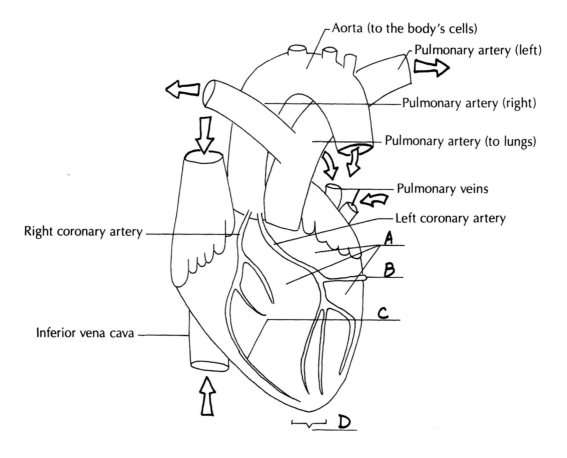

Clench your fist. Your heart, which is about the size of your fist, is perfectly designed to pump your blood. To understand how the heart works, you must understand its outside structure.

Statements and Questions

1. The top of your heart, also called the "superior end," has large tubes on it.

   a. Count the tubes on the superior end of the heart (do not include the branches of these blood vessels). How many tubes are there?

   _____

2. The tubes that direct blood toward and into the heart are called "veins," and the tubes that direct blood away from the heart are called "arteries." The arrows on the diagram show the direction of the blood flow through these tubes.

   b. How many veins are on the superior end of the heart? _____

   c. How many arteries are on the superior end of the heart? _____

    d. The artery that directs blood from the heart to the lungs carries deoxygenated blood (blood that has left its oxygen molecules in many cells so that it is now "oxygen-poor"). Name the artery that carries deoxygenated blood.

    e. The artery that directs blood to the body's cells carries oxygenated blood (blood that has recently picked up oxygen molecules from the lungs). Name the artery that carries oxygenated blood.

3. The bottom or lower part of the heart is called the "inferior end." From the inferior end, a large blood vessel can be seen directing blood toward the heart.

    f. Is the blood vessel on the inferior end of the heart an artery or a vein?

    g. Name the blood vessel that can be seen on the inferior end.

4. The main structure of the heart is made of muscle tissue; in fact, the heart is really one large muscle. The contracting heart muscle provides the force that squeezes the blood through both pumps of the heart.

    h. Which arrow on the diagram points to muscle tissue?

       A   B   C   D   (Circle one.)

    i. What provides the force that squeezes blood through the heart?

5. Like all other cells of the body, the cells that make up the heart's muscle tissue need substances that are delivered by the blood. The arteries that direct blood to the heart muscle lie on the surface of the heart.

    j. Name the two arteries that direct blood to the heart's muscle tissue.

    k. What large artery do these arteries branch from?

6. The circumflex branch of the left coronary artery travels around the heart.

    l. Which arrow points to the circumflex branch of the left coronary artery?

       A   B   C   D   (Circle one.)

7. Arrow C points to the branch of the right coronary artery that directs blood along the lower margin of the heart. This branch is called the "marginal artery."

    m. Why is the branch that arrow C points to called the "marginal artery"?

8. The inferior (lower) end of the heart is pointed. The pointed end of the heart is called the "apex."

    n. Which arrow points to the apex of the heart? A   B   C   D   (Circle one.)

Name _____ Date _____

6–5. THE INTERNAL ANATOMY OF THE HEART

Instructions: (1.) Read the statements. (2.) Use the statements to help you to label the diagram and answer the questions.

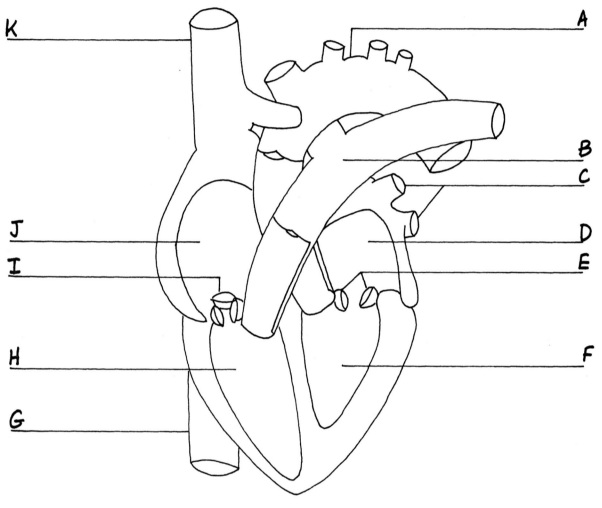

Statements

1. Inside the heart are four spaces or chambers. Each chamber in the top half of the heart is called an "atrium"; the plural form is "atria." Arrows D and J point to the atria. Label arrow D "left atrium," and label arrow J "right atrium."

2. The two chambers directly below the atria are called "ventricles." Arrows H and F point to the ventricles. Label arrow F "left ventricle," and label arrow H "right ventricle."

3. Two large veins bring deoxygenated blood to the right atrium. The large vein on the superior (top) end of the heart is called the "superior vena cava," and the large vein on the inferior end (bottom) is called the "inferior vena cava." Find the arrows that point to the superior and inferior venae cavae (plural). Label these arrows.

4. A large artery sends deoxygenated blood from the right ventricle to the lungs. This artery is called the "pulmonary artery." Arrow B points to the pulmonary artery. Label arrow B "pulmonary artery."

5. A large valve with three cup-shaped flaps lies between the right atrium and the right ventricle. (*Note:* To make the diagram easier to understand, the flaps have been drawn to look more like cups than they really would.) This valve is called the "tricuspid valve." When it opens, blood leaves the right atrium and empties into the right ventricle. When it closes, blood is prevented from flowing back into the right atrium. Arrow I points to the tricuspid valve. Label arrow I "tricuspid valve."

6. Two small veins bring oxygen-rich blood from the lungs to the left atrium. These veins are called "pulmonary veins." Find the arrow that points to the pulmonary veins. Label that arrow "pulmonary veins."

7. The bicuspid valve lies between the left atrium and the left ventricle. When it opens, blood leaving the left atrium flows into the left ventricle. When it closes, it prevents the blood from flowing back into the left atrium. Arrow E points to the bicuspid valve. Label arrow E "bicuspid valve."

8. Oxygen-rich blood leaves the left ventricle through a large artery called the "aorta." The aorta is the largest artery in your body. Arrow A points to the aorta. Label A "aorta."

Level One Questions:

1. How many chambers are inside the human heart? _____

2. What are the top chambers called? _____

3. What are the bottom chambers called? _____

4. Name the two large veins that bring blood into the right atrium.

   _____

5. What is the job of the pulmonary artery?

   _____

6. What is the job of the pulmonary vein?

   _____

7. Where is the tricuspid valve?

   _____

8. Where is the bicuspid valve?

   _____

9. Is the blood leaving the right ventricle oxygenated or deoxygenated? _____

10. Is the blood leaving the left ventricle oxygenated or deoxygenated? _____

11. What is the job of the aorta?

   _____

   _____

6–6. VOCABULARY: THE INTERNAL ANATOMY OF THE HEART

Part I: Crossword Puzzle

Instructions: Use the last project, "The Internal Anatomy of the Heart," to help you to find the answers to this puzzle. (*Note:* If the answer has two or more words, do not leave spaces between the words.)

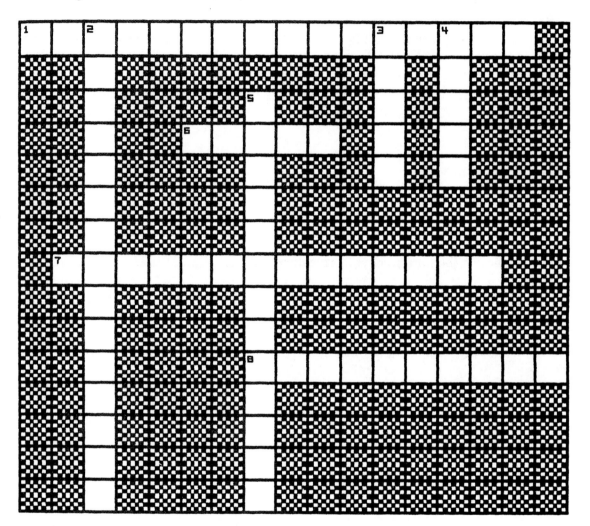

Across

1. large vein that directs blood to the right atrium
6. The pulmonary _____ (plural) bring blood to the heart.
7. This valve is located between the right atrium and the right ventricle.
8. the inferior (bottom) chambers of the heart (use the plural form)

Down

2. This artery sends blood to the lungs.
3. the superior (top) chambers of the heart (use the plural form)
4. the largest artery in the body
5. This valve is located between the left atrium and the left ventricle.

Part II: Flash Cards

Instructions: (1.) Cut out the cards. (2.) Use the clues from the crossword puzzle to help you to write the definitions on the back of these cards. (3.) Study these cards until you know the definitions on them.

ATRIA	BISCUSPID VALVE
TRICUSPID VALVE	VENTRICLES
PULMONARY ARTERY	SUPERIOR VENA CAVA
PULMONARY VEINS	THE INTERNAL ANATOMY OF THE HEART Name _____ Date _____

6–7. THE HEART CYCLE

Instructions: (1.) Read the text. (2.) Complete the project. (3.) Use the text and your observations to help you to answer the questions.

In this project, you will follow the flow of blood through the heart.

Your heart has two jobs to do, and its two sides have separate responsibilities: The left side pumps oxygen-enriched blood from your lungs to your body's cells, and the right side pumps oxygen-poor, waste-carrying blood back from your body's cells to your lungs.

When blood has made one "round trip," it has completed one "heart cycle." Although this project will guide you through the heart cycle by examining what happens in one chamber at a time, it is important for you to know that blood flows through both sides of the heart simultaneously (at the same time). That is, when the right atrium contracts and pumps its blood, the left atrium contracts at the same time. The same is true for the ventricles—both the right and left ventricles contract and pump blood at the same time.

In biological drawings, it is standard to use blue to represent deoxygenated blood and red to represent oxygenated blood. (This practice is not just to make your drawing colorful; oxygen-rich blood actually looks bright red, and oxygen-poor blood looks bluish or purple.) You will, therefore, use blue circles to follow deoxygenated blood through the right side of the heart and red circles to follow oxygenated blood through the left side of the heart.

Obtain the following materials:

☐ ten blue circles and ten red circles (you can make them by using a hole punch on blue and red construction paper)

☐ color pencils or markers

Procedure

1. Each stage will instruct you to place colored circles on the "number" diagram. Be sure to place the circles on the correct numbers and to use the correct color (red or blue).

2. On the "heart sequence" page, sketch and color the circles for each stage.

3. Before going to the next stage, remove the circles from the "number" diagram so that they can be reused for the next stage. The idea, of course, is to show the movement of the blood in successive stages.

Stage one: Deoxygenated blood enters the right atrium through the superior and inferior venae cavae. Place blue circles on numbers 1, 2, 3, 4, 5, 6, 7, and 8. Sketch and color these circles on Diagram A.

Stage two: When the right atrium is full, it contracts and forces blood through the tricuspid valve and into the right ventricle. Remove the blue circles from stage one and place them on numbers 9, 10, 11, 12, and 13. Sketch and color these circles on Diagram B.

Stage three: After the blood passes into the right ventricle, the tricuspid valve slams shut. The muscular wall of the right atrium contracts, forcing the blood through the pulmonary artery and to the lungs. Remove the blue circles from stage two and place them on numbers 14, 15, 16, 17, 18, 19, 20, 21, 22, and 23. Sketch and color these circles on Diagram C.

Stage four: The blood returns from the lungs to the left atrium through the pulmonary veins. While in the lungs, the red blood cells become saturated with oxygen and change from a bluish color to a bright red. Remove the circles from stage three. Place *red* circles on numbers 24, 25, 26, 27, 28, 29, 30, and 31. Sketch and color these circles on Diagram D.

Stage five: When the left atrium is full, it contracts and forces blood through the bicuspid valve and into the left ventricle. Remove the red circles from stage four and place them on numbers 32, 33, 34, 35, 36, 37, and 38. Sketch and color these circles on Diagram E.

Stage six: The last stage of the heart cycle occurs when the bicuspid valve slams shut and the oxygen-enriched blood is pumped out of the left ventricle through the aorta. From the aorta, the blood is directed to the body's cells. Remove the red circles from stage five and place them on numbers 39, 40, 41, 42, 43, 44, 45, 46, and 47. Sketch and color these circles on Diagram F.

Level One Questions:

1. Through which veins does deoxygenated blood enter the right atrium?

   _____

2. What structure must the blood pass through before it enters the right ventricle?

   _____

3. Where is the blood pumped after it leaves the right ventricle?

   _____

4. What is the job of the pulmonary veins?

   _____

5. What happens when the left atrium is full?

   _____

6. Describe the last stage of the heart cycle.

   _____

   _____

   _____

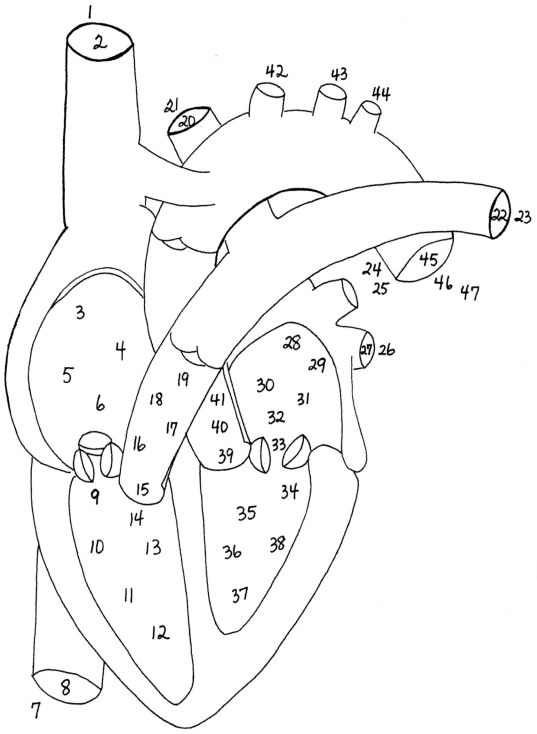

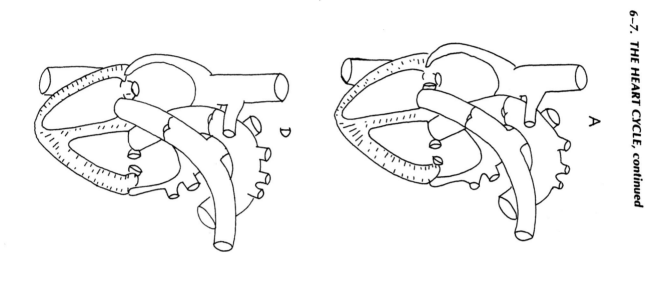

A

D

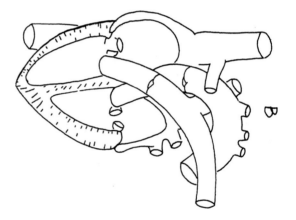

B

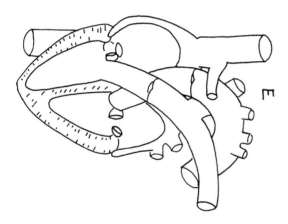

E

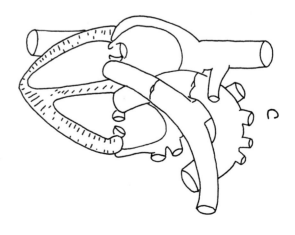

C

F

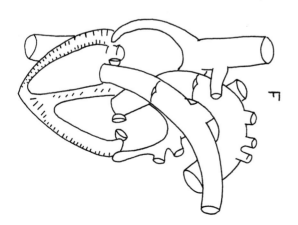

6–8. INVESTIGATING CARDIAC MUSCLE

Instructions: (1.) Read the text. (2.) Complete the investigation. (3.) Use the text and your observations to help you to answer the questions.

Heart muscle is called "cardiac muscle." In certain ways, cardiac muscle is similar to the muscles that allow you to move the bones of your skeleton.

The cells that make a skeletal muscle are striated (have parallel stripes or bands). Cardiac muscle is also made of striated cells, but since its job is to squeeze blood through the heart and not to pull the bones of the skeleton, its cells are shaped differently.

The cells of the skeletal muscles are long and slender so that they can reach out and attach to the bones. The cells that make cardiac muscle, on the other hand, are short and branched; when a cardiac muscle cell contracts (shortens), its branches pull on other muscle cells that they attach to. These muscle cells, in turn, will contract and pull on other muscle cells. This is like tightening a net. When cardiac muscle contracts, the overall effect is a tightening or squeezing action.

Procedure

1. Obtain the following materials:
   - ☐ prepared microscope slide of cardiac muscle
   - ☐ microscope
2. Carefully watch and listen as your teacher shows you how to complete this investigation.
3. Using a microscope, focus the prepared microscope slide to 100X magnification.

   To complete this project—

☐ In the circle, accurately sketch what you see in one field of vision.

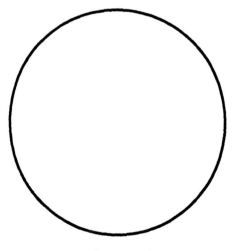

Cardiac Muscle

Level One Questions:

1. Heart muscle is called _____ muscle.

2. The cells that make cardiac muscle are _____ and branched.

3. When a cardiac muscle cell contracts, its branches _____ on the muscle cells to which they are attached.

4. When cardiac muscle contracts, the overall effect is a _____ or _____ action.

Level Two Questions:

5. Describe the ways in which cardiac muscle is similar to and different from skeletal muscle.

_____

_____

_____

6. Why are cardiac muscle cells shaped differently from skeletal muscle cells?

_____

_____

_____

6–9. THE PARTS AND FUNCTION OF THE FROG'S HEART

Part I: External Structures

Instructions: (1.) Read the text. (2.) Use the text and the statements to help you to label the diagram and answer the questions.

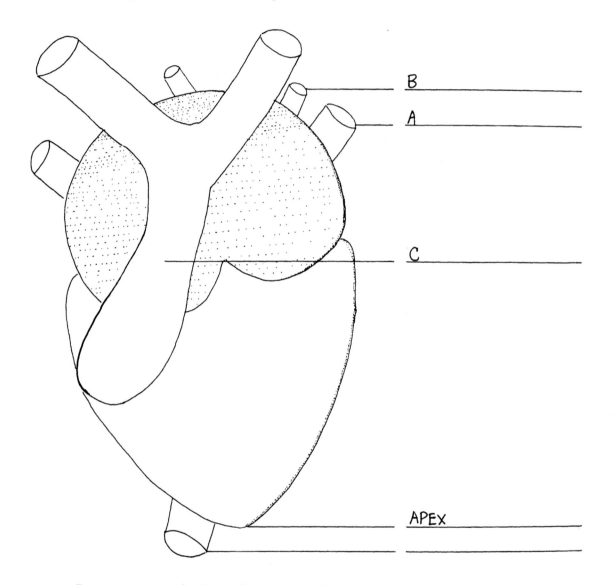

In many ways, the frog's heart is similar to the human heart. Both are roughly triangular organs located in the center of the chest, and their primary job is to pump blood that contains oxygen, chemicals, nutrients, and wastes.

Unlike the human heart, the frog's has only three chambers. The frog's heart contains two atria (like the human heart), but only one ventricle.

It is easy to see where the chambers of the frog's heart are located. The superior (upper) end of the frog's heart is dark brown; the atria are located here. The light tan inferior (lower) end of the heart contains the single ventricle.

The following statements will help you to learn the parts and functions of the frog's heart.

Statements

1. As in the human heart, there are many tubes that direct blood. Two large veins, called the "anterior venae cavae," bring blood from the upper part of the body. Arrow A points to the left anterior vena cava. Label arrow A "left anterior vena cava."

2. Another large vein, called the "posterior vena cava," brings blood to the heart from the lower parts of the body. On the diagram, this large vein can be seen near the apex of the heart. Find the arrow that points to the posterior vena cava. Label that arrow "posterior vena cava."

3. A smaller pair of veins brings oxygenated blood from the lungs. These veins are called "pulmonary veins." Arrow B points to the left pulmonary vein. Label arrow B "pulmonary vein."

4. When the heart contracts, blood is pushed out of the heart through a large artery called the "conus arteriosis"; it divides into smaller arteries as it directs blood throughout the body. Arrow C points to the conus arteriosis. Label arrow C "conus arteriosis."

Part II: Observing the External and Internal Structures

Instructions: (1.) Carefully watch and listen as your teacher shows you how to expose the frog's heart. (2.) Use your observations to help you to answer the questions.

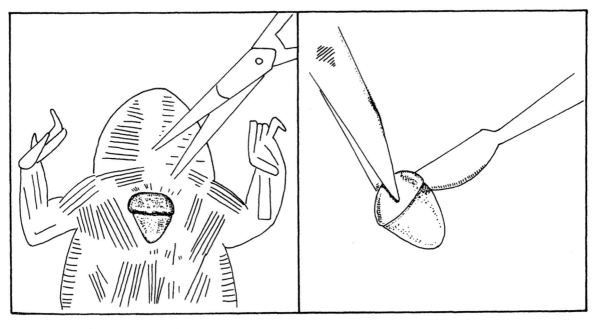

Procedure A   Procedure B

Special note to the student: While removing the muscle and bone tissue to expose the frog's heart, be careful not to cut too deeply; you might damage the heart and the other organs.

Procedure A

1. Obtain the following materials:
   - [ ] preserved frog
   - [ ] dissecting kit
   - [ ] Petri dish
   - [ ] dissecting pan
2. Lay the preserved frog on its dorsal (back) side in the dissecting pan.
3. Using scissors and forceps (tweezers), carefully remove the pectoralis (chest muscle) and the other muscles in the chest area. This will expose the sternum or breast bone.
4. Carefully insert the tip of your scissors beneath the sternum and cut the bone. Use the forceps to remove the bone and the remaining tissue. This will expose the frog's heart.

   To complete procedure A—

- [ ] Carefully study the structure of the heart; on the diagram, sketch what you see.
- [ ] Notice that the superior end (top) of the frog's heart is a dark brown. Draw an arrow to this area of the heart and label it "atrium."
- [ ] The inferior end (bottom) of the heart is a light tan. Draw an arrow to this area of the heart and label it "ventricle."

Procedure B

1. Use scissors to cut away the tissue and blood vessels from both the superior and inferior ends of the heart. Use forceps (tweezers) to remove the heart.
2. Use forceps and a scalpel to section the heart by making a lateral cut (from the side). Study the diagram carefully before you do this.
3. Rinse the inside of the heart with water.
4. Place the heart in the petri dish so that the open end is up. You may add water to the petri dish to help to support the tissues.

   To complete procedure B—

- [ ] In the box provided, sketch the frog's heart.

Human Heart	Frog Heart
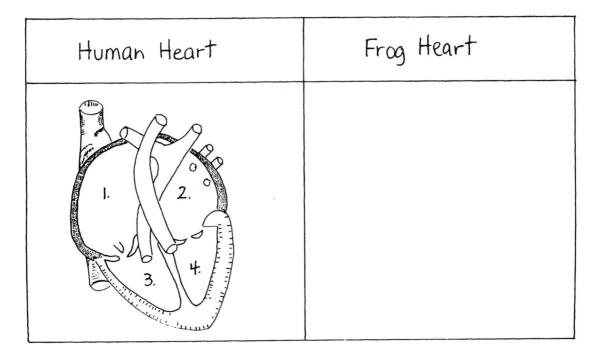	

Level One Questions:

1. How many chambers does the frog's heart have? _____

2. How many chambers does the human heart have? _____

3. How many atria does the frog's heart have? _____

4. How many atria does the human heart have? _____

5. How many ventricles does the frog's heart have? _____

6. How many ventricles does the human heart have? _____

7. The large veins that bring blood from the upper part of the frog's body are called the

   _____ .

8. The veins that bring oxygenated blood from the frog's lungs are the _____

   _____ veins.

9. Describe the job of the conus arteriosis.

   _____

   _____

   _____

   _____

   _____

6–10. THE POWER STATION OF THE HUMAN HEART

Instructions: (1.) Read the text and study the diagrams. (2.) Use the text and the diagrams to help you to answer the questions.

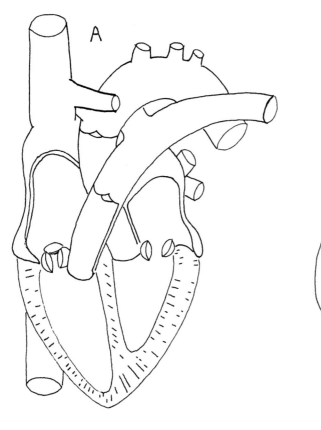

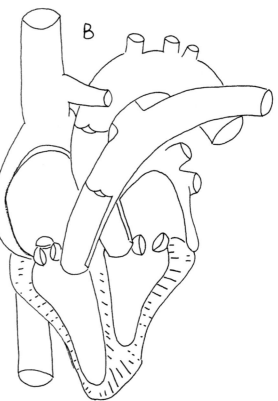

The brain serves as the body's control center: it sends electrochemical impulses through the central nervous system to control the organs and systems of the body. The heart, however, is an exception; it is not entirely controlled by the nervous system. In fact, if you were to remove the heart from a living animal such as a frog and place it in a liquid that is similar to blood plasma, the heart would continue to beat for several minutes.

The human heart has a small band of specialized tissue on the back wall of its right atrium; this band of tissue, called the "sinoatrial node," acts like a power station. It produces electrochemical impulses that cause the cardiac muscle (the heart's muscle) to contract. Scientists are not sure how the sinoatrial node generates its own impulses; they think it has something to do with its ability to soak up sodium ions. The sinoatrial node fires about 72 times a minute, and these electrochemical impulses quickly spread through the interconnected cells in the walls of the atria, causing the atria to contract.

The electrochemical impulses from the sinoatrial node cannot pass freely from the atria to the ventricles. Instead, they collect at another node called the "atrioventricular node." This node, which lies above the ventricles, directs these impulses through a special bundle of fibers called the "bundle of His." These fibers travel downward through the muscular walls of the ventricles, and both ventricles contract at the same time.

Level One Questions:

1. Is the contraction of the heart directly controlled by the brain? _____

2. What structure produces the heart's electrochemical impulses?

   _____

3. Where on the heart is its power station located?

   _____

4. Scientists think that the sinoatrial node's ability to soak up _____ ions makes it possible for the heart to generate its own electrochemical impulses.

5. About how many times a minute does the sinoatrial node fire? _____

6. What does the sinoatrial node release when it fires? _____

7. What happens when electrochemical impulses spread through the atria?

   _____

8. Where is the atrioventricular node located?

   _____

9. What is the job of the atrioventricular node?

   _____

10. What is the job of the bundle of His?

    _____

11. What happens when electrochemical impulses travel through the ventricles?

    _____

Level Two Questions:

Look at the two diagrams at the beginning of this activity.

12. A contraction of the atria is called an "atrial systole." Which heart in the diagrams shows an atrial systole?   A   B   (Circle one.)

13. When the atria are relaxed, they are in "atrial diastole." Which heart in the diagrams shows atrial diastole?   A   B   (Circle one.)

14. Ventricular systole occurs when the ventricles are contracted. Which heart in the diagrams shows ventricular systole?   A   B   (Circle one.)

15. Ventricular diastole occurs when the ventricles are relaxed. Which heart in the diagrams shows ventricular diastole?   A   B   (Circle one.)

Level Three Question:

16. The sinoatrial node is nicknamed the "pacemaker of the heart." Why is this an appropriate nickname?

_____

_____

To complete this project—

☐ On Diagram C, label the following structures:
   a. the sinoatrial node
   b. the atrioventricular node
   c. the bundle of His

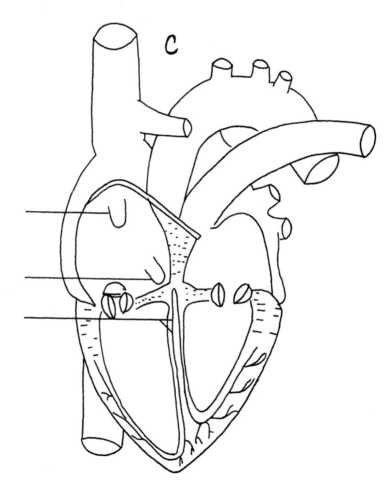

6–11. HOW MUCH BLOOD DOES YOUR HEART PUMP IN A MINUTE?

Instructions: (1.) Read the text. (2.) Use the text to help you to do the calculations and answer the questions.

Your "heart rate" is the number of times your heart beats or contracts in one minute. Since the job of your heart is to send oxygen to your cells, one major factor that determines how fast your heart beats is the amount of oxygen your cells need. While resting, the average person has a heart rate of about 72 beats (contractions) a minute. When you exercise, however, the cells of your body are working harder and use more oxygen; obviously, this means that your heart must beat faster to deliver more oxygen to the working cells.

Your "stroke volume" is the amount of blood pumped out of your heart each time it contracts. Each time the left ventricle contracts, about 80 milliliters of blood is sent out of the heart through the aorta (the artery that directs oxygenated blood to the body's cells), and a shock wave of blood pressure passes through the arteries of your body. When you count your pulse by putting a finger on one of the "pulse spots" (on your wrist, perhaps, or on your throat), you are really feeling this shock wave at a spot where the major arteries pass close to your skin.

While doing this project, you will determine how much blood is pumped out of your left ventricle each minute. You will first determine your heart rate by taking your pulse and then use this figure to determine the amount of blood your heart pumps. To do this, you simply multiply your pulse rate—which is the same as your heart rate—by 80 ml of blood. You may use a calculator, if you like.

Procedure

1. Watch carefully as your teacher shows how to locate your pulse in your left wrist. To insure accuracy, you will do this three times and then figure the average.

2. Count your pulse for one minute, and record it on line A.

3. Count your pulse rate two more times. Record these pulse rates on lines B and C.

4. Add lines A, B, and C. Write the sum on line D.

   A. _____

   B. _____

   C. _____

   D. _____

5. Divide the sum on line D by 3. This will give you your average heart rate. Record it below.

   My average pulse rate is _____ beats per minute.

6. Write your pulse rate on line E and multiply by 80. Write your answer on line F.

   E. _____
       × 80
   F. _____

Use line F to answer the question that follows.

Since I know that my heart pumps about _____ ml (milliliters) of blood with each contraction, and my heart contracts _____ times each minute, I know that my heart pumps about _____ ml in one minute.

Level One Questions:

1. How many times your heart beats (contracts) in one minute is your _____

   _____

2. What major factor determines how fast your heart beats?

   _____

3. While resting, the average person has a heart rate of about _____ beats per minute.

4. The amount of blood pumped out of the aorta each time the left ventricle contracts is the _____ volume.

Level Two Questions:

5. Why does your heart beat faster when you exercise?

   _____

   _____

6. What causes your pulse?

   _____

Level Three Questions:

7. Most trained athletes have lower-than-average heart rates. What might be an explanation for this?

   _____

   _____

   _____

8. If your heart rate is about 80 beats per minute, does this mean that your heart rate is abnormal? Explain your answer.

   _____

   _____

   _____

9. Your body contains about 5 liters of blood. Is the entire volume of your blood pumped through your heart in less than a minute or more than a minute?

   _____

6–12. THE BLOOD VESSELS

Instructions: (1.) Read the text carefully. (2.) Use the text and the diagrams to help you to answer the questions.

Blood travels through a network of arteries (which send blood away from the heart) and veins (which return blood to the heart).

When the heart contracts, blood is pumped into the aorta under pressure. This pressure, which causes the walls of the aorta to bulge slightly, helps to push blood through this large artery.

The aorta, the main passageway through which blood travels, leaves the heart through the left ventricle and curves upward to form a large arc called the "aortic arch." Smaller arteries called "distributing arteries" branch from the aortic arch and carry blood to the upper parts of the body (brain, arms, etc.).

(*Note:* Every section of every artery has its own name, so that a scientist can be extremely accurate in his or her descriptions. But nonscientists use a somewhat simpler approach and think of an entire branch that sends blood to the brain, for example, as a "carotid artery," and the branch that sends blood to the right arm as the "right subclavian artery.")

The aorta then curves downward behind the heart to form the descending aorta; distributing branches from the descending aorta travel to the stomach, liver, spleen, and so forth. Then the aorta divides to send blood to the legs. The branches travel through the pelvic region as the iliac arteries, branching further as they go; the large branch that travels through the thigh is called the "femoral artery."

The distributing arteries, in turn, branch into still smaller blood vessels called "arterioles"; they direct blood into the capillaries, where the most important work of the circulatory system is done. With the high power of magnification of an electron microscope, a capillary looks like a net made of extremely small tubes. The thin walls of these tiny tubes allow two-way traffic: oxygen and nutrients leave the blood and go to the cells, while carbon dioxide and other cellular wastes leave the cells and combine with the blood.

The waste-carrying, deoxygenated blood then leaves the capillary through an exit tube called a "venule." The venule will carry the blood a short distance before joining a larger branch called a "vein." This vein will eventually drain into the vena cava, which in turn will direct the blood into the right side of the heart; there it is pumped to the lungs, where it is replenished with oxygen. The wastes travel in the blood until they reach other specialized organs and tissues that remove them from the body.

While completing this worksheet, you will learn the names of some of the major arteries and veins of the human body.

To complete this project—

☐ Obtain your map pencils.

☐ Use a red pencil to color the arteries on the artery diagram.

☐ Use a blue pencil to color the veins on the vein diagram.

Level One Questions:

1. _____ are tubes that send blood away from the heart.

2. _____ are tubes that return blood to the heart.

3. The _____ serves as the main passageway through which blood travels.

4. Branches of the aorta are collectively called _____.

5. Distributing arteries branch to make smaller arteries called _____.

6. Arterioles direct blood into the _____.

7. Where is the real work of the circulatory system done?

   _____

8. What does a capillary look like?

   _____

9. Blood leaves the capillary through a tube called a _____.

   Use the diagram to help you answer the following Level One questions:

10. Name the arteries that send blood to the brain.

    _____

    _____

11. Name the veins that return blood from the brain.

    _____

    _____

12. Name the artery that sends blood to the left arm.

    _____

13. Name the vein that returns blood from the left arm.

    _____

14. Name the artery that sends blood to the left leg.

    _____

15. Name the vein that returns blood from the left leg.

    _____

16. Which arrow indicates the gastric artery, which sends blood to the stomach?

    A   B   C   (Circle one.)

17. Which arrow indicates the hepatic artery, which sends blood to the liver?

    A   B   C   (Circle one.)

18. Which arrow indicates the splenic artery, which sends blood to the spleen?

    A   B   C   (Circle one.)

Level Two Questions:

19. What does the blood entering the capillary contain?

_____

20. What does the blood leaving the capillary contain?

_____

21. What is the difference between a vein and a venule?

_____

_____

Level Three Questions:

22. Why are the arteries that branch from the aorta called "distributing" arteries?

_____

_____

23. Explain the name of the femoral artery.

_____

_____

24. Blood leaves the heart under pressure. When the blood reaches the capillary, this pressure has been greatly reduced. Why is this reduction of pressure important?

_____

_____

25. The following diagram is a stylized representation of the human circulatory system. Use the diagram showing the veins and arteries and what you have learned about the circulatory system to help you to write the labels.

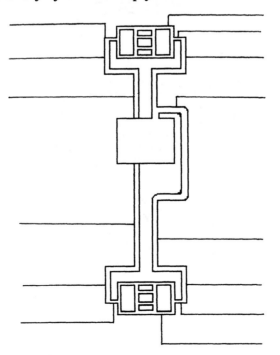

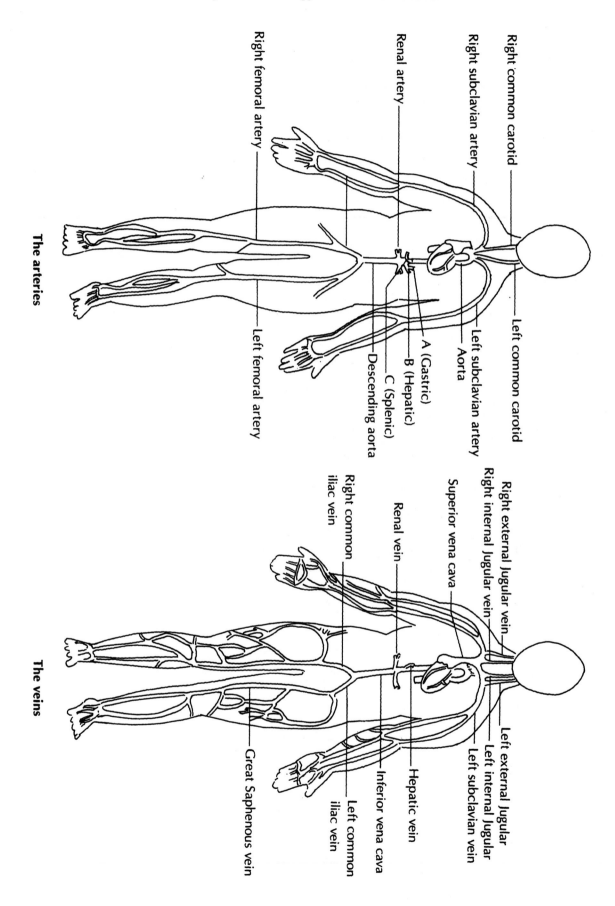

The arteries

Right common carotid
Right subclavian artery
Renal artery
Right femoral artery

Left common carotid
Left subclavian artery
Aorta
A (Gastric)
B (Hepatic)
C (Splenic)
Descending aorta
Left femoral artery

The veins

Right external Jugular vein
Right internal Jugular vein
Superior vena cava
Renal vein
Right common iliac vein

Left external Jugular
Left internal Jugular
Left subclavian vein
Hepatic vein
Inferior vena cava
Left common iliac vein
Great Saphenous vein

6–13. MICROSCOPIC OBSERVATION OF A VEIN AND AN ARTERY

Instructions: (1.) Read the text and study the diagrams. (2.) Do the investigation. (3.) Use the text and your observations to help you to answer the questions.

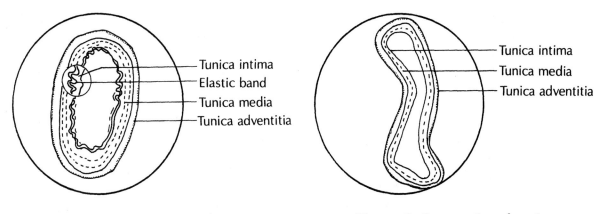

Diagram A: Cross-section of an artery   Diagram B: Cross-section of a vein

By observing cross sections of veins and arteries through the microscope, you can see their similarities and differences. Both have three layers: an inner layer called the "tunica intima," which forms the inside wall of the blood vessel; a middle layer called the "tunica media"; and an outer layer called the "tunica adventitia." In both veins and arteries, the tunica intima contains elastic fibers and a smooth inner layer of cells called "endothelium"; the tunica media contains circular layers of smooth muscle cells; and the tunica adventitia is composed of long, nonelastic fibers called "collagen."

Because veins and arteries have different jobs to do, they are designed differently. Compare Diagram A with Diagram B and notice that

1. the artery is open and the vein is collapsed;
2. the tunica media of the artery is thicker than the tunica media of the vein; and
3. only the artery has a dark band of elastic tissue.

Your arteries are designed to withstand pressure. A band of elastic tissue in the tunica intima allows an artery to expand or stretch each time the heart contracts and releases blood into the aorta. If this band of elastic tissue were not present, your arteries could rupture from the resulting shock wave of pressure. This elasticity also allows an artery to shrink to its original size after the blood has been distributed.

The smooth muscle cells of your arteries help them to regulate your blood pressure. The tunica media has three or more layers of circularly arranged smooth muscle cells. Smooth muscles, unlike skeletal and cardiac muscles, contract slowly and can remain in the contracted state for long periods.

You can compare an artery to a garden hose, and the smooth muscle to your hand; if you squeeze the hose with your hand, the water will come out with more force because the pressure on the hose has been increased. When the smooth muscles that surround an artery contract, the diameter of the artery gets smaller, and this causes an increase in your blood pressure.

   Smooth muscles also help arterioles to distribute your blood to the organs where it is needed most. For example, after you eat a large meal, more blood is needed around your stomach and intestines. Arterioles act like on-and-off valves; each one has a band of smooth muscle that can completely shut off the flow of blood to the capillary and can redirect blood to other areas of the body.

   Blood leaving a capillary is under reduced pressure; in fact, there is not enough pressure to return the blood to the heart. Fortunately, contracting skeletal muscles help to move the blood. When the skeletal muscles are doing work, such as moving the bones of the skeleton, nearby veins are compressed and the blood inside is then pushed toward the heart. There is one problem with this kind of pumping action: When the skeletal muscles relax, gravity can make the blood flow backward through the vein. To prevent this, many veins, especially those in the lower parts of your body, contain one-way valves that allow the blood to flow in only one direction—toward the heart.

   While doing this investigation, you will learn to identify, describe, and compare the parts of veins and arteries.

Step one: Obtain the following materials:

   ☐ microscope

   ☐ prepared microscope slides of a vein and an artery

Step two: Using 100X magnification, sketch the vein and artery in the indicated circles.

Step three: Use Diagrams A and B to help you to label your sketches.

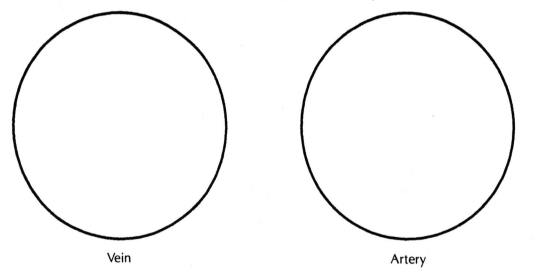

Vein   Artery

Level One Questions:

   1. Both veins and arteries have _____ layers.

   2. What is the innermost layer called? _____

   3. What is the middle layer called? _____

   4. What is the outermost layer called? _____

   5. What two tissues are found in the tunica intima?

   _____

6. What tissue is found in the tunica media?

_____

7. What is collagen? In which layer is it found?

_____

8. Your arteries are designed to withstand _____.

9. A band of _____ tissue in the tunica intima allows the artery to expand or stretch.

10. Elasticity also allows the artery to _____ to its original size after the blood has been distributed.

11. The structure of your arteries helps them to regulate your blood _____.

12. Where is blood most needed after you eat a large meal?

_____

13. _____ act like shut-off valves that can redirect blood to other areas of your body.

14. Blood leaving a capillary is under _____ pressure.

15. Contracting _____ muscles help to move the blood.

16. Many veins contain one-way _____ to prevent blood from flowing

_____.

17. Diagrams C and D show how the valves in a vein prevent the back flow of blood. What do the small circles in these diagrams represent?

_____

18. Which diagram shows the valve open?

C   D   (Circle one.)

19. Which diagram shows the valve closing?

C   D   (Circle one.)

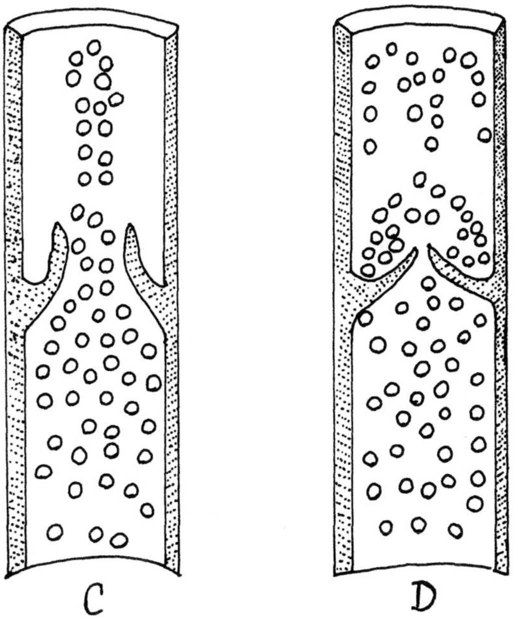

C   D

Level Two Questions:

20. How does the structure of your arteries help to regulate your blood pressure?

_____

_____

21. How do the arterioles help to redistribute your blood?

_____

_____

22. How do skeletal muscles help to pump the blood toward the heart?

_____

_____

23. Study Diagrams C and D. How does the valve inside the vein work?

_____

_____

Level Three Question:

24. Not all veins have valves. In which area of the body do you think valves are not needed? Explain your answer.

_____

_____

_____

_____

_____

Unit **7**

The Immune System

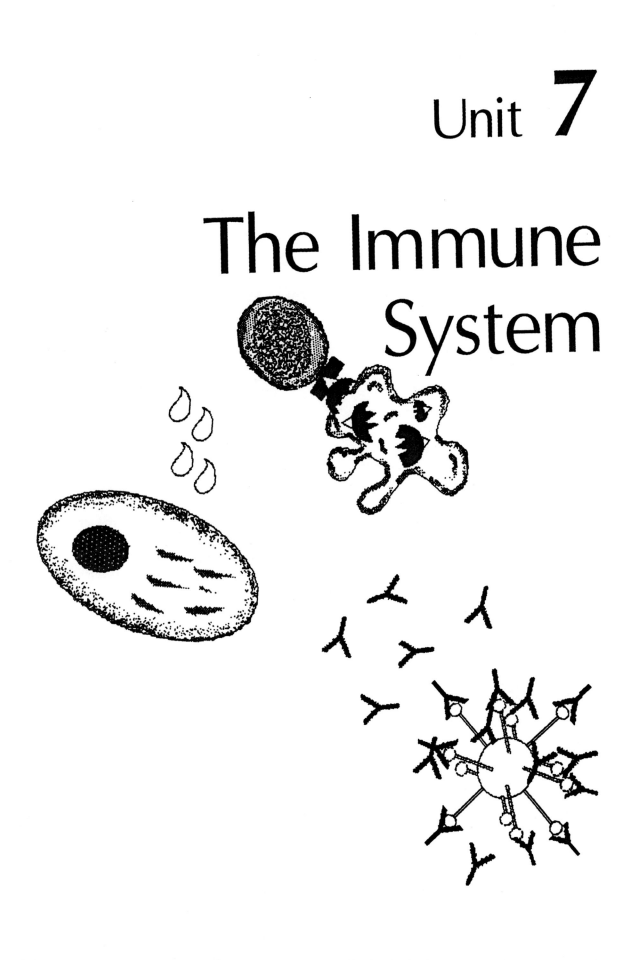

7–1 HAVING A HEALTHY IMMUNE SYSTEM IS IMPORTANT

Note: This is a self-directed activity.

Answers to the Questions:

Level One

1. microorganisms
2. through broken skin, mouth, nose (and others that are not mentioned in the text)
3. generally enters through your nose or mouth
4. mucous cells
5. monocytes
6. shapeless blobs
7. monocytes

Level Two

8. serves as a barrier that prevents pathogenic (disease-causing) organisms from entering the body
9. Both are "cell eaters" or phagocytes, and they are the first white blood cells to defend the body.

7–2 WHITE BLOOD CELLS

Teaching Suggestions:

1. If available, use an optical disk player to show a short movie about the amoeba.
2. It is often difficult to see the granules and their colors and to distinguish the cytoplasm on many commercially prepared microscope slides, especially if they have been sitting in a cupboard for a while. Consider the colors you see, and if they vary from the descriptions, explain to your students.

Answers to Statement Questions:

a. C
b. D
c. E
d. B
e. A

Answers to the Questions:

Level One

1. through broken (injured) skin, nose, mouth, and other ways not mentioned in the text

2. leucocytes
3. phagocytosis
4. erythrocytes, monocytes
5. basophils
6. eosinophils

Level Two

7. Answers will vary. Essentially, either can move by throwing out a jellylike arm and pulling the rest of its body toward it.
8. Answers will vary. In phagocytosis, the leukocyte surrounds a foreign invader with its jellylike body and eats it.
9. Answers will vary. Not all foreign invaders are destroyed by the digestive processes. Food unfortunately contains bacteria, viruses, and other invaders, and eating conditions are not necessarily sanitary. So there are more invaders after a meal, requiring more white blood cells.

7–3 MAKE AN ACTION CARTOON

Teaching Suggestions:

1. Remind your students to make sure that the bottom edges of their cartoons are even before stapling them.
2. Make an overhead transparency of an uncut cartoon. Use this transparency to help you to describe the action of a white blood cell.

Answers to the Questions:

Level One

1. one
2. round with spines
3. The macrophage surrounds it with its body and eats it.
4. The pathogen sketched should be round with spines.
5. The macrophage should look like a jelly creature.

7–4 THE ANATOMY OF THE VIRUS

Note: This is a self-directed activity.

Answers to the Questions:

Level One

1. shape
2. particle
3. crystal, tissue

4. genetic strand

5. a needlelike structure called the tail sheath

6. land

7. landing gear

Level Two

8. No. Its tail fibers will allow it to land only on a certain kind of bacteria and not on human cells.

7–5 LANDING GEAR AND LANDING PADS

Note: This is a self-directed worksheet.

Teaching Suggestion:

Make an overhead transparency of the diagram to show your students the lock-and-key mechanism used by viruses to attach to cells.

Answers to the Questions:

Level One

1. about 750,000
2. cell
3. design, shape
4. shapes on all cell membranes that match the inscribed patterns on a virus
5. landing, landing
6. three
7. mucous cell, liver cell, skin cell
8. #3
9. yes
10. #2
11. no

Level Two

12. Virus one has triangular landing feet (gear) that cannot fit (lock) into the round landing pad on the mucous cell.

7–6 REVIEWING THE PARTS OF THE CELL

Note: In order for your students to understand how viruses affect a cell, it is important that they understand the mechanism that cells use to assemble proteins.

Teaching Suggestion:

Use a cell model to help you to conduct a review of the structure and function of the cell.

Answers to the Questions:

Level One

1. DNA
2. deoxyribonucleic acid
3. directs all the cell's activities
4. the chromosomes
5. instructions that direct the cell to make chemicals (proteins)
6. ribosomes
7. ribosomes

Level Two

8. No. Answers will vary. On ribosomes, proteins (digestive chemicals in this case) are produced. If liver cells did not contain ribosomes, they would not have "assembly lines."

7–7 THE VIRUS TAKES OVER

Note: This is a self-directed worksheet.

Answers to the Questions:

Level One

1. no
2. Viruses can enter the body through the nose and mouth. If you are around a person suffering from the flu and he sneezes or coughs, you could inhale the virus.
3. It drifts.
4. The infected cell changes into a virus factory.
5. no
6. no
7. viruses

Level Two

8. A virus can enter the body only by chance because it has no specialized structures for moving.
9. A phage virus uses a needlelike structure to inject its genetic material. A human pathogenic virus first sinks into the cell; next, its envelope partially breaks open to release its genetic material.
10. Answers will vary. Essentially, the nucleus (computer control room in a factory) of a cell (factory) contains chromosomes (computers) that send instructions to the ribosomes (assembly-line robots).

7–8 LYMPHOCYTES

Note: This is a self-directed activity.

Teaching Suggestion:

Make an overhead transparency of the diagram to help you to conduct a discussion.

Answers to the Questions:

Level One

1. surrounds, eats
2. fragments
3. membrane
4. key, lymphocyte
5. recognition sites
6. lock
7. viral
8. three
9. yes
10. lymphocyte 3
11. C

Level Two

12. Yes. You can see the capsule fragments.
13. No. There are no broken capsule fragments.

7–9 TURNING ON THE IMMUNE SYSTEM

Note: This is a self-directed activity.

Answers to the Questions:

Level One

1. lock and key
2. A T4 lymphocyte is readied for action.
3. turns on other kinds of white blood cells
4. B-lymphocytes grow and divide into other types of cells.
5. produce specific antibodies against the virus
6. small Ys
7. lock onto the virus's landing gear

Level Two

8. Memory cells remain circulating in the blood for years; they will remember the shape of the virus and begin producing antibodies before the invader infects the cells.

Level Three

9. Answers will vary. There are different varieties of flu viruses with different shapes on their envelopes. (This question really deals with new pathogens, but students may also mention that viruses can change their shapes so that the memory cells may not recognize the new shape.)

7–10 HOW CHEMICALS CAN STIMULATE A CELL

Notes:

1. BECAUSE OF THE HAZARDS OF WORKING WITH MERCURY, THIS ACTIVITY WILL BE A TEACHER DEMONSTRATION ONLY.
2. If students are to benefit from this teacher-directed demonstration, they should have completed the previous worksheet, "Turning on the Immune System."

Answers to the Demonstration Questions:

1. round
2. yes
3. The answer depends on how many crystals the teacher used.
4. eating the crystals (viruses)
5. At this point, the mercury is inactive.
6. Yes. The mercury became active and surrounded (ate) the crystals.
7. Yes. The nitric acid (which represents interleukin-2) somehow activated the mercury (B lymphocyte).
8. Answers will vary.

7–11 THE T8 LYMPHOCYTES

Note: This is a self-directed worksheet.

Answers to the Questions:

Level One

1. cell
2. virus
3. cytotoxic killer, suppressor cells
4. They use a poison to destroy cells that have already been invaded by viruses.
5. They release a chemical that signals the T4 lymphocytes to stop producing interleukin-2.

Level Two

6. This part of the immune system has the ability to destroy virus factories (cells that have already been invaded by a virus).

Level Three

7. A newborn has not yet established a strong immune system. The presence of a large thymus gland enables him to produce more T4 and T8 lymphocytes.

7–12 THE MODERN-DAY PLAGUE: AIDS

Note: This is a self-directed worksheet.

Answers to the Questions:

Level One

1. immune system
2. Human Immunodeficiency Virus
3. Certain pathogenic microorganisms (which are usually kept at bay by white blood cells and antibodies) take hold in the body.
4. Pneumocystis carinii
5. Karposi's sarcoma
6. Acquired Immune Deficiency Syndrome (AIDS)
7. AIDS cannot be transmitted in most of the usual ways. It can be prevented. You should recognize the symptoms, but if you have some of them you do not necessarily have AIDS; and so forth.

7–13 THE CASE OF JOHN DOE

Note: This is a self-directed worksheet.

Answers to the Questions:

Level One

1. A syndrome is a group of related symptoms produced by a pathological condition.
2. no

Level Two

3. AIDS weakens the body's defenses by weakening the immune system.

Level Three

4. Answers will vary. This frequently used term seems to be connected most with the word *opportunity;* the virus strikes when conditions are "suitable, appropriate, favorable." It also has some of the pejorative connotations of *opportunist,* of course.

7–14 HOW THE HIV ATTACKS A T4 LYMPHOCYTE

Note: This is a self-directed activity.

Answers to the Questions:

Level One

1. protecting, diseases
2. no
3. Some viruses change their outside structures so that antibodies cannot recognize them as enemies.
4. T4 lymphocytes
5. cytotoxic killer cells, B-lymphocytes

7–15 HOW AIDS IS SPREAD

Note: This is a self-directed worksheet.

Answers to the Questions:

Level One

1. yes
2. If an infected person sneezes, small droplets can carry the virus through the air and infect a healthy person.
3. liver
4. yes
5. Hepatitis can be spread from a shared glass or eating utensil.
6. no
7. having sex with an infected person, sharing a hypodermic needle with another drug abuser

Level Two

8. The HIV is unstable in air.

Level Three

9. The HIV is spread when body fluids from an infected person mix with the body fluids of a healthy person. This can occur from a razor cut or from sharing toothbrushes, especially if there is a cut or a sore in the infected person's mouth. This is not likely to occur through the sharing of hand towels and soaps.

7–16 INTRAVENOUS DRUG ABUSE

Note: This is a self-directed worksheet.

Teaching Suggestion:

Use question 7 to conduct a class discussion.

Answers to the Questions:

Level One

1. hypodermic
2. share, reuse
3. transmitted
4. ten

Level Two

5. Since AIDS symptoms may not appear for up to ten years, a person engaging in high-risk behavior may not know that he or she is infected with the HIV.

Level Three

6. Answers will vary. Since the HIV is transmitted by sexual contact and by the sharing of needles, such high-risk activity is obviously to be avoided. Some students will mention the need to investigate the care with which blood banks screen blood, and they may think of other blood-to-blood risks.

7. Answers will vary. One hopes that students would think first of educating the populace about the risks and the avenues of transmission; some may consider making blood tests mandatory. (Note: At some point you may wish to discuss the students' answers and help them to strive for balance. For example, my dental hygienist, aware of the sentiment in favor of testing health-care professionals, says wistfully that she wishes all the patients could be tested, too.)

7–1. HAVING A HEALTHY IMMUNE SYSTEM IS IMPORTANT

Instructions: (1.) Read the text. (2.) Use the text to help you to answer the questions.

Your skin is a barrier that protects you from many pathogenic (disease-causing) organisms. If your skin is broken, microorganisms can come into your body and multiply. Even a very small cut will allow hundreds to enter.

Microorganisms also get into your body through your nose and mouth. A flu virus, for example, generally enters through your nose or mouth, then attaches itself to the lining of your throat and destroys mucous cells. Thousands of persons with weak immune systems die each year from the flu. (Flu is a short way to say "influenza"—an unspecific "umbrella" term for many respiratory infections and digestive problems.)

A person with a healthy immune system seldom dies from the flu because the immune system destroys viruses shortly after they enter the body. Neutrophils and monocytes (white blood cells) destroy viruses by eating them. Scientists call these guardian cells "phagocytes," meaning "cell eaters." They look like large shapeless blobs as they travel through the circulatory system keeping watch.

The most powerful of the phagocytes, the monocytes, can eat about five times as many microorganisms as the neutrophils.

Level One Questions:

1. If your skin is broken, _____ can come into your body and multiply.

2. In what ways do microorganisms generally enter your body?

   _____

   _____

   _____

3. How does the flu virus enter your body?

   _____

4. What kind of cell does the flu virus destroy? _____

5. Neutrophils and _____ destroy viruses by eating them.

6. Phagocytes look like large _____ as they travel through the circulatory system.

7. The most powerful of the phagocytes are the _____.

Level Two Questions:

8. How does the skin help the immune system?

   _____

   _____

9. How are neutrophils and monocytes similar?

   _____

   _____

7–2. WHITE BLOOD CELLS

Instructions: (1.) Read the text and the statements. (2.) Use the text, the statements, and the diagram to help you to answer the questions.

Every moment, your body is under attack. Bacteria, viruses, fungi, protozoa, and other microorganisms can enter your body through your nose and mouth, through cuts in your skin, and through the pores of your intestines. If your body did not have white blood cells to protect it, you would be sick all the time. White blood cells help you to stay well by destroying foreign invaders.

While doing this project, you will learn that by comparing the size of the cell, observing the nucleus, and examining the cytoplasm, you can identify five different types of leukocytes. You will also learn the ways in which leukocytes can help you to stay healthy.

White blood cells (which do not have hemoglobin, as red blood cells do) are called "leukocytes"; *leuki* means "white," and *cyte* means "cell." About ⅔ to ¾ of all leukocytes are also called "granulocytes," because they contain fine granules; neutrophils, eosinophils, and basophils are granulocytes.

Neutrophils (the most numerous granulocytes) have very fine granules, which do not absorb dyes well; when a dye is used, the granules of a neutrophil turn only a pale lavender color. The nucleus of a neutrophil is divided into three to five lobules. The granules of eosinophils are much coarser and turn a bright reddish color when dyed. An eosinophil's nucleus has only two lobes. Basophils are quite rare (only .5 of all blood cells); their granules stain a bluish purple, and their nuclei have two lobes.

The remainder of the leukocytes are called "agranulocytes" (*a* means "not"). The agranulocytes are lymphocytes and monocytes. A lymphocyte has a single nucleus; it turns very dark under stain and has a thin blue edge. A monocyte is usually larger than a lymphocyte and stains a lighter blue color than lymphocytes do; its nucleus is roughly bean-shaped. The phagocytes (cell-eaters), the neutrophils and monocytes, are attracted to the site of a foreign invasion—probably by some kind of chemical action set up by the degeneration of the tissues that are being destroyed by the invader. There they surround and digest the invader. After the phagocyte digests the invading material, the phagocyte dies—but in doing so, it makes more chemicals to attract more phagocytes. Lymphocytes can become monocytes when necessary and can help to destroy invaders.

Basophils secrete heparin; it is a normal part of the blood, and it is important in keeping blood from clotting in the blood vessels.

Granulocytes

	granules	stained	nucleus	% of leuc.	capabilities
neutrophils	fine	pale lav.	3 to 5 lobes	65 to 75	phagocytes
eosinophils	coarse	or. to red	bi-lobed	2 to 5	probably help defense
basophils	irregular	blue-purp.	bi-lobed	about .5	secrete heparin

Agranulocytes

	stained	nucleus	% of leuc.	capabilities
lymphocytes	rim is lt. blue	large, dark	25 to 30	help in defense
monocytes	blue-grey	bean-shaped	3 to 8	phagocytes

Statements

1. The most common type of white blood cell is the neutrophil; it is chemically attracted to any foreign matter that enters your body. While searching for foreign matter such as bacteria and viruses, it can move about like an amoeba. That is, it can move by throwing out a jellylike arm and pouring the rest of its body toward it. A neutrophil can leave the blood and circulatory system by squeezing through the pores of small blood vessels.

   Neutrophils are easy to identify because their nuclei have three or more lobes, connected to one another by thin strands.

   a. On the diagram, which white blood cell is a neutrophil?

      A B C D E (Circle one.)

2. Like neutrophils, monocytes destroy foreign invaders by a process called "phagocytosis." In phagocytosis, the leukocyte surrounds a foreign invader with its jellylike body and digests it. A monocyte has a large nucleus and can reach a diameter of 20 microns.

   b. On the diagram, which white blood cell is a monocyte?

      A B C D E (Circle one.)

3. Lymphocytes look similar to monocytes, and both have large nuclei. But a monocyte is much larger; it may be 20 microns in diameter, whereas a lymphocyte is only about 8 microns in diameter—about the size of an erythrocyte.

   Lymphocytes are unusual because they can change into other types of blood cells. Lymphocytes can change into erythrocytes, monocytes, and other types of white blood cells.

   c. On the diagram, which white blood cell is a lymphocyte?

      A B C D E (Circle one.)

4. Basophils release a chemical called "heparin," which appears to prevent blood from clotting in the arteries and veins. A basophil is about 12 microns in diameter and has a bilobed (two-lobed) nucleus. The cytoplasm of the basophil is filled with large, irregularly shaped granules.

   d. On the diagram, which white blood cell is a basophil?

      A B C D E (Circle one.)

5. Eosinophils are easy to identify because their nuclei are bi-lobed; they look rather like stereo headphones. Scientists think that these leukocytes help you to stay healthy by removing poisonous substances from your tissues.

   e. On the diagram, which white blood cell is an eosinophil?

      A B C D E (Circle one.)

   To complete this project—

☐ Use the diagram and the statements to help you to sketch (in the circles) the five types of leukocytes.

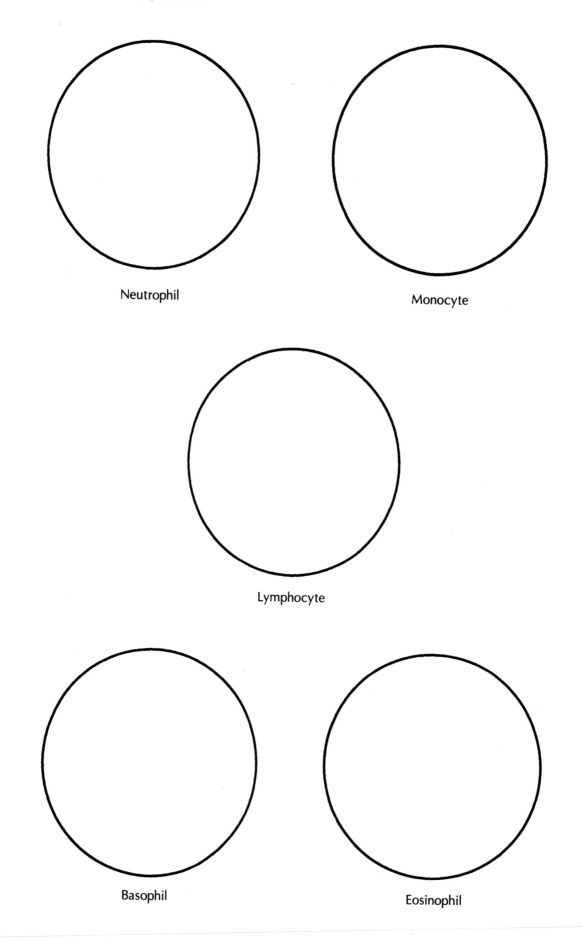

Neutrophil

Monocyte

Lymphocyte

Basophil

Eosinophil

Level One Questions:

1. List three ways in which disease-causing microorganisms can enter your body.

   _____

   _____

   _____

2. White blood cells are also called _____.

3. Neutrophils and monocytes can destroy foreign invaders by a process called ____

   _____.

4. Lymphocytes can change into _____, _____,
   and other kinds of blood cells.

5. Which leukocyte probably helps to prevent blood from clotting? _____

   _____

6. Which leukocyte probably absorbs poisonous substances from the tissues?

   _____

Level Two Questions:

7. Neutrophils and monocytes can move about like amoebas. Describe this kind of movement.

   _____

   _____

   _____

8. Neutrophils and monocytes can eat foreign invaders by a process called "phago-cytosis." Describe this process.

   _____

   _____

   _____

   _____

Level Three Question:

9. The number of leukocytes in the blood increases after a heavy meal. Why do you think this happens?

   _____

   _____

   _____

   _____

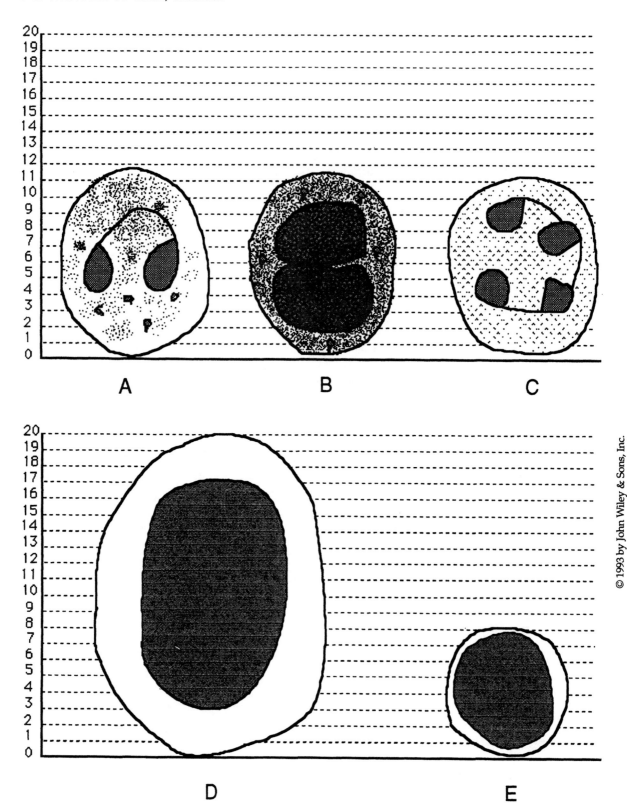

Name _____   Date _____

7–3. MAKE AN ACTION CARTOON

Instructions: (1.) Follow these procedures to help you to cut out and assemble the cartoon. (2.) Use the cartoon and the text to help you to answer the questions.

A macrophage moves by shooting out a fingerlike extension of its body and pouring the rest of its jellylike mass toward it. In this way, it can attack and eat an invading microorganism. After you assemble the cartoon, carefully watch the action of the macrophage to see how it digests a virus.

Step one: Using scissors, carefully cut out the squares of the cartoon.

Step two: Put the squares in numerical order to make a booklet. Square number one should be on top.

Step three: Make sure the bottom edges of the little pages line up with one another.

Step four: Staple, or have your teacher help you staple, the cartoon booklet at the top.

Step five: Riffle through the booklet and watch the action.

Level One Questions:

1. How many pathogens did you see in the cartoon? _____

2. Describe the shape of a pathogen.

   _____

3. Describe the macrophage's method of eating the pathogen.

   _____

   _____

4. In the space here, sketch the pathogen.

5. In the space here, sketch the macrophage.

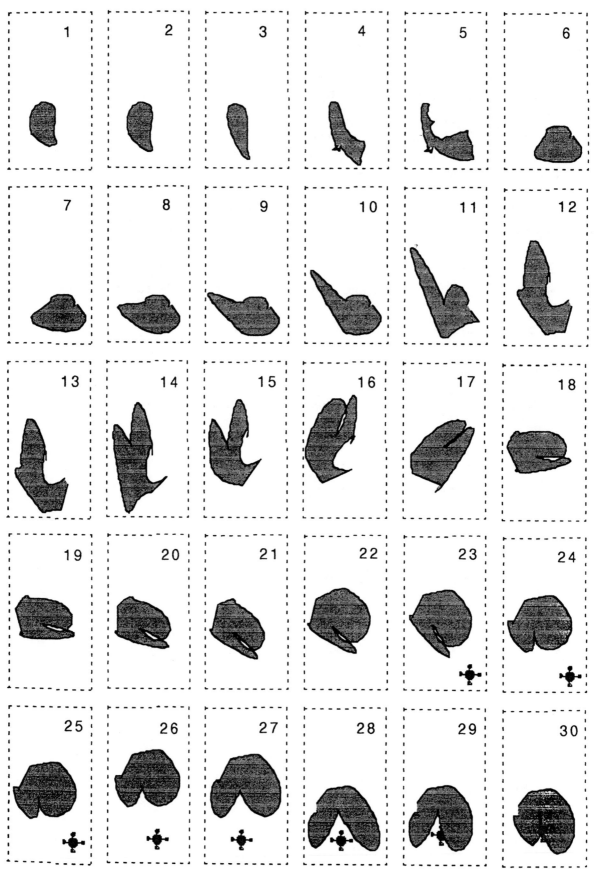

7–4. THE ANATOMY OF THE VIRUS

Instructions: (1.) Read the text and the descriptions. (2.) Use both to help you to label the diagram and answer the questions.

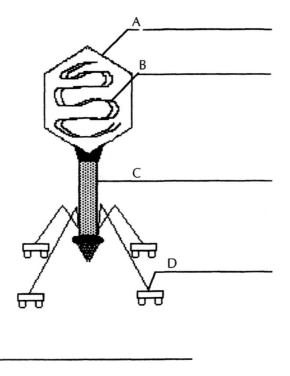

Title

Macrophages are the first line of defense against viruses and other pathogens. Macrophages alone, however, can seldom defend the body. After eating a pathogen, a macrophage signals the lymphocytes for help.

A lymphocyte can recognize an invader only by its shape. To help you to learn how lymphocytes do this, the shape of the virus is described here.

Since the phage virus has an easy shape to understand, it will be our example. It is important for you to know that this virus is harmless to humans: Its tail fibers will allow it to land only on a certain kind of bacteria and not on human cells.

Descriptions

1. The virus is a very small particle. Because it acts like a nonliving particle most of the time, scientists are not sure whether it should be classified as a living or a non-living substance. The diagram shows a typical virus; on the title line, write "A Typical Virus."

2. The body of the virus looks more like a crystal than like living tissue. This crystal-like structure is called the "envelope." Arrow A points to the envelope. Find arrow A and label it "envelope."

3. Inside the envelope is a genetic strand. It has a chemical code that orders an attacked cell to make more viruses. Arrow B points to the genetic strand. Label arrow B "genetic strand."

4. To inject the genetic strand into a cell, the virus uses a needlelike structure called the "tail sheath." Arrow C points to the tail sheath. Find arrow C and label it "tail sheath."

5. The tail fibers act like landing gear and help the virus to land on a cell. Arrow D points to the tail fibers. Find arrow D and label it "tail fibers."

Level One Questions:

1. A lymphocyte can recognize an invader only by its _____.

2. The virus is a very small _____.

3. The body of the virus looks more like a _____ than like living _____.

4. What is located inside the envelope? _____

5. What does the virus use to inject its genetic strand?

   _____

6. The tail fibers help the virus to _____ on a cell.

7. The tail fibers act like _____.

Level Two Question:

8. Is the phage virus harmful to humans? Explain your answer.

   _____

   _____

   _____

   _____

7–5. LANDING GEAR AND LANDING PADS

Instructions: (1.) Read the text. (2.) Use the text and the diagram to help you to answer the questions.

No one knows just how many types of viruses there are. Some experts think that at least 750,000 different kinds of viruses are pathogenic to humans.

It is interesting to notice that any one type of virus can land only on one kind of cell. For example, the flu virus can land only on mucous cells, the hepatitis virus only on liver cells, and the AIDS virus only on specific types of white blood cells.

You may remember that the tail fibers of a virus serve as landing gear and that the tip of each tail fiber has inscribed on it a unique design that only a certain shape can fit.

Cell membranes have viral receptor sites; these are shapes made from large molecules that match the inscribed patterns on a virus. If the shape on a cell does not match a virus's landing gear perfectly, the virus cannot land and therefore cannot harm the cell.

Level One Questions:

1. About how many types of viruses are harmful to humans? _____

2. One type of virus can land on only one type of _____.

3. The tip of each tail fiber has a unique _____ that

   only a certain _____ can fit.

4. What are viral receptor sites?

   _____

   _____

5. The virus can land only on a cell where its _____

   gear matches the viral _____ pads.

   Use the diagrams to help you to answer the remaining Level One questions.

6. How many viruses do you see on the diagram? _____

7. Name the different kinds of cells on the diagram.

   _____

   _____

   _____

8. Which virus can land on the liver cell? _____

9. Can virus 2 land on the mucous cell? _____

10. The flu virus attacks mucous cells. Which virus causes flu? _____

11. The virus that causes hepatitis lands on liver cells. Can virus 1 cause hepatitis?

    _____

Level Two Question:

12. Explain the answer to question #11.

_____

_____

_____

_____

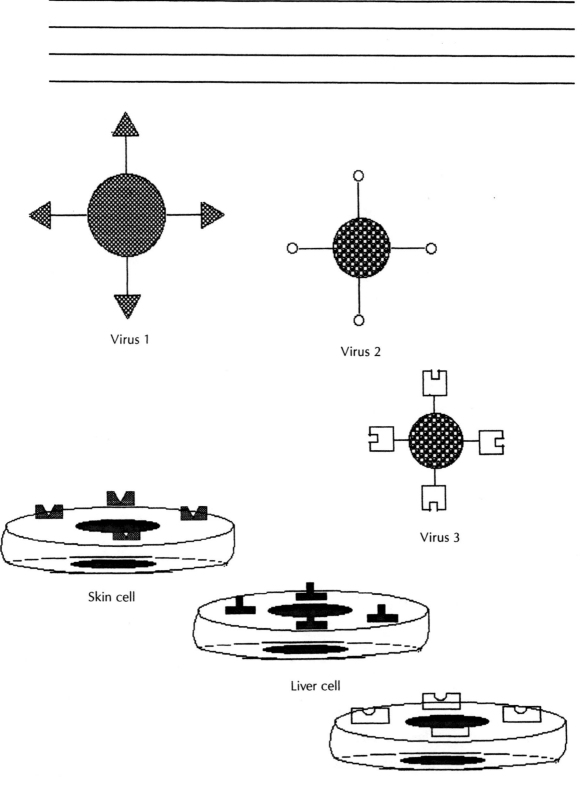

Virus 1

Virus 2

Virus 3

Skin cell

Liver cell

Mucous cell

7–6. REVIEWING THE PARTS OF THE CELL

Instructions: (1.) Read the text. (2.) Use the text and the diagram to help you to answer the questions.

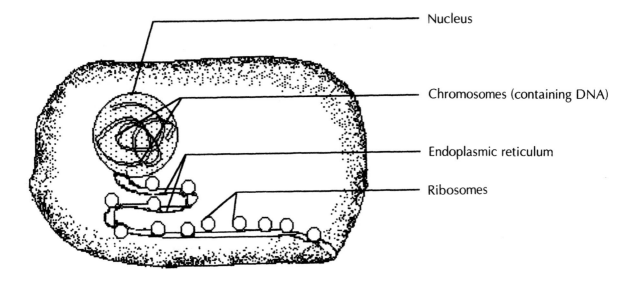

Inside the nucleus of every cell is "deoxyribonucleic acid" or "DNA"; it directs all of the cell's activities. Under the direction of DNA, for example, liver cells make chemicals that help the small intestine to digest food. This occurs when instructions are sent to the ribosomes on the endoplasmic reticulum. On these ribosomes, digestive chemicals are put together in an assembly-line fashion.

To complete the project—
Carefully study the diagram and use colored pencils as follows:

☐ Color the nucleus brown.

☐ Color the chromosomes yellow.

☐ Color the ribosomes blue.

☐ Color the endoplasmic reticulum orange.

Level One Questions:

1. Inside the nucleus of every cell is _____.

2. What do the letters DNA stand for?

   _____

3. What does DNA do?

   _____

4. Where in the nucleus is DNA located? _____

   5. What instructions are sent to the cell?

      _____

   6. What is located on the endoplasmic reticulum? _____

   7. Where on the liver cell are digestive chemicals put together? _____

      _____

Level Two Question:

   8. Liver cells are often described as small chemical factories. Do you think the liver cells' chemical-producing activities would be possible if the cell did not have ribosomes? Explain your answer.

      _____

      _____

      _____

      _____

7–7. THE VIRUS TAKES OVER

Instructions: (1.) Read the text. (2.) Use the text and the diagrams to help you to answer the questions.

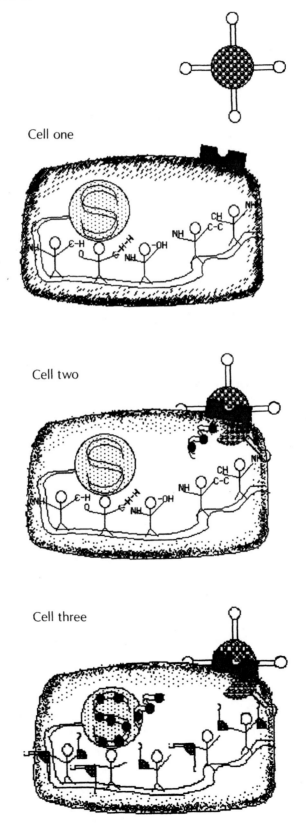

Cell one

Cell two

Cell three

A virus has no specialized structures for moving. This means that it has no fins for swimming, legs for walking, or wings for flying; it enters your body merely by chance. You can become infected with the flu virus if, for example, you happen to be near an ill person who sneezes or coughs.

Not all viruses are transmitted this way. Some viruses are transmitted by casual contact such as shaking hands, hugging, or kissing. Some viruses can be transmitted from dirty dishes and by animal bites; others are transmitted only by sexual contact or hypodermic needles.

Since it can't swim, walk, or crawl, even after a virus enters your body it must drift along until, by chance, it finds a cell that it can land on.

Unlike the phage virus, a virus that is pathogenic to humans does not use a needlelike structure to inject its genetic code. Instead, it partially sinks into the cell; the cell envelope breaks, and genetic material then empties into the cell's cytoplasm, passes into the nucleus, and combines with the cell's DNA. At this stage, the infected cell becomes a "virus factory." Instead of sending instructions that direct the cell's normal activities, the virus's genetic material reprograms the host cell's nucleus to send instructions for making new viruses.

Level One Questions:

1. Do viruses have special structures for moving about? _____

2. How can a virus enter the body by chance? Give one example.

   _____

3. After a virus enters the body, how does it move about until it locates a cell it can land on?

   _____

4. What happens after the virus combines its genetic material with the cell's DNA?

   _____

   Use the diagrams to help you to answer the remaining Level One questions.

5. On cell one, has the virus particle landed? _____

6. On cell two, the virus has landed and has released its genetic material into the cytoplasm. Has the genetic strand completely entered the nucleus?

   _____

7. In cell three, the dots on the DNA show that the virus's genetic material has combined with it. What has this caused the stick-figure men (the ribosomes) to make?

   _____

Level Two Questions:

8. Explain the statement, "A virus can enter your body only by chance."

_____

_____

_____

9. A phage virus injects its genetic material in one way, and a virus pathogenic to humans releases its genetic material in another. Explain the difference.

_____

_____

_____

10. Many automobile companies have updated their factories by using computers to operate assembly-line robots. Compare such an updated factory with the workings of the cell.

_____

_____

_____

_____

7–8. LYMPHOCYTES

Instructions: (1.) Read the text. (2.) Use the text and the diagrams to help you to answer the questions.

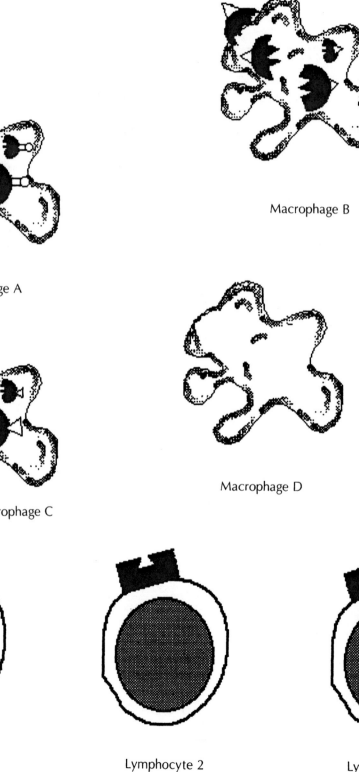

Macrophage B

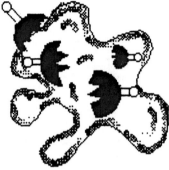

Macrophage A

Macrophage C

Macrophage D

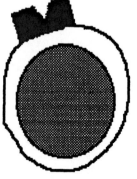

Lymphocyte 1

Lymphocyte 2

Lymphocyte 3

Lymphocytes and macrophages work together to protect your body from a virus attack.

After a macrophage encounters a virus, it surrounds and eats it. Chemicals inside this white blood cell help to break the virus apart; at least one small fragment of the broken virus is placed on the macrophage's membrane where it acts like a key that can activate a resting lymphocyte.

On the membrane of a certain kind of lymphocyte is a recognition site that acts like a lock. This lock (recognition site) is specific because only one kind of viral fragment fits into it. For example, a piece of flu virus displayed on a macrophage's membrane can only attach to and activate those lymphocytes that carry a specific recognition site for it.

Level One Questions:

1. After a macrophage encounters a virus, it _____ and _____ it.

2. The chemicals in the macrophage help to break the virus into _____.

3. One small fragment of the virus is placed on the macrophage's outer _____.

4. The fragment acts like a _____ that activates a resting _____.

5. What is on the membrane of every lymphocyte? _____

6. A recognition site acts like a _____.

7. A lock carried on the lymphocyte can be activated by only one kind of _____ fragment.

   Use the diagrams to help you to answer the remaining Level One and Level Two questions.

8. Macrophage A has eaten a flu virus. How many capsule fragments remain inside its body? _____

9. Does macrophage A have a capsule fragment displayed on its membrane? _____

10. Which lymphocyte carries a recognition site for the flu virus? _____

11. Which macrophage has a capsule particle that can attach to lymphocyte 2? _____

Level Two Questions:

12. Has macrophage C eaten a virus? Explain how you know this.

   _____

   _____

   _____

13. Has macrophage D eaten a virus? Explain how you know this.

   _____

   _____

   _____

7–9. TURNING ON THE IMMUNE SYSTEM

Instructions: (1.) Read the text. (2.) Use the text and the diagrams to help you to answer the questions.

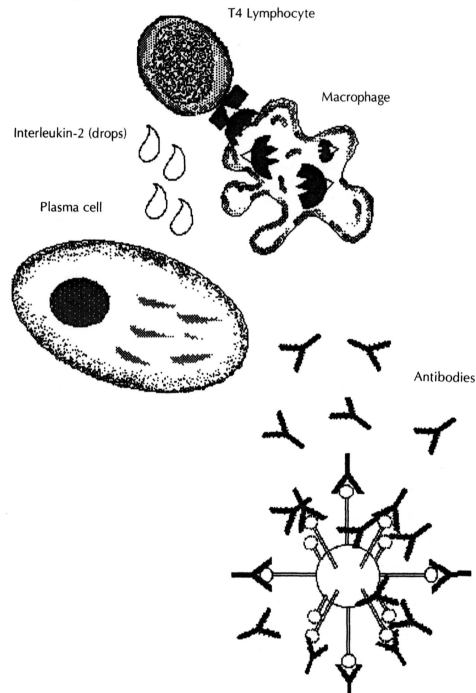

T4 Lymphocyte

Macrophage

Interleukin-2 (drops)

Plasma cell

Antibodies

A "lock-and-key" mechanism mobilizes the immune system. When a macrophage inserts a broken envelope fragment into the receptor site of a special kind of white blood cell called a "T4 lymphocyte," the whole immune system is readied for action. Like a key turning a lock, the virus fragment turns on the T4's machinery to make a chemical called "interleukin-2." When released into the blood, interleukin-2 turns on other kinds of white blood cells.

B lymphocytes are affected by interleukin-2 in a strange way: Interleukin-2 causes B lymphocytes to grow and to divide into other types of cells. Two of these newly formed cells are

a. plasma cells

b. memory cells

Plasma cells have an important job to do: They produce specific antibodies against the virus. Antibodies look like small Y's. At the forked ends of each Y are receptor sites that can lock onto the virus's landing gear. With its landing gear covered, the virus cannot land on a healthy cell and use its genetic material to turn the cell into a virus factory.

After you recover from an illness caused by a virus, you may become immune. This means you will never catch the same disease again. Memory cells are responsible for making you immune; they remain circulating in your blood for years, and if the same virus should enter your body again, memory cells will remember the shape of the virus and immediately start producing antibodies before the invader gets a chance to infect the cells.

Level One Questions:

1. A _____ mechanism gets the immune system ready for action.

2. When a macrophage inserts a broken envelope fragment into a receptor site, what happens?

   _____

3. What happens when interleukin-2 is released into the blood?

   _____

4. How does interleukin-2 affect B lymphocytes?

   _____

5. What do plasma cells do?

   _____

6. What do antibodies look like?

   _____

7. What do the receptor sites on an antibody do to a virus's landing gear?

   _____

Level Two Question:

8. How do memory cells help you to become immune?

   _____

Level Three Question:

9. If memory cells make a person immune from the flu, why is it possible for a person with a healthy immune system to catch the flu every year?

   _____

   _____

   _____

7–10. HOW CHEMICALS CAN STIMULATE A CELL

Note: **BECAUSE OF THE HAZARDS OF WORKING WITH MERCURY, THIS ACTIVITY WILL BE A TEACHER DEMONSTRATION ONLY.**

Instructions: (1.) Watch as your teacher demonstrates the chemical stimulation of cells. (2.) Use what you have observed to help you to answer the questions.

Special Caution: Mercury is a highly toxic substance; avoid any contact with your skin.

In this demonstration, your teacher will use an overhead projector and certain chemicals to show you how interleukin-2 stimulates white blood cells. A small drop of mercury will represent a white blood cell, small orange crystals of potassium dichromate will be used for viruses, and dilute nitric acid will act like interleukin-2.

Step one: Your teacher will place a small drop of mercury on a clean Syracuse dish and project this image on the overhead screen.

1. Describe the shape of the mercury as it appears on the overhead screen.

   _____

2. Does the shape you described remind you of the shapes of the white blood cells you

   saw through the microscope? _____

Step two: Your teacher will place a few orange crystals near the mercury.

3. Count the crystals. How many crystals did you see projected on the screen?

   _____

4. If the mercury represents a white blood cell and the crystals represent viruses, what should the mercury be doing?

   _____

5. Describe the action of the mercury.

   _____

   _____

Step three: Your teacher will carefully place a drop of dilute nitric acid on the mercury.

6. Describe the action of the mercury.

   _____

   _____

7. Does the nitric acid act like interleukin-2? _____

8. This demonstration only simulates how interleukin-2 helps the body to fight viruses, but it should enable you to draw some conclusions. In a real immune system, what do you think would happen to a person if his or her T4 lymphocytes did not produce interleukin-2? Explain your answer on the back of this sheet.

Name _____ Date _____

7–11. THE T8 LYMPHOCYTES

Instructions: (1.) Read the text. (2.) Use the text to help you to answer the questions.

Antibodies and macrophages can destroy viruses only before they enter a cell. In many infections, however, viruses slip past this first line of defense and enter cells, changing them into virus factories. Unless the immune system has a way of destroying these factories, the body can be severely weakened.

Fortunately, interleukin-2 stimulates a group of white blood cells called the "T8 lymphocytes." Two important kinds of T8 lymphocytes are the cytotoxic killer cells and the suppressor cells.

The term *cyto* means "cell," and the term *toxic* refers to poison. As their name implies, cytotoxic killer cells use a poison to destroy cells. Once cytotoxic killer cells have been stimulated, they seek out and destroy cells that have already been invaded by viruses.

By the combined efforts of the plasma cells (which create antibodies) and the cytotoxic killer cells, the immune system can fight off most virus attacks. But after the battle is won and the memory cells have established immunity against more attacks, the activity of the immune system must be slowed down. Slowing down the immune system is the job of the suppressor cells; they release a chemical that signals the T4 lymphocytes to stop producing interleukin-2. Without interleukin-2, the plasma cells and the cytotoxic killer cells once again become inactive. The memory cells, however, continue to circulate, keeping watch, and the macrophages continue their job of eating new viruses that enter the body.

Level One Questions:

1. Antibodies and macrophages can destroy viruses only before they enter a _____.

2. In many infections, viruses slip past the first line of defense and enter cells, changing them into _____ factories.

3. Two important T8 lymphocytes are the _____ and _____.

4. What is the job of the cytotoxic killer cell?

   _____

5. What is the job of the suppressor cell?

   _____

Level Two Question:

6. Explain why the job of the cytotoxic killer cell is important.

   _____

   _____

Level Three Question:

7. The thymus is a small gland that releases T4 and T8 lymphocytes. It is very large in newborn babies and begins to shrink when a child is about six years old. Why do you think it is important for newborns to have a larger thymus gland than adults have? Explain your answer on the back of this sheet.

7–12. THE MODERN-DAY PLAGUE: AIDS

Instructions: (1.) Read the text. (2.) Use the text to help you to answer the questions.

In the 1980s a new and deadly disease appeared, and the world suddenly became aware of the importance of the immune system. This disease is commonly referred to as AIDS. Since it is always fatal, it is sometimes called the "modern-day plague."

The term *AIDS* is an acronym (a word made of the first letters of several other words) for Acquired Immune Deficiency Syndrome. These words mean that AIDS is a collection of symptoms (syndrome) that result from a breakdown (deficiency) of the immune system; it is not something that you were born with, but something that you can acquire.

It is important for you to know that AIDS cannot be transmitted in most of the usual ways. It can be transmitted only by sexual contact, by sharing an unsterilized hypodermic needle with someone who has the disease, or by having infected blood somehow introduced into your bloodstream. It is a very serious disease, but you will not catch it by any kind of casual contact. It is, however, also important for you to know that a person who has been infected with the virus that causes AIDS may not have any symptoms for up to ten years. Unless he or she happens to be tested for AIDS during that time, the person will be unaware of the infection and may spread the disease to others. To protect yourself, you need to understand what the disease is and exactly how it may be spread.

The virus that causes this disease is called the "Human Immunodeficiency Virus," or HIV; it does its deadly work by weakening the immune system.

By destroying certain white blood cells, the HIV allows certain pathogenic microorganisms (which are usually kept at bay by white blood cells and antibodies) to take hold in the body. Pneumocystis carinii, for example, is a rare form of pneumonia that commonly infects persons whose immune system has been weakened by HIV. Karposi's sarcoma, a cancer of the small blood vessels, is another example; once only rarely seen in elderly persons or in patients whose immune systems had been suppressed by certain drugs, it now appears frequently among victims of the HIV.

Level One Questions:

1. In the 1980s the world suddenly became aware of the importance of the _____

   _____.

2. What do the letters *HIV* stand for?

   _____

3. What happens when the HIV weakens the immune system?

   _____

4. What is the name of the rare form of pneumonia that infects persons whose immune system has been weakened by the HIV?

   _____

5. What is another disease that frequently appears among victims of the HIV?

   _____

6. Name the "modern-day plague" that is caused by the HIV.

   _____

7. What is important for you to know about AIDS?

   _____

   _____

   _____

7–13. THE CASE OF JOHN DOE

Instructions: (1.) Read the story.   (2.) Use the story to help you to answer the questions.

In 1982, while working on an oil platform off the coast of Rio de Janeiro, John Doe (not his real name) began to have severe diarrhea and to run a high fever. He was obviously very ill, and so he was sent to Houston for medical treatment. Doctors were able to relieve his symptoms to some extent, but many things about his condition continued to puzzle them.

Even though John never completely recovered from the diarrhea, he seemed fairly healthy for three years. But in 1985 he returned to the hospital with a rare and severe form of pneumonia called "pneumocystic carinii."

Again, he seemed to improve with treatment, but within six months he developed Canadian thrush—a yeast infection of the mouth and gums. Symptoms of tuberculosis appeared. And this was only the beginning; he began to lose weight and was always tired. Many trips to the hospital followed.

John's immune system had been weakened by the HIV. Without a healthy immune system, he contracted diseases that normally would have been controlled before they had a chance to become established in his body. In 1986, John's condition worsened, and he died. The direct cause of his death was pneumonia, but he had contracted pneumonia because his immune system had been seriously weakened by the HIV.

In 1982, AIDS and the HIV were almost entirely new phenomena; doctors knew little about the disease and its cause and were helpless to treat it. There is still no cure for AIDS, but intensive research has developed some medicines that can improve an AIDS patient's general condition and lengthen his or her life. Most important, doctors now recognize the HIV and understand most of the mechanisms involved in AIDS.

As its name implies, Acquired Immune Deficiency Syndrome (AIDS) is characterized by a group of related symptoms (a syndrome). Some of the symptoms that AIDS patients develop are actually those of the conditions that attack after the patients' immune systems have been weakened, and of course those symptoms may vary widely. But some symptoms seem to be characteristic of AIDS itself.

Following is a list of symptoms that most AIDS victims develop. It is important for you to know that most of these symptoms can be caused by other diseases and conditions, including ordinary ones like colds and flu; IF YOU HAVE A FEW OF THE SYMPTOMS, DON'T WORRY; YOU DON'T HAVE AIDS.

List of Symptoms

a. a persistent dry cough

b. flulike symptoms that hang on

c. unexplained tiredness

d. excessive weight loss

e. night sweats

f. purple splotches on the skin

g. swollen lymph nodes

h. diarrhea

Level One Questions:

1. What is a syndrome?

2. If you have a few of the AIDS symptoms, does it mean that you have AIDS?

Level Two Question:

3. A person with AIDS catches many diseases. Explain why this happens.

Level Three Question:

4. The diseases that occur in persons with AIDS are often called "opportunistic infections." Use the dictionary, and explain why this is an appropriate term.

7–14. HOW THE HIV ATTACKS A T4 LYMPHOCYTE

The human immune system does a good job of protecting the body against diseases. Unfortunately, it is not always successful, because pathogenic organisms have ways of tricking the immune system. Some viruses, for example, constantly change their outside structures so that antibodies cannot recognize them as enemies. This is why you can catch the flu again even after you have built up an immunity against it.

The HIV, the virus that causes AIDS, also uses this trick and goes one step further. To protect itself from being destroyed, it attacks and weakens the body's most important defenders—the T4 lymphocytes.

When the T4 lymphocytes are attacked, the immune system loses its power to defend the body. When the T4 lymphocytes are unable to release interleukin-2, the cytotoxic killer cells and the B-lymphocytes remain inactive. This is why a person with AIDS can catch many diseases that a person with a healthy immune system will not catch.

The following steps describe how the HIV attacks a T4 lymphocyte.

Step one: The HIV enters the blood and floats in the circulatory system until it finds a T4 lymphocyte.

Step two: The landing gear of the HIV matches the recognition sites or landing pads on the T4's membrane. This allows the virus to land and release its genetic material.

Step three: The genetic material travels through the cells to the nucleus.

Step four: The HIV's genetic material combines with the DNA of a T4 lymphocyte.

Step five: The T4 lymphocyte can no longer do its job of protecting the body, and the virus's genetic material has reprogrammed the T4 lymphocyte cell to make new viruses.

Step six: The new viruses leave the cell ready to attack other T4 lymphocytes.

To complete this project—

☐ Use scissors to cut out the pictures.
☐ Paste them in the proper sequence on the boxes.

Level One Questions:

1. The immune system does a good job of _____ the body against _____.

2. Is the immune system always effective? _____

3. How do some viruses trick the immune system?

   _____

4. What part of the immune system does the HIV attack?

   _____

5. When the T4 lymphocytes do not release interleukin-2, the _____

   cells and the _____ are never called into action.

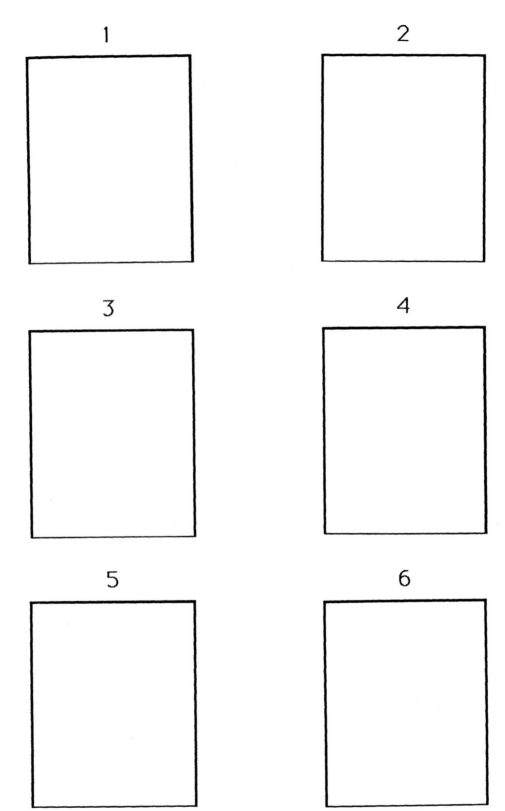

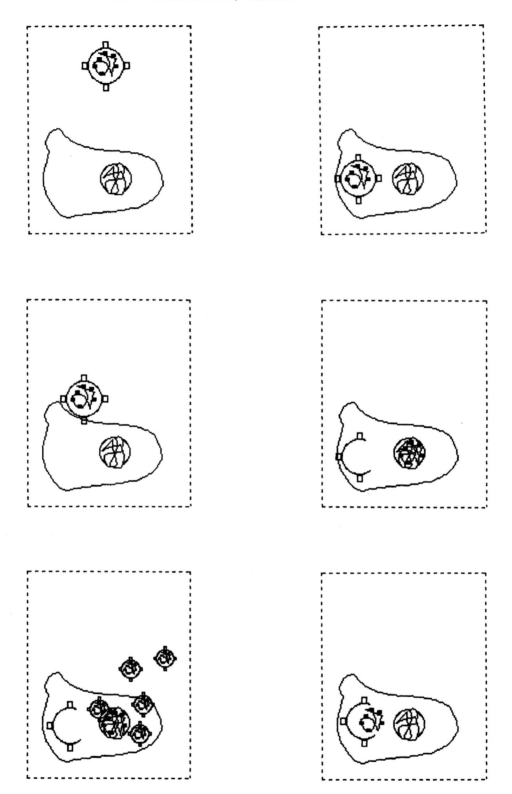

7–15. HOW AIDS IS SPREAD

Instructions: (1.) Read the text. (2.) Use the text to help you to answer the questions and complete the chart.

Activity	Can spread AIDS	Cannot spread AIDS
1. Shaking hands		
2. Hugging		
3. Sneezing		
4. Eating in a restaurant		
5. Casual sex		
6. Using public restrooms		
7. Swimming		
8. Sharing hypodermic needles		

Many viruses are easily spread from person to person. The flu virus, for example, can be spread simply by a sneeze. If an infected person doesn't cover his or her mouth when he or she sneezes, small droplets can carry the virus through the air and can infect a healthy person. The virus that causes hepatitis—a virus that attacks liver cells—can be spread from a shared glass or an eating utensil.

The HIV, fortunately, isn't spread so easily, because it is unstable in air. It cannot be spread by shaking hands, hugging, or by any other forms of casual contact. You cannot catch AIDS in swimming pools, by eating in restaurants, or by using public restrooms. The two most common ways in which the HIV is transmitted are by having sex with an infected person and by sharing a hypodermic needle with another drug abuser.

Level One Questions:

1. Is it easy for the flu virus to spread from person to person? _____

2. Describe how the flu virus is spread.

    _____

    _____

3. What kind of cells does the hepatitis virus attack? _____

4. Is the hepatitis virus easily spread? _____

5. What is one way in which the hepatitis virus can be spread?

    _____

6. Can you catch AIDS by hugging someone or by shaking hands? _____

7. What are the two most common ways in which the HIV is transmitted?

    _____

    _____

Level Two Question:

8. Why is it not possible for the HIV to be transmitted through the air or by the sharing of eating utensils with an infected person?

    _____

Level Three Question:

9. The American Red Cross recommends that persons living with AIDS patients should not share razor blades and toothbrushes. It is safe, however, to share bar soaps and hand towels. Explain the difference.

    _____

    _____

    _____

7–16. INTRAVENOUS DRUG ABUSE

Instructions: (1.) Read the text. (2.) Use the text to help you to answer the questions.

A person abusing illegal drugs may sometimes use a hypodermic needle to inject a drug directly into his or her circulatory system. This is called "mainlining."

It is common practice for drug abusers to share and reuse needles. In a newspaper interview, a police officer said,

> Dopers don't care about AIDS. They got a needle, they don't care where the needle came from. They pass the needles around. They go to dope houses, they use the old needles that are already there. They never wash them off. Never.

If a needle is contaminated with the HIV, the virus can be transmitted to the next user of the needle, and the next, and the next. Since the symptoms for AIDS *may not appear for up to ten years,* newly infected persons will unknowingly spread the HIV virus to other drug abusers and also to those with whom they have sexual contact. All these persons become carriers who can spread the disease.

Level One Questions:

1. A person abusing illegal drugs sometimes uses a _____ needle

   to inject a _____ directly into his or her circulatory system.

2. It is common practice for drug abusers to _____ and _____ needles.

3. If a needle is contaminated with the HIV, the virus can be _____
   to the next user of the needle.

4. The symptoms of AIDS may not appear for up to _____ years.

Level Two Question:

5. Explain how it is possible for a person with the HIV to spread this virus without knowing it.

   _____

   _____

Level Three Questions:

6. How do you plan to protect yourself against being infected by the HIV?

   _____

   _____

   _____

7. If you were in charge of disease control in your community, what steps would you take or recommend to protect its citizens against AIDS? Use the back of this sheet for your answers. Be prepared to discuss your answers.

Unit **8**

The Respiratory System

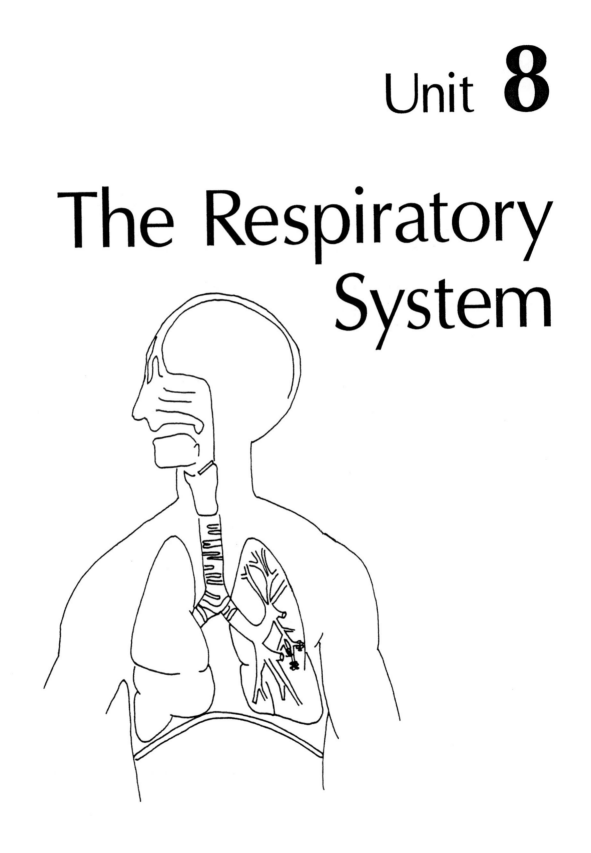

8–1 THE ANATOMY OF THE RESPIRATORY SYSTEM

Teaching Suggestion:

Use a model of the human torso or anatomical charts to demonstrate the anatomy of the respiratory system.

Answers to the Questions:

Level One

1. lungs
2. trade places
3. thoracic, abdominal
4. The muscle fibers of the diaphragm contract and bulge downward.
5. tubes, spaces
6. Small, stiff hairs trap dust and other foreign particles.
7. Mucus and the mucous membrane help to warm and moisturize the air.
8. They form channels that direct air into a space called the "pharynx."
9. voice box
10. vocal cords
11. trachea or windpipe
12. rings of cartilage
13. bronchioles
14. cilia
15. respiratory membrane

Level Two

16. When the diaphragm contracts, it bulges downward, creating more space (or creating a void or vacuum). To fill this empty space, air rushes in through the nose.
17. Swelling of the mucous membranes sometimes prevents the sinuses from draining. The resulting pressure may cause a sinus headache.
18. because respiratory gases diffuse through the membranes of these thin sacs as they (the gases) enter and leave the blood

Level Three

19. The cilia help to trap and remove foreign particles from the respiratory pathway.
20. Answers will vary. Tar from cigarettes (and other tobacco products) absorbs pollutants; tar collects in the lungs and remains there, holding the pollutants in the lungs until they (the pollutants) become concentrated.
21. Answers will vary. The lungs inflate because of a vacuum created when the diaphragm drops and the rib cage expands; such a hole would make it impossible for this vacuum to form.

8–2 VOCABULARY: THE RESPIRATORY SYSTEM

Note: This is a self-directed activity.

Answers to the Puzzle:

Across

4. concha
6. epiglottis
8. trachea

Down

1. bronchi
2. pharynx
3. alveoli
5. diaphragm
7. larynx

8–3 INSPIRATION

Answers to the Questions:

Level One

1. breathing in
2. about half a liter
3. Oxygen must dissolve in water before it can pass through the thin walls of the alveoli.
4. high, low
5. a. 110 mm
   b. 40 mm

Level Two

6. a. 110 mm of mercury
   b. 40 mm of mercury
7. It will diffuse into the capillary. Explanations will vary; essentially, since the partial pressure of oxygen inside the alveolus is higher than the partial pressure inside the capillary, and since diffusion occurs from an area of high concentration to an area of low concentration, oxygen will pass from the alveolus into the capillary.

Level Three

8. Yes. The length of the shafts (lines) of the arrows in the diagram indicates air pressure (or force) in millimeters of mercury. The arrowheads indicate the direction in which the force is exerted against the walls of the alveoli.

8-4 TESTING FOR CARBON DIOXIDE DURING EXHALATION

Teaching Suggestion:

Demonstrate all lab procedures.

Answers to the Questions:

Level One

1. breathing out
2. carbon dioxide
3. carbonic acid
4. acid
5. no
6. yes
7. yes
8. Lighter blue. If students are having a hard time observing this color change, add a pinch of baking soda to the cabbage water after it has cooled.

Level Two

9. The purpose is to make sure that the distilled water is uncontaminated by acid. Any contamination can alter the pH and therefore the color of the water; if the color does not change, the water is uncontaminated.

10. Yes. The color change indicates that carbon dioxide has reacted with the cabbage juice; it shows the presence of an acid. Carbonic acid is formed as soon as carbon dioxide mixes with water.

11. Answers will vary. Exercising causes more carbon dioxide to be produced and to be exhaled, so that more carbon dioxide is dissolved in the water and the cabbage juice becomes more acid. A higher concentration of acid causes the cabbage juice to change to an entirely different color.

8–1. THE ANATOMY OF THE RESPIRATORY SYSTEM

Instructions: (1.) Read the text and the statements. (2.) Use the text and the statements to help you to label the diagram and answer the questions.

The lungs are the main organs of respiration; their job is to help gases (mainly oxygen and carbon dioxide) to trade places. When you inhale, your lungs take in the oxygen that your cells need; blood circulating in the tissues of the lungs take the oxygen to cells all over your body. At the same time, the blood has been collecting carbon dioxide waste from your cells. That waste goes into your lungs, and you expel it when you exhale (breathe out).

In this gas-exchange process, the lungs need help from the muscles around the ribs, from a specialized muscle called the "diaphragm," and from other structures and organs. All together, the lungs and these muscles and other structures and organs make up the respiratory system. The following statements will help you to learn more about this system.

Statements

1. The diaphragm is a large sheetlike muscle that divides the body cavity into two smaller cavities: the thoracic (chest) cavity, which contains the lungs and heart (the heart is not shown in the diagram); and the abdominal cavity, which houses the organs and glands of digestion, excretion, and reproduction. Arrow A points to the thoracic cavity, and arrow B points to the abdominal cavity. Locate these arrows on the diagram and label them.

2. As you inhale (breathe in), the muscle fibers of the diaphragm contract and "bulge" downward and the ribs move outward; both of these actions expand the thoracic cavity. To fill this empty space, air rushes in through your nose. Red blood cells pick up oxygen from the "new" air, and carbon dioxide leaves the blood and mixes with the air in the lungs.

3. As you exhale (breathe out), the diaphragm and the rib muscles relax; the diaphragm assumes its convex "at rest" shape (it now bulges upward) and the ribs move inward. Both of these actions compress the air and force it out through the nose, expelling the carbon dioxide from the lungs. Arrow N points to the diaphragm. Label arrow N "diaphragm."

4. To reach the lungs, air from the atmosphere follows a system of tubes and spaces called the "respiratory pathway," which begins at the nose. On either side of the nose are small openings called "nostrils." As incoming air passes through the nose itself, small, stiff hairs trap dust and other foreign particles. Arrow C points to the nose. Label arrow C "nose."

5. Directly behind the nose, within the bone of the skull, is a space called the "nasal cavity"; it is lined with a membrane containing specialized cells that release a thick, clear liquid called "mucus." Mucus and the mucous membrane help to warm and moisturize the air. Arrow D points to the nasal cavity. Label arrow D "nasal cavity."

6. Additional fluid drains into the nasal cavity from the sinuses, which are also lined with mucous membrane. Like the nasal cavity, the sinuses are spaces in the bones of the skull; there are sinuses above and below the eyes. (If you have allergies, you

know that sometimes your mucous membranes can swell and prevent your sinuses from draining, causing pressure to build up and giving you a sinus headache.) Arrow E points to the frontal sinus. Label arrow E "frontal sinus."

7. On the walls of the nasal cavity are three rounded plates that look like scrolls; they are called "conchae" (plural for "concha"). Their job is to form channels that direct air into a space called the "pharynx." When you open your mouth and look at your throat in a mirror, you will see a dangling piece of tissue called the "uvula"; the space behind the uvula is the oral pharynx. Arrow F points to the conchae, and arrow G points to the pharynx. Locate these arrows on the diagram and label them.

8. The pharynx directs air into the larynx. When you swallow, you can see the larynx move in your neck; this protruding part of the larynx is sometimes called the "Adam's apple." Another name for the larynx is the "voice box"; inside it are the vocal cords—thin bands of tissue that vibrate when exhaled air rushes past them; this enables you to make sounds when you speak or sing. Arrow H points to the larynx. Label arrow H "larynx."

9. The larynx has a flap of tissue called the "epiglottis" that protects its opening. When you swallow, this flap closes, making a slight noise that you can hear. The purpose of this flap is to prevent food from entering and blocking the respiratory pathway. Arrow I points to the epiglottis. Label arrow I "epiglottis."

10. From the larynx, air passes into a large tube called the "trachea" or "windpipe." The trachea is about 4½ inches long. It is protected by rings of cartilage that help to keep it open so that air can travel through it freely. Arrow J points to the trachea. Label arrow J "trachea."

11. The trachea branches to make two smaller tubes called "bronchi" (the plural of "bronchus"), which direct air into the lungs. Arrow K points to the left bronchus. Label arrow K "left bronchus."

12. The bronchi divide to make smaller tubes called "bronchioles." The bronchioles, the trachea, and the bronchi are lined with small hairlike structures called "cilia." Cilia wave back and forth as they trap foreign particles and push them back toward the throat or pharynx. Arrow L points to the bronchioles. Label arrow L "bronchioles."

13. The bronchioles continue to divide, making smaller and smaller tubes; they may divide up to twenty times before becoming air ducts. (Because these divisions are so small, they have not been included on the diagram.) Air ducts are minute tubes that direct air into small, thin sacs called "alveoli" (the plural of "alveolus"). Collectively, the alveoli are sometimes called the "respiratory membrane" because respiratory gases diffuse through these thin sacs while entering and leaving the blood. Arrow M points to the alveoli. Label arrow M "alveoli."

Level One Questions:

1. The _____ are the main organs of respiration.

2. The function of the lungs is to help gases _____.

3. The body cavity above the diaphragm is the _____ cavity;

   below the diaphragm is the _____ cavity.

4. What happens in the diaphragm when you breathe in?

   _____

5. To reach the lungs, air follows a system of _____ and _____ called the "respiratory pathway."

6. What happens to incoming air as it passes through the nose?

   _____

7. How is the air warmed and moistened as it passes through the nasal cavity?

   _____

8. What is the job of the conchae?

   _____

9. The larynx is also called the _____.

10. What structures are in the larynx?

    _____

11. From the larynx, air passes into a tube about 4½ inches long called the _____.

12. What keeps this tube open so that air can pass freely through it?

    _____

13. The bronchi divide to make smaller tubes called _____.

14. These smaller tubes are lined with hairlike structures called _____.

15. Collectively, the alveoli are sometimes called the _____ membrane.

Level Two Questions:

16. How does the diaphragm help to bring air into the lungs?

    _____

    _____

17. What causes sinus headaches?

    _____

    _____

18. Why are the alveoli sometimes called the "respiratory membrane"?

    _____

    _____

Level Three Questions:

19. Smoking tobacco products destroys the cilia in the respiratory pathway. Why is the absence of cilia harmful?

   _____

20. Tar from cigarettes and other tobacco products can absorb gases that are known to be harmful when we encounter them as factors in air pollution. Can you make some assumptions about why this contributes to lung disease?

   _____

   _____

   _____

21. Imagine a hole through the skin and muscle into the thoracic cavity. Can you explain why it would make the lungs collapse?

   _____

   _____

   _____

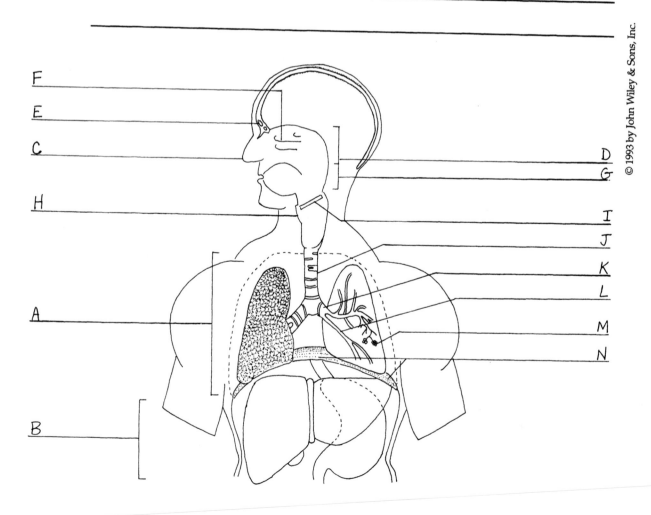

8–2. VOCABULARY: THE RESPIRATORY SYSTEM

Part I: Crossword Puzzle

Instructions: Use the last project, "The Anatomy of the Respiratory System," to help you to find the answers to this puzzle.

Across

4. scroll-like structure in the nasal cavity that directs air into the pharynx
6. a flap of tissue that protects the opening of the larynx
8. the tube that directs air from the larynx (also called the "windpipe")

Down

1. branches of the trachea that direct air into the lungs (use the plural form)
2. the space in the throat behind the uvula
3. the sacs where gas is exchanged (use the plural form)
5. a sheetlike muscle that helps to bring air into the lungs
7. a structure that is also called the voice box

Part II: Flash Cards

Instructions: (1.) Cut out these cards. (2.) Use the clues from the crossword puzzle to help you to write the definitions on the backs of these cards. (3.) Study these cards until you have learned the terms on them.

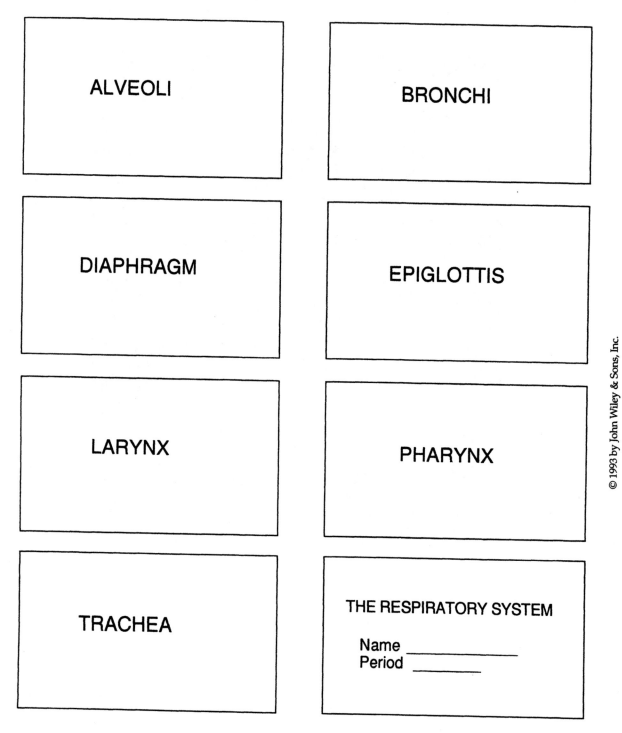

ALVEOLI

BRONCHI

DIAPHRAGM

EPIGLOTTIS

LARYNX

PHARYNX

TRACHEA

THE RESPIRATORY SYSTEM

Name _____
Period _____

8–3. INSPIRATION

Instructions: (1.) Read the text. (2.) Complete the project. (3.) Use the text and the project to help you to answer the questions.

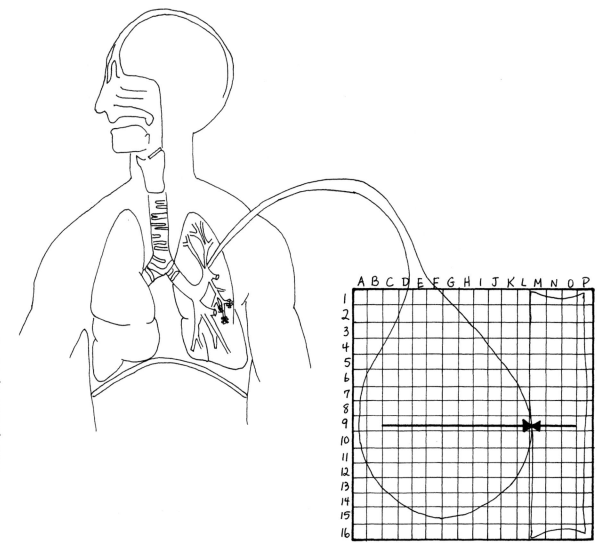

Statements

1. The term *inspiration* means "breathing in." When the diaphragm flattens and the rib cage expands, air rushes through the respiratory pathway and fills the alveoli. During normal inspiration, about half a liter (slightly more than half a quart) of air enters the alveoli of the lungs with each breath.

2. Oxygen must dissolve before it can pass through the thin walls of the alveoli. Oxygen dissolves in water; a microscopically thin layer of water on the lining of the inner wall of the alveoli makes this possible.

   Gas pressure is very important in this process. As the alveoli fill with air, the pressure inside them increases. Oxygen molecules dissolve faster under high pressure, and the number of molecules builds up rapidly in the water linings of the alveoli. Another way to say this is that "their concentration increases" in the water linings.

3. "Molecules always diffuse from an area of high concentration to an area of low concentration." That means that when a substance goes through a membrane, it tends to go from the side where there are *more* molecules of the substance to the side where there are *fewer* molecules of the substance.

    When the concentration of dissolved oxygen is higher in the alveoli than it is in the capillaries, oxygen molecules quickly leave the alveoli (lungs) and enter the capillaries (blood).

4. Carbon dioxide must also dissolve before it can pass into the alveoli from the capillaries, but it is already dissolved in the blood and is ready for diffusion. Since the concentration of carbon dioxide is always higher in the capillaries than it is in the alveoli, it quickly leaves the capillaries (blood) and enters the alveoli (lungs).

    To complete this project—

☐ 1. Use the grid to help you to enlarge the diagram.
☐ 2. Enlarge the arrows accurately. You will measure them to determine how much pressure is exerted against the wall of the alveolus. (*Note:* Use a metric ruler.)

Level One Questions:

1. What does the term *inspiration* mean?

    _____

2. When you breathe in, about how much air goes into your lungs?

    _____

3. Why is it important for a thin layer of water to line the walls of the alveoli?

    _____

4. Molecules always diffuse from an area of _____ concentration

    to an area of _____ concentration.

    Use the diagram that you enlarged to help you to answer the remaining questions.

5. Using a metric ruler, measure the lengths of the arrows in the enlarged diagram. Record this data in millimeters (mm).

    a. The length of the arrow inside the alveolus is _____ mm.

    b. The length of the arrow inside the capillary is _____ mm.

Level Two Questions:

6. If the arrows that you measured represent partial pressures of oxygen, and each mm that you measured represents one mm of mercury, what is the pressure of oxygen gas in:

    a. the alveolus? _____

    b. the capillary? _____

7. Where do you think the oxygen molecules will diffuse? Explain your answer.

_____

_____

_____

_____

Level Three Question:

8. When arrows are used to show force and direction, they are called "vectors." Are the arrows in the diagram vectors? Explain your answer.

_____

_____

_____

_____

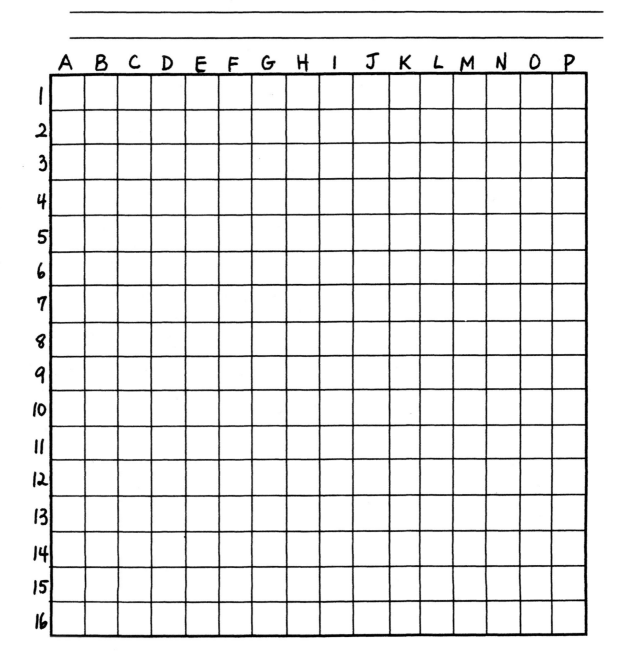

8–4. TESTING FOR CARBON DIOXIDE
DURING EXHALATION

Instructions: (1.) Read the text. (2.) Complete the investigation. (3.) Use the text and your observations to help you to answer the questions.

Procedure 2   Procedure 7

The term *exhalation* means "breathing out." As you have already learned, carbon dioxide is removed from your body when you exhale.

When carbon dioxide dissolves in water, it combines with hydrogen to form carbonic acid. This chemical change makes it possible for you to perform an experiment that will detect the presence of carbon dioxide gas in the air that you exhale.

In the presence of an acid, a pH indicator changes color. To make your own pH indicator, you will boil red-cabbage leaves in distilled water; as you might expect, you will have red water when you finish. You will then blow air bubbles into the water. If the bubbles contain carbon dioxide, carbonic acid will form when the air meets the water, and the color of the water will change.

Note: Because preparation, boiling, and cooling the liquid take considerable time, your teacher may prefer to boil the cabbage before you begin the experiment. If so, adjust the supply list and procedures accordingly.

Obtain the following materials:

☐ two 250 ml beakers
☐ 400 ml of distilled water
☐ one large red-cabbage leaf
☐ safety goggles
☐ clock or watch with second hand
☐ four inches of masking tape

☐ drinking straw
☐ eyedropper
☐ four test tubes
☐ test tube rack
☐ lab apron
☐ hot plate

Test tube	Describe color change
A	
B	
C	
D	

Procedure

☐ 1. Pour equal amounts of water into the beakers; set one beaker on the hot plate.

☐ 2. Break the cabbage leaf into pieces and drop them into the beaker as it heats; bring the water to a boil, and let it boil about ten minutes or until your teacher tells you that the proper color has been obtained.

☐ 3. Remove the pieces of cabbage leaf and allow the water to cool.

☐ 4. Using the masking tape, label each test tube with a letter—A, B, C, D.

☐ 5. Pour equal amounts of cabbage water into the test tubes. For best results, each test tube should be half filled.

☐ 6. Using the eyedropper, add four drops of clean distilled water to test tube A. After twenty seconds (your teacher will time you if you do not have a watch), check to see if the distilled water has caused the cabbage water to change color. On the data table, record what you observe.

☐ 7. Using the straw, blow gently for twenty seconds into the cabbage water in test tube B. Check to see if the water has changed color. On the data table, record what you observe.

☐ 8. Rinse the straw in the second beaker (filled with distilled water) and repeat step seven by blowing gently into the cabbage water in test tube C. Remember to blow for only twenty seconds and to record what you observe.

☐ 9. While your teacher is timing you, exercise by running in place for thirty seconds. (With your teacher's permission, you may substitute another form of vigorous exercise.)

☐ 10. Quickly rinse the straw in the clean distilled water. Blow gently into the cabbage water in test tube D. Remember to blow for only twenty seconds and to record what you observe.

Level One Questions:

1. The term *exhalation* means _____.

2. As you breathe out, _____ is expelled from your body.

3. When carbon dioxide dissolves in water, it combines with the hydrogen in the

   water to form _____ _____.

4. Cabbage water will change color when an _____ is added to it.

   Use your data chart and your observations to help you to answer the remaining questions.

5. Did the four drops of distilled water cause the cabbage water in test tube A to

   change color? _____

6. Did the cabbage water change color in test tube B? _____

7. Compare the color change that occurred in test tube B with the color change that

   occurred in test tube C. Are the colors the same? _____

8. Compare the color change that occurred in test tube C with the color change that

   occurred in test tube D. Are the colors the same? _____

Level Two Questions:

9. In step six you tested the distilled water to see whether it caused the cabbage water to change color. Why do you think this test was advisable?

   _____

   _____

10. Do your observations show that carbonic acid is in your exhaled air? _____

11. Do your observations show that carbon dioxide is removed from your lungs when you exhale? Explain.

    _____

    _____

    _____

Unit 9

The Digestive System

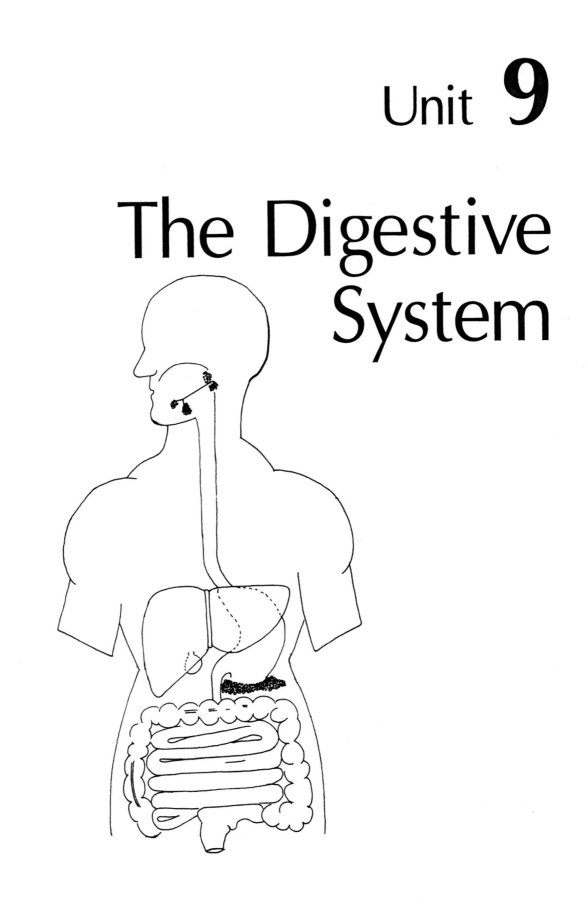

TEACHER'S GUIDE TO UNIT 9 _____

9–1 NUTRITION AND THE DIGESTIVE SYSTEM

Note: This is a self-directed worksheet. You may wish to have your students research pellagra or other deficiency diseases. Pellagra in particular will acquaint them with a time—not so terribly long ago—when knowledge about nutrition was almost unbelievably primitive.

Answers to the Questions:

Level One

1. substances
2. nutrients
3. proteins, carbohydrates, fats, minerals, and vitamins
4. an improper diet
5. Sores may develop on the skin; the skin on the hands and feet may turn black; the mucous linings of the throat and intestines become inflamed, causing diarrhea and loss of appetite; the ability to think clearly may be impaired.
6. nicotinic acid
7. so that it would not be confused with nicotine
8. how important it is for us to eat a healthful diet

Level Two

9. With the addition of nicotinic acid (niacin) to their diets, pellagra patients improved in just a few days.

Level Three

10. After years of research, scientists found that the cure was very easily obtainable from ordinary foods such as beans, fresh vegetables, eggs, and lean meat. The irony lies in their search for a miracle cure that proved to be right under their noses.

9–2 THE ANATOMY OF THE HUMAN DIGESTIVE SYSTEM

Note: This is a self-directed worksheet.

Teaching Suggestions:

1. Use a model of the human torso or an anatomical chart to demonstrate the parts of the digestive system.
2. The National Geographic Society film, *Digestive System,* contains actual footage of the entire digestive process. (Be sure to show it before lunch!) This seventeen-minute film is in the NG series, The Human Body.

Answers to the Questions:

Level One

1. beginning
2. tearing, grinding, and chewing of food
3. in the mouth
4. in the mouth
5. three
6. amylase
7. sugar
8. The esophagus serves as a tubular passageway that directs food from the mouth to the stomach.
9. The stomach squeezes, sloshes, and mixes the food, and adds two important chemicals: hydrochloric acid and pepsin.
10. small intestine
11. Chemical substances break complex sugars into simple sugars, break proteins into amino acids, and emulsify fats.
12. to change into small drops
13. small intestine
14. Bile is a chemical produced in the liver and stored in the gallbladder. Its job is to emulsify fats.
15. a sac
16. by a small tube
17. to add digestive chemicals to the small intestine
18. breaks proteins into amino acids
19. They enter the circulatory system where they are transported to the liver for storage or to the cells.
20. stores them
21. to make new proteins
22. wastes
23. removes water from the wastes and returns it to the body
24. stores dehydrated wastes until they are removed from the body

Level Two

25. Answers will vary. Mechanical digestion, chemical digestion, absorption, and reabsorption should be mentioned.
26. storage, producing digestive chemicals (These are not the only functions of the liver, of course.)

Level Three

27. Answers will vary. The analogy of the spool should be obvious; the thread passing through the hole does not penetrate the wood of the spool. The channels of the body, beginning with the mouth and ending with the anus, are like the hole passing through the spool; and as long as nutrients remain within these channels they have

not penetrated the organs of the body. But once in the blood stream, they enter the body proper.

28. Answers will vary. During diarrhea, wastes pass through the large intestine before the water can be removed and returned to the body.

9–3 VOCABULARY: THE DIGESTIVE SYSTEM

Note: This is a self-directed activity.

Answers to the Puzzle:

Across

1. salivary glands
4. gallbladder
7. esophagus
8. stomach

Down

2. small intestine
3. rectum
5. liver
6. pancreas

9–4 A WINDOW IN THE STOMACH

Note: This is a self-directed activity.

Answers to the Questions:

Level One

1. light pink
2. Small points of fluid can be seen arising from the walls of the stomach.
3. A
4. acid
5. B
6. The food breaks apart and becomes a thick paste.
7. C
8. It is a thick paste.
9. D
10. They continually contracted in a slow, regular order.
11. about three hours

Level Two

12. Answers will vary. The acid helps to break down the food. Since most bacteria cannot survive the strong acid in the stomach, some potential pathogens are killed before they can enter the body. Stomach acid also prevents the food from spoiling while it is in the stomach.

Level Three

13. Answers will vary. As the cells and tissues of the stomach become more active, more blood is needed to provide the extra oxygen and nutrients required for this increased activity, and the color of the stomach tissues changes from pink to red.

14. Answers will vary. The fibers of pork roast are denser and less fatty than those in pig's feet; dry cooking does not break down fibers as quickly as boiling does; pig's feet may have been pickled in vinegar or brine, which would also break down fibers. Cellulose is slow to digest, and in the human system it is never completely digested.

9–5 DIGESTION IN THE SMALL INTESTINE

Note: This is a self-directed worksheet.

Suggestion:

If you have not shown the National Geographic Society film *Digestive System,* this would be a good time. (See note on "The Anatomy of the Digestive System.")

Answers to the Questions:

Level One

1. to the small intestine
2. B
3. about 25 feet long
4. A
5. F
6. nutrients
7. E
8. C
9. D
10. nutrients: proteins, carbohydrates, and fats
11. proteins into amino acids
12. absorption
13. villi
14. three villi
15. artery, vein, capillary net, lacteal
16. capillary

17. yes
18. no
19. yes
20. Special chemicals and enzymes process them before they are sent to the cells.

9–6 SIMULATING THE STEPS OF DIGESTION

Notes:

1. Step four, boiling chopped carrot in alcohol to remove the pigment from the carrot, takes about ten to fifteen minutes. Because of the obvious risks, you may wish to perform this step at your demonstration table.
2. This investigation takes two lab periods to complete. In step five, the chromatography paper should be left in the alcohol mixture overnight. Before returning them to the students for the second lab session, these strips should be removed and allowed to dry.

Teaching Suggestions:

1. Read the safety precaution aloud to the students.
2. Demonstrate all lab procedures.

Answers to the Questions:

Level One

1. I chopped a piece of carrot.
2. stomach
3. digestive chemicals
4. A warm temperature helps digestive chemicals to break down food.
5. Heat helps the alcohol to remove the carrot's pigments.
6. the strip of chromatography paper
7. Answers will vary. There should be orange, greens of various shades, and possibly brown.
8. Answers will vary, depending on how many colors the students saw on their chromatography papers.
9. Answers will vary. Most will answer yes.
10. Most will answer yes.
11. Answers will vary, depending on which of the colors passed the arrow.

9–7 IDENTIFYING THE DIGESTIVE STRUCTURES OF THE FROG

Teaching Suggestions:

1. Demonstrate all lab procedures.
2. Discuss the similarities in and differences between the human and frog digestive systems.

Answers to the Questions:

Level One

1. Answers will vary. Essentially, mouth tissues in both frog and human contain three pairs of salivary glands; a short tube (esophagus) directs food into the stomach; the stomach releases hydrochloric acid and enzymes; the small intestine receives enzymes and digestive chemicals from the pancreas and liver; absorption occurs in the small intestine; the primary job of the large intestine is to reabsorb water.

2. Answers will vary. Differences in size and shape should be mentioned. Also, the frog's body has a single opening, the cloaca, where the urinary, digestive, and reproductive systems empty.

9–8 ENERGY FROM FOOD

Note: This is a self-directed worksheet.

Teaching Suggestion:

Discuss various ways in which machines obtain, use, and transform energy. Make a comparison between the way a machine uses energy with the way the human body uses energy.

Answers to the Questions:

Level One

1. energy
2. carbohydrates, fats, and proteins
3. breaking food into nutrients

Level Two

4. Answers will vary. Both use energy; initial sources of fuel (foods/crude oil), except for simple sugars, must be broken down before they can be used to produce energy.

9–9 CARBOHYDRATES

Note: This is a self-directed activity.

Answers to the Questions:

Level One

1. because sugar and starch molecules are made of carbon, oxygen, and hydrogen atoms
2. Answers will vary. Table sugar (sucrose), jelly, candy, fruits, certain vegetables, and milk may be mentioned.
3. glucose
4. enzymes
5. in salivary glands, pancreas, walls of the small intestine, the liver

6. liver

7. when the glucose level of the blood is low

Level Two

8. Glucose can be used directly, while other simple sugars must be rearranged to form glucose; complex sugars must be broken into simple sugars and eventually into glucose.

Level Three

9. Answers will vary. Students should say that sugars are needed for energy to perform gross motor activities and chemical activities, including those of the brain, and that low glucose levels produce hunger pangs. Also, after sugar stores are depleted, protein begins to be converted into sugars (which happens in anorexia nervosa). They may also say that it would be impossible to eliminate all sugars because they are contained in most foods, in one form or another.

9–10 CARBOHYDRATES LAB

Notes:

1. Students generally enjoy this lab.
2. This investigation requires advance preparation.
3. Use glucose and sucrose for the unknown sugars.

Teaching Suggestions:

1. Discuss and review the safety precautions.
2. Demonstrate all lab procedures.

Answers to the Questions:

Level One

1. a substance that changes color during a chemical test
2. Benedict's solution
3. iodine
4. to a different color
5. purple

Level Two

6. Yes. When boiled, the Benedict's solution did not change color.
7. No. Benedict's solution changed color, indicating simple sugars.
8. Answers depend on which test tube the teacher placed the unknown sugars in.
9. Answers depend on which test tube the teacher placed the unknown sugars in.

9–1. NUTRITION AND THE DIGESTIVE SYSTEM

Instructions: (1.) Read the text. (2.) Use the text to help you to answer the questions.

Your body requires certain substances for producing new cells, repairing worn and damaged tissues, and for maintaining your health. These substances are called "nutrients"; they are proteins, carbohydrates, fats, minerals, and vitamins. To obtain these nutrients, you must eat the right kinds of foods and your digestive system must be healthy.

Malnutrition is a general term used to describe what happens when your body does not get enough nutrients. You can become malnourished if you do not eat the right things or if your digestive system is not working properly. Malnutrition may cause problems in growth and development; it may cause general poor health, or "failure to thrive"; it is now known to be the cause of many diseases.

Pellagra is an example of a disease caused by an improper diet. Someone suffering from pellagra develops sores on his or her skin; in severe cases, the skin on the hands and feet may turn black. The mucous linings of the throat and intestines become inflamed, causing diarrhea and loss of appetite. The neurons in the brain may also be affected, so that the person loses the ability to think clearly. Until a cure was discovered, some mental hospitals were filled with patients suffering from pellagra.

In 1937 a scientist found that patients suffering from pellagra would improve in just a few days with the addition to their diets of a substance called "nicotinic acid"; it seemed to be a miracle cure. At that time it was made in the laboratory, but researchers later discovered that nicotinic acid can be found in many foods such as beans, fresh vegetables, eggs, and lean meat. After this discovery, nicotinic acid was classified as vitamin B. So that it would not be confused with nicotine (a drug found in tobacco), it was renamed "niacin."

By studying pellagra, scientists learned just how important it is for us to eat a healthful diet. While completing this unit you will learn more about the foods you eat. You will also learn about the structure of the digestive system and how this system breaks the foods you eat into the nutrients your body needs.

Level One Questions:

1. Your body requires certain _____.

2. These substances are called _____.

3. List the five kinds of nutrients.

   a. _____   b. _____   c. _____

   d. _____   e. _____

4. What causes pellagra?

   _____

   _____

5. Describe what happens to the body of a person suffering from pellagra.

   _____

   _____

   _____

6. What substance was found to be a cure for pellagra?

   _____

7. Why was this substance renamed?

   _____

8. What important fact did scientists learn while studying pellagra?

   _____

   _____

Level Two Question:

9. Why was nicotinic acid considered a miracle cure?

   _____

   _____

Level Three Question:

10. Look up the word *irony* in a dictionary. Why was it ironic when nicotinic acid was found in a variety of foods?

    _____

    _____

    _____

9–2. THE ANATOMY OF THE HUMAN DIGESTIVE SYSTEM

Instructions: (1.) Read the text and the descriptions. (2.) Use the text and the descriptions to help you to label the diagram and to answer the questions.

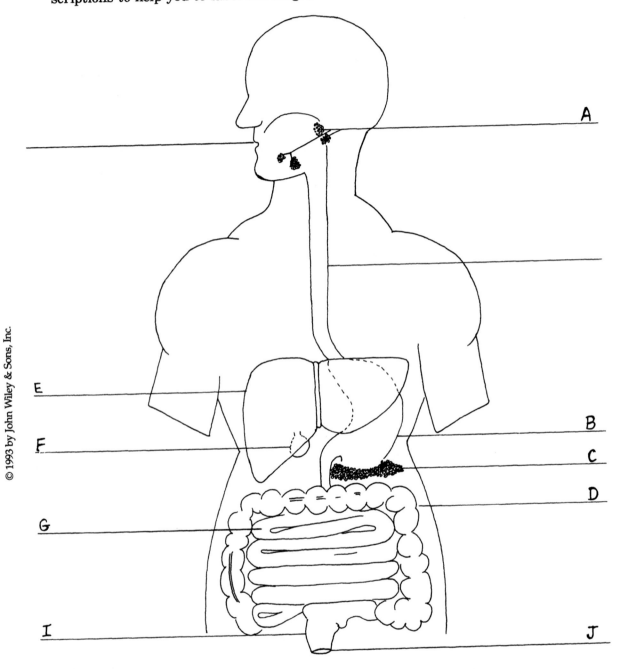

The job of your digestive system is to take nutrients from the foods you eat so that the cells of your body can use them. If for some reason your digestive system could not do this, you would become malnourished and your health would deteriorate.

While completing this project, you will learn to name the different parts of the digestive system and learn how these parts work together to utilize the nutrients in the foods you eat.

Descriptions

1. The mouth is the beginning of the digestive system. Its job is to tear and grind food into pieces small enough to swallow. This tearing, grinding, and chewing process is called "mechanical digestion"; the mouth has thirty-two teeth and strong jaws to accomplish it. Find the arrow that points to the mouth. Label that arrow "mouth."

2. Chemical digestion also begins in the mouth. In the tissues within the mouth are three pairs of glands called "salivary glands"; they release a liquid called "saliva." Saliva moistens the food and helps you to swallow, and it has another important job to do: It contains a digestive enzyme called "amylase," which breaks starch molecules into sugar. (You may have noticed that a cracker—composed mostly of starch—tastes sweet after you have chewed it for a few seconds.) Arrow A points to the salivary glands. Label arrow A "salivary glands."

3. After food has been mechanically digested and moistened by saliva and after chemical digestion has begun, the tongue pushes the pulpy mass to the back of the throat and you swallow. Swallowing pushes the food into the esophagus, a tubular passageway to the stomach. Find the arrow that points to the esophagus. Label that arrow "esophagus."

4. At its lower end, the esophagus widens into a pouch called the "stomach." The stomach squeezes, sloshes, and mixes the food, and adds two important chemicals: hydrochloric acid and pepsin. These chemicals change food into a thick liquid called "chyme." On the diagram, arrow B points to the stomach. Label arrow B "stomach."

5. The chyme leaves the stomach and passes into the small intestine where chemical digestion continues. Specific chemical substances break complex sugars into simple sugars, break proteins into amino acids, and emulsify fats. Arrow G points to the small intestine. Label arrow G "small intestine."

6. The term *emulsify* means "to change into small drops." During emulsification, fats are broken into tiny drops that can pass through the wall of the small intestine. The small intestine uses a substance called "bile" to do this job. Bile is produced by the liver and is stored in the gallbladder.

   The gallbladder is a sac connected to the small intestine by a small tube. Arrow E points to the liver, and arrow F points to the gallbladder. Locate these arrows and label them.

7. The pancreas is a gland that adds more digestive chemicals to the chyme as the chyme travels through the small intestine. One such chemical is trypsin, which breaks proteins into amino acids. These amino acids enter the circulatory system where they are transported to the liver for storage. (A few of these amino acids are sent directly to the cells, where they are used to make new protein.) Arrow C points to the pancreas. Label arrow C "pancreas."

8. The last step of digestion is called "absorption"; it occurs when nutrients pass through the wall of the small intestine and enter the circulatory system.

   Only wastes remain in the small intestine after absorption has occurred. They enter the large intestine, where water is removed from the wastes and returned to the body; this process is called "reabsorption." Arrow D points to the large intestine. Label arrow D "large intestine."

9. After reabsorption, wastes collect in the last four to six inches of the large intestine. This part of the large intestine is called the "rectum"; it has nerve endings that, when stretched, are responsible for the urge to defecate. Defecation occurs when wastes are removed from the rectum through an opening called the "anus." Arrow I points to the rectum, and arrow J points to the anus. Locate and label these arrows.

Level One Questions:

1. The mouth is the _____ of the digestive system.

2. What is mechanical digestion?

   _____

3. Where does mechanical digestion take place?

   _____

4. Where does chemical digestion begin?

   _____

5. How many pairs of salivary glands are within the tissues of the mouth? _____

6. Name the digestive enzyme in saliva. _____

7. Amylase breaks starch molecules into _____.

8. What is the job of the esophagus?

   _____

9. What is the job of the stomach?

   _____

10. Where does chyme go after it leaves the stomach?

    _____

11. What happens to chyme in the small intestine?

    _____

12. What does the term *emulsify* mean?

    _____

13. Where are fats emulsified?

    _____

14. What is bile?

    _____

15. What does the gallbladder look like?

    _____

16. How is the gallbladder connected to the small intestine?

    _____

17. What is the job of the pancreas?

    _____

18. How does trypsin digest protein?

    _____

19. After proteins have been broken down into amino acids, where do the amino acids go?

    _____

20. What does the liver do with amino acids?

   _____

21. How do the cells use amino acids?

   _____

22. What remains in the small intestine after all the nutrients have passed through its walls?

   _____

23. What is the job of the large intestine?

   _____

24. What is the job of the rectum?

   _____

Level Two Questions:

25. Write a short report on the back of this sheet that describes how food passes through the digestive system.

26. From what you have learned, name two functions of the liver.

   _____

   _____

Level Three Questions:

27. The following statement is true, although it may not appear to be. Can you explain why scientists consider it to be accurate?

   > Nutrients are not really inside the body until they have passed through the wall of the small intestine.

   As you consider your answer, you might think about a spool of thread. If you pass a length of thread through the center hole, is the thread inside the spool?

   _____

   _____

   _____

   _____

28. Persons suffering from severe diarrhea may become dehydrated. Look up "dehydration" in a dictionary, consider the eighth step in the digestive process, and explain what the term means and why it happens.

   _____

   _____

   _____

   _____

   _____

9–3. VOCABULARY: THE DIGESTIVE SYSTEM

Part I: Crossword Puzzle

Instructions: Use the last project, "The Anatomy of the Human Digestive System," to help you to find the answers to this puzzle.

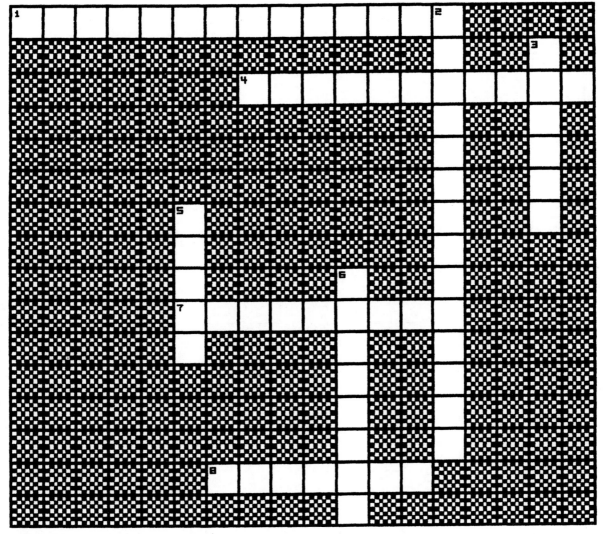

Across

1. glands near the mouth that release amylase
4. a saclike structure that stores bile
7. a tube that directs food from the mouth to the stomach
8. a pouchlike structure that changes food into chyme

Down

2. Nutrients pass through the wall of this structure to enter the circulatory system.
3. the last four to six inches of the large intestine
5. a large gland that produces bile and other digestive chemicals and enzymes
6. a gland that produces trypsin and other digestive enzymes

Part II: Flash Cards

Instructions: (1.) Cut out these cards. (2.) Use the clues from the crossword puzzle to help you to write the definitions on the backs of these cards. (3.) Study these cards until you have learned the terms on them.

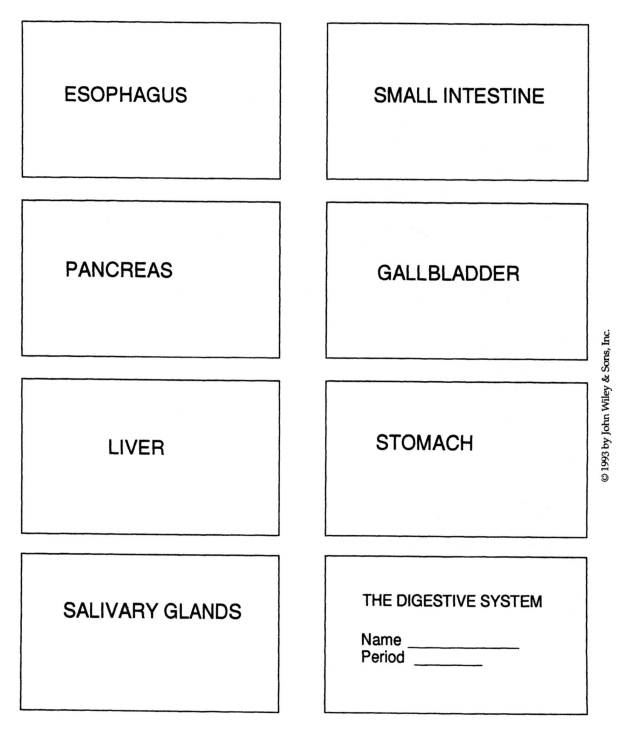

ESOPHAGUS

SMALL INTESTINE

PANCREAS

GALLBLADDER

LIVER

STOMACH

SALIVARY GLANDS

THE DIGESTIVE SYSTEM

Name _____
Period _____

9–4. A WINDOW IN THE STOMACH

Instructions: (1.) Read the text. (2.) Use the text and the diagrams to help you to answer the questions.

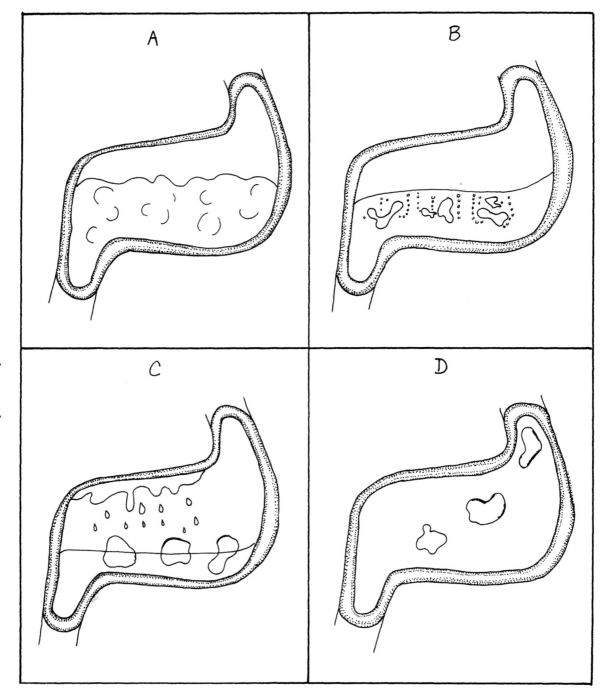

Very little was known about digestion until 1833, when a remarkable combination of circumstances enabled Dr. William Beaumont, an army doctor, to watch food being digested inside a human stomach.

Eleven years earlier Alexis St. Martin, a fur trapper, had been accidentally shot at close range. Dr. Beaumont saved St. Martin's life, but the wound left a permanent hole in St. Martin's stomach. From mucous tissue Dr. Beaumont fashioned a covering for the hole, but he arranged it so that it could be opened and closed; he paid St. Martin to let him look through the hole at frequent intervals.

Dr. Beaumont made careful notes as he watched different kinds of foods being digested, and in 1833 his accurate descriptions of a human stomach digesting food were published in a book called *A Window in the Stomach.*

To complete this project—

☐ Read the quotations from Dr. Beaumont's book.

☐ Study the diagrams (which are not Dr. Beaumont's).

☐ Answer the questions that follow.

From *A Window in the Stomach:*

> The interior of the stomach, in its healthy state, is a light pink color, varying in its shades according to its full and empty state.
> When food enters the stomach, small points of fluid can be seen arising from the walls of the stomach. This fluid is distinctly acid.
> The fluid mingles with the food. This fluid begins to break the food apart until the food becomes a thick paste.
> During digestion, the stomach muscles are continually contracting in a slow, regular order. These contractions continue until the stomach is perfectly empty and not a particle of food remains.
> The average time required to digest an ordinary meal is about three hours.

Level One Questions:

1. What color is the stomach in its healthy state? _____

2. What happens when food enters the stomach?

   _____

3. Which diagram (A, B, C, D) shows food entering the stomach? _____

4. Is the "fluid" produced by the walls of the stomach acid or alkaline? _____

5. Which diagram shows fluid dripping from the walls of the stomach? _____

6. What happens when the fluid mingles with the food?

   _____

7. Which diagram shows the fluid at work on the food? _____

8. When the fluid finishes its work, in what state is the food in the stomach?

   _____

9. Which diagram shows the final state of the food in the stomach? _____

10. What did Dr. Beaumont notice about the motions of the muscles in the stomach?

_____

_____

11. According to Dr. Beaumont's observations, what is the average time required to digest an ordinary meal?

_____

Level Two Question:

12. Why do you think it is necessary for the "fluid" in the stomach to be acid?

_____

_____

Level Three Questions:

13. Can you make some guesses about what the difference in color may be when a stomach is empty and when it is full? What might cause such changes?

_____

_____

_____

14. Dr. Beaumont noted that the digestion of different foods required different lengths of time: pork roast (mostly protein) required five hours; boiled pig's feet (also mostly protein) required one hour; rice (mostly starch) required one hour; and boiled cabbage (mostly cellulose) required four hours. Can you draw some conclusions about why these foods required different lengths of time?

_____

_____

_____

_____

_____

_____

_____

_____

9–5. DIGESTION IN THE SMALL INTESTINE

Instructions: (1.) Read the text. (2.) Study the diagrams. (3.) Use the text and the diagrams to help you to answer the questions.

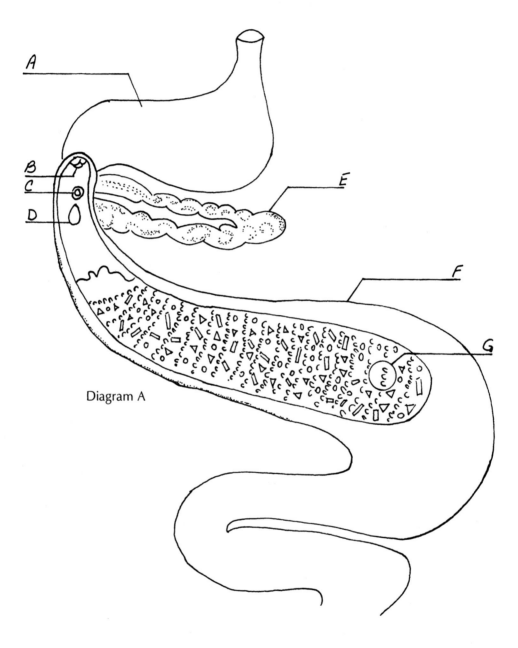

Diagram A

After the stomach changes food into chyme, the pyloric valve opens and the contents of the stomach empty into the small intestine. On Diagram A, arrow B points to the pyloric valve. Label arrow B "pyloric valve."

The small intestine is a tube about twenty-five feet long and about one inch in diameter. Enzymes and other digestive chemicals from the liver, pancreas, and other glands pour into the small intestine where they break chyme into nutrients. Arrow A (on Diagram A) points to the stomach, and arrow F points to the small intestine. Find these arrows and label them. (Notice that a long window has been cut from the wall of the small intestine so you can see inside.)

As you have already learned, the last step of digestion is called "absorption"; it occurs when the nutrients pass through the wall of the small intestine and enter the circulatory system. To help you remember the kinds of nutrients present, triangles have been used to represent fats, dots to represent sugars, and rectangles to represent amino acids. A special lining in the small intestine helps with absorption. On its inner wall are small fingerlike structures called "villi," which aid absorption by greatly increasing the surface area of the intestinal lining. To help you to identify these structures in Diagram A, the small circle indicated by arrow G encloses three villi.

Each villus (singular form of villi) is formed of a single layer of cells; because its walls are so thin, certain substances such as water can pass freely through them. (Some substances first attach to a carrier molecule that pulls them through.)

Diagram B shows three greatly enlarged villi. Notice that inside each villus are four kinds of vessels: an artery, a vein, a capillary net, and a lacteal (a tiny lymph vessel). Blood enters the villus through the artery. As the artery divides into smaller branches, it forms the capillary; most nutrients enter the circulatory system through this capillary. From the capillary, the blood leaves the villus through the vein.

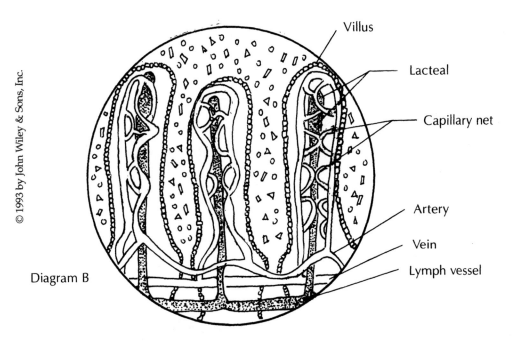

Villus

Lacteal

Capillary net

Artery

Vein

Lymph vessel

Diagram B

In Diagram B, each villus is surrounded by nutrients. Notice that some of these nutrients have already passed into the capillary and are leaving the villus through the vein. The job of this vein is to carry these nutrients from the intestine to the liver, where special chemicals and enzymes will further process them before they are sent to the cells.

Level One Questions:

1. Where does chyme go after the pyloric valve opens?

2. Which arrow points to the pyloric valve? _____

3. About how long is the small intestine? _____

4. Which arrow points to the stomach? _____

5. Which arrow points to the small intestine? _____

6. Enzymes and other digestive chemicals from the liver, pancreas, and other glands break chyme into _____.

7. On Diagram A the pancreas, which produces many digestive chemicals, is just below the stomach. Which arrow points to the pancreas? _____

8. The pancreas drains its digestive enzymes through a hole called the "pancreatic duct." Which arrow points to the pancreatic duct? _____

9. Trypsin, an enzyme produced in the pancreas, drains into the small intestine. Locate the drop of trypsin on Diagram A. Which arrow points to the drop of trypsin?

   _____

10. On the diagram, dots, triangles and rectangles have been used to represent three kinds of _____; they are _____, _____, and _____.

11. Trypsin breaks _____ into _____.

12. What is the last step in digestion? _____

13. On the inner wall of the small intestine are small fingerlike structures called

    _____.

14. What does arrow G point to? _____

15. List the different kinds of vessels in a villus.

    _____

    _____

16. Most nutrients enter the circulatory system through the _____.

17. On Diagram B, have any amino acids entered the capillary? _____

18. Have any fats entered the capillary? _____

19. Have any sugars entered the capillary? _____

20. What happens to the nutrients after they are carried to the liver?

    _____

    _____

    _____

9–6. SIMULATING THE STEPS OF DIGESTION

Instructions: (1.) Read the text. (2.) Use the text to help you to answer the questions.

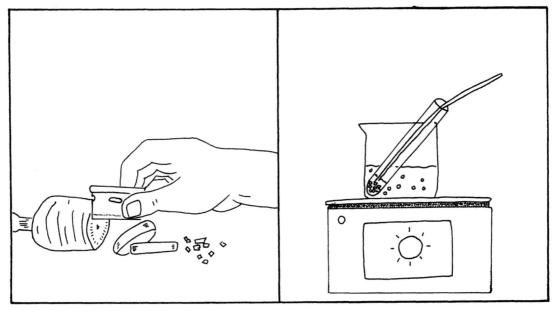

Procedure 2   Procedure 5

You have learned that digestion occurs in three steps. While doing this investigation, you will simulate mechanical digestion, chemical digestion, and absorption. Carefully follow the steps listed here.

Special Precautions: While doing this investigation, you will be using a hot-water bath to boil a mixture of 70 percent ethyl alcohol (rubbing alcohol may be substituted) and chopped carrot. Because this could splatter and cause burns, your teacher may prefer to heat this mixture for you. Be careful while you are working around the hot plate.

Avoid breathing the alcohol fumes; they may irritate your sinus passages.

Use caution while working with the safety razor blade.

Procedure

1. Obtain the following materials:
   - ☐ scalpel (or single-edged razor blade)
   - ☐ test tube
   - ☐ 500 ml beaker
   - ☐ hot plate
   - ☐ chromatography paper about ¼ inch wide and 8 inches long (white copy-machine paper may be substituted)
   - ☐ 40 ml of 70% ethyl alcohol (rubbing alcohol may be substituted)
   - ☐ #2 pencil
   - ☐ clear tape (paste or glue may be substituted)
   - ☐ safety goggles

2. Mechanical digestion takes place in the mouth, where strong jaws and teeth tear and grind food into small pieces. You will use a scalpel (or a safety razor blade) to represent teeth. Your hand will represent the strong jaw muscles. Carefully chop the carrot into pieces small enough to fit inside the test tube.

3. After the food has been mechanically digested by the teeth, it passes into the esophagus, which carries the food to the stomach. In this step, your hand will be the esophagus and the test tube will represent the stomach. Put enough pieces of the chopped carrot into the test tube to fill it about one quarter full.

4. Chemical digestion begins in the mouth and continues in the stomach and small intestine. In the stomach, hydrochloric acid and pepsin break food into a thick paste called "chyme." In this step the test tube will represent the stomach, and alcohol will take the place of the digestive chemicals. Pour the alcohol over the carrot pieces until the test tube is about one half full.

5. Body heat in the stomach helps the digestive chemicals to break down food. To help the alcohol to remove the carrot's pigments (colors), the hot plate will be used to boil the carrot and alcohol mixture. Study the picture for this step (at the beginning of this worksheet). Fill the beaker about one quarter full of water and place the test tube in it. Put on your safety goggles. Turn on the hot plate to medium heat, place the beaker on it, and watch the contents of the test tube carefully; the alcohol will boil before the water does.

   After the alcohol comes to a boil, turn the temperature down and let the alcohol simmer for at least fifteen minutes.

6. In the small intestine, absorption takes place; nutrients pass through the intestinal wall, leaving waste behind. In this step the orange liquid in your test tube will represent food nutrients, and the strip of chromatography paper will represent the intestinal wall. Carefully place the chromatography paper in the test tube so that its bottom edge touches the carrot pieces.

   Special notes: 1. Before you place the strip in the alcohol, use your pencil to write your name on the end that will not be in the alcohol.

   2. Leave the chromatography paper in the alcohol overnight before doing step seven.

7. Nutrients absorbed through the intestinal walls are picked up by tiny blood vessels, which carry them to the liver and the body's cells. Position the chromatography paper on the long rectangle here and use clear tape to anchor it at each end.

intestine   blood vessels

Level One Questions:

1. Describe your simulation of mechanical digestion.

_____

_____

2. In step three, what did the test tube represent?

   _____

3. In step three, what did the alcohol represent?

   _____

4. Why is the warmth of the stomach important in digestion?

   _____

5. Why did you apply heat to the alcohol and carrot mixture?

   _____

   _____

6. What did you use to represent the wall of the intestine?

   _____

7. Closely examine your chromatography paper. What colors do you see?

   _____

8. If each color represents a nutrient, how many nutrients are represented on your chromatography paper?

   _____

   Use the arrow on the diagram that you taped to your chromatography strip (step seven) to help you to answer the remaining questions.

9. The area to the left of the arrow represents the small intestine. Did any of the nutrients (colors on your chromatography paper) remain inside the small intestine?

   _____

10. The nutrients that passed to the right of the arrow have entered the circulatory system. Did any of the nutrients (colors on your chromatography paper) pass into the circulatory system?

    _____

11. If the different colors on your chromatography paper represent nutrients, which food nutrients (name the colors) passed into the circulatory system?

    _____

    _____

9–7. IDENTIFYING THE DIGESTIVE STRUCTURES OF THE FROG

Instructions: (1.) Read the text. (2.) Complete the investigation. (3.) Use the text and your observations to help you to answer the questions.

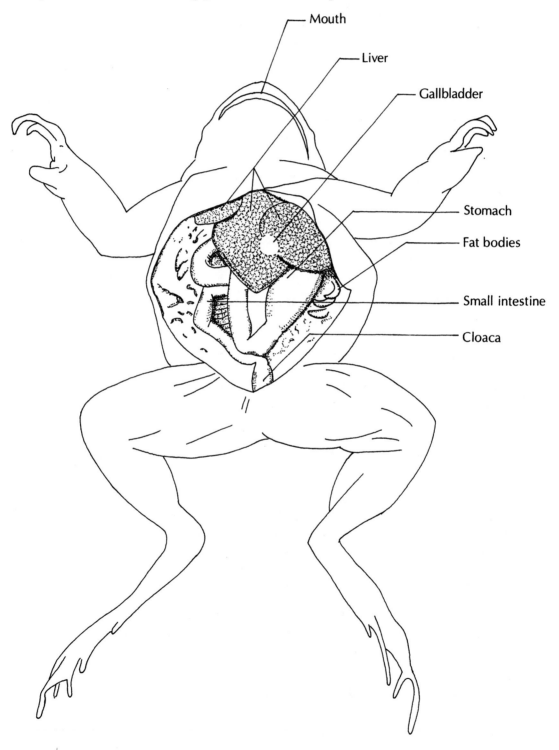

Mouth

Liver

Gallbladder

Stomach

Fat bodies

Small intestine

Cloaca

The frog's digestive system is remarkably similar to our own:

1. Its mouth tissues contain three pairs of salivary glands;

2. a short tube (esophagus) directs food into its stomach;

3. its stomach releases hydrochloric acid and enzymes;

4. its small intestine receives enzymes and digestive chemicals from the pancreas and liver to complete chemical digestion;

5. absorption occurs in its small intestine; and

6. the primary job of the frog's large intestine is to allow water to be reabsorbed.

Everything on this list is also true of the human digestive system.

One major difference between the frog's digestive system and our own is the way in which wastes are removed. The human body has separate openings for the urinary and digestive systems, and entirely different openings for the reproductive system; the frog's body has a single opening, the cloaca, where the urinary, digestive, and reproductive systems empty.

While completing this investigation, you will use the preserved frog to identify the major structures of the frog's digestive system.

Obtain the following materials:

☐ preserved frog

☐ dissecting kit

☐ dissecting pan

☐ colored pins

Procedure

1. Lay the frog on its dorsal (back) side in the dissecting pan.

2. Remove any remaining muscle tissue that may be covering the digestive structures. At the end of this step, your frog should look like the frog in the diagram.

To complete this project—

☐ Compare your specimen with the diagram.

☐ Stick the pins into the specimen as follows:

1. Stick the red pin into the liver.

2. Stick the green pin into the gallbladder. (*Hint*—You may have to separate the lobes of the liver to uncover the gallbladder.)

3. Stick the yellow pin into the stomach.

4. Stick the blue pin into the small intestine.

5. Stick the orange pin into the large intestine.

Level One Questions:

1. List the ways in which the frog's digestive system is similar to your own.

   _____

   _____

   _____

   _____

   _____

2. In what ways is the frog's digestive system different from your own?

   _____

   _____

   _____

   _____

   _____

9–8. ENERGY FROM FOOD

Instructions: (1.) Read the text. (2.) Use the text to help you to answer the questions.

You use machines every day. An alarm clock tells you when to get up, a toaster contributes to your breakfast, and a bus or a car may take you to school. These machines have one thing in common: They all use energy.

The energy that operates these machines comes from different sources. The alarm clock and the toaster use electricity produced at large generating stations and sent to your house through power lines. The bus and the car use gasoline or diesel fuel from crude oil that has been pumped from the ground and then refined into these fuels (and other substances).

You can think of your body as a complex machine; like all machines, it needs energy to operate. The carbohydrates, fats, and proteins that your body uses for fuel come from the foods you eat. Like crude oil, food must be broken down into these nutrients before it can be used by your body as energy. This is the job of the digestive system.

Level One Questions:

1. Like all machines, your body needs _____ to operate.

2. List the three nutrients your body uses for fuel.

   _____

   _____

   _____

3. What is the job of the digestive system?

   _____

   _____

   _____

Level Two Question:

4. Write a short paragraph about the ways in which the human body is similar to a machine.

   _____

   _____

   _____

   _____

   _____

9–9. CARBOHYDRATES

Instructions: (1.) Read the text. (2.) Use the text to help you to answer the questions.

Sugar and starch molecules are made of carbon, oxygen, and hydrogen atoms; it is easy to see why sugars and starches are called "carbohydrates."

You may not be aware of all the sugars in your diet. Table sugar (sucrose) is the easiest to identify and is present in other things like jelly and candy; but you get other sugars from fruits and vegetables, from milk and other dairy products, and from starches like potatoes, beans, and cereal grains.

Scientists divide sugars into "simple sugars" and "complex sugars." Some of the simple ones can be used by your body without being chemically changed or may require some slight rearrangement, but the complex ones must be broken down into the chief energy-producing sugar, called "glucose." Enzymes are the major agents in the complicated process of extracting sugars from starches and separating or rearranging sugar molecules; some of these enzymes are in the saliva, and some are produced by the pancreas, the walls of the small intestine, and the liver.

All of the body's cells, especially the muscle cells, can store glucose to some extent; but the liver is the most important "storehouse" and the only one that can regulate the glucose level of the blood.

Most of the glucose produced in the liver is released into the blood and transported to the cells, where it is used for the energy that your body requires for performing its many essential jobs. The remaining glucose molecules are bonded into a long chainlike molecule called "glycogen" and stored in the liver until the glucose level of the blood is low; then they are released into the blood.

Level One Questions:

1. Why are sugars and starches called "carbohydrates"?

   _____

   _____

2. List six sources of carbohydrates in your diet.

   _____

   _____

   _____

   _____

3. What is the name of the chief energy-producing sugar?

   _____

4. Some sugars must have their molecules separated or rearranged before they can be used by the body. What are the "chief agents" in these processes?

   _____

5. Where are these "agents" produced?

_____

6. What is the chief storehouse of glucose?

_____

7. When does it undo its glycogen chain and release glucose into the blood?

_____

Level Two Question:

8. In what way is the body's use of simple sugars different from its use of complex sugars?

_____

_____

Level Three Question:

9. Anyone on a reducing diet knows that candy is a no-no. What would happen if he or she decided to extend this concept and eliminate all sugars from the diet?

_____

_____

_____

9–10. CARBOHYDRATES LAB

Instructions: (1.) Read the text. (2.) Use the text to help you to answer the questions.

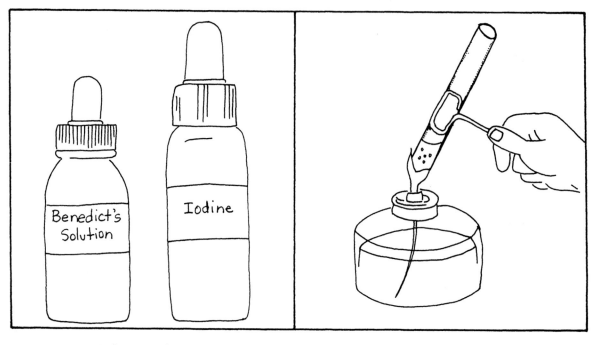

Indicator Solutions   Procedure 5

© 1993 by John Wiley & Sons, Inc.

Most of the foods you eat contain only complex carbohydrates. That is, they contain either complex sugars or starches. Your digestive system must break these into simple sugars before your cells can use them.

Only a few foods contain simple sugars. These sugars are already in a form that your cells can use, and they do not need to be broken down by your digestive system.

To test foods to see if they contain simple sugars, scientists use a color indicator—a substance that changes color during a chemical test. Benedict's solution is an example of a color indicator. It begins as a blue solution, and when it is boiled with a complex sugar it remains blue; but when it is boiled with a simple sugar, it changes to a different color.

Iodine, another chemical indicator, changes to purple when it is mixed with a starch.

This lab involves making two chemical tests. In the first test, Benedict's solution will be used to test five samples for simple sugars; in the second test, iodine will be used to test an identical set of samples for starch.

Because the indicators (Benedict's solution and iodine) *must not be mixed,* you will work with a lab partner who will be responsible for conducting the second test.

Special Precautions: Follow these safety precautions while heating your samples or when you are around anyone else who is conducting the experiment.

If you have long hair, tie your hair back.

Wear safety goggles and a lab apron.

When you are heating a test tube, prevent dangerous splatters by pointing your test tube away from other people.

Iodine is poisonous, and MUST NOT be allowed to get into your mouth or eyes. If you suspect that any iodine has reached your mouth or eyes, TELL YOUR TEACHER IMMEDIATELY.

Each lab partner will obtain the following materials:

- ☐ five test tubes
- ☐ test tube rack (a can may be substituted)
- ☐ test tube holder
- ☐ wax pencil
- ☐ safety goggles and apron

Only the person testing for simple sugars will need

- ☐ an alcohol burner
- ☐ a bottle of Benedict's solution

The following samples to be tested will be on the demonstration table or some other suitable location. Do not add them to the test tubes until your teacher gives you specific instructions for obtaining them.

- ☐ two unknown sugar samples—about a pinch of each
- ☐ a piece of lettuce about the size of a penny
- ☐ a banana sample about the size of a penny
- ☐ a piece of potato about the size of a penny

The person testing for starch will need

- ☐ a dropper bottle of iodine

(The person testing for starch also obtains samples.)

Procedure

1. Use the wax pencil to label your test tubes as follows:
   a. Label one test tube "US-1" for "unknown sugar 1."
   b. Label one test tube "US-2" for "unknown sugar 2."
   c. Label one test tube "B" for "banana."
   d. Label one test tube "L" for "lettuce."
   e. Label one test tube "P" for "potato."
2. Place the test tubes in the test tube rack and add the samples to them. Be careful that you put the samples in appropriately labeled test tubes.
3. The person who is testing for SIMPLE SUGARS will then pour about an inch of Benedict's solution over each sample.
4. After you have completed the preceding steps, return to your work area and wait for your teacher to light your alcohol burner.

5. Use the test tube holder to hold the test tubes while you heat them. One at a time, heat each test tube until the contents boil.

6. After you heat each test tube, check to see if the Benedict's solution has changed color. Return each test tube to the rack and record your observations on the data table.

7. The person who is testing for STARCHES will then place two drops of iodine on his or her samples.

8. Check to see if the iodine drop turns purple after it touches the sample.

9. Record your observations on the data table.

Data chart for the sugars test			
TEST TUBE	COLOR CHANGE YES	NO	DESCRIBE COLOR CHANGE
US-1			
US-2			
B			
L			
P			

Data chart for the starch test			
TEST TUBE	COLOR CHANGE YES	NO	DESCRIBE COLOR CHANGE
US-1			
US-2			
B			
L			
P			

Level One Questions:

1. What is a color indicator?

2. What color indicator is used to test for simple sugars?

   _____

3. What color indicator is used to test for starch?

   _____

4. When boiled with simple sugars, Benedict's solution changes _____.

5. When a drop of iodine touches starch, its color changes to _____.

   Use your data to help you to answer the remaining questions.

Level Two Questions:

6. Do the sugars in lettuce need to be broken down by the digestive system? Explain how you know this.

   _____

   _____

   _____

7. Do the sugars in banana need to be broken down by the digestive system? Explain how you know this.

   _____

   _____

   _____

8. Sucrose is a complex sugar. Which test tube (US-1 or US-2) contained sucrose?

   _____

   How did you determine this?

   _____

   _____

9. Glucose is a simple sugar. Which test tube (US-1 or US-2) contained glucose?

   _____

   How did you determine this?

   _____

   _____

Unit 10

The Excretory System

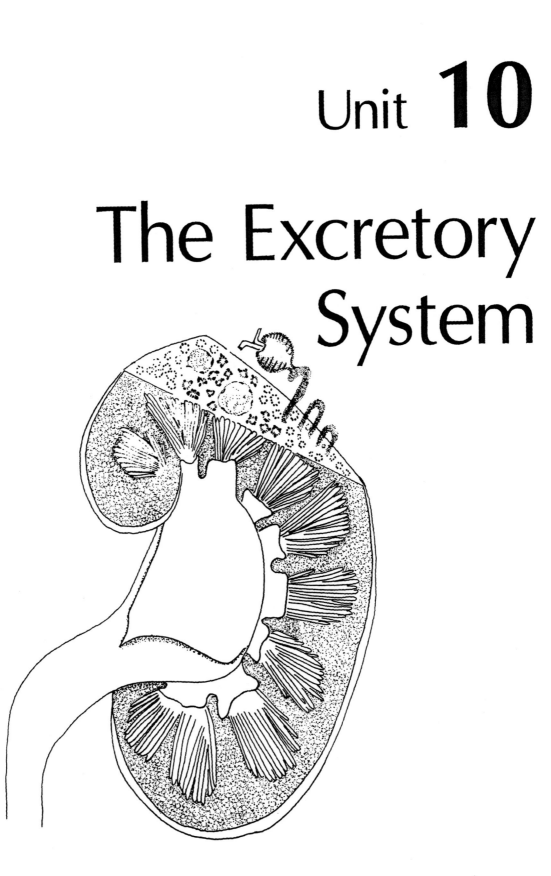

TEACHER'S GUIDE TO UNIT 10 _____

10–1 EXCRETION

Note: This is a self-directed worksheet.

Answers to the Questions:

Level One

1. removed
2. skin, lungs, kidneys
3. kidneys, skin, metabolism
4. urea, ammonia
5. kidneys
6. because of the way the liver is situated
7. the right kidney (Students may be confused when they look at the diagram because the left side of the body appears on the right side of the paper. Remind them, if necessary, to imagine that they are holding the diagram against their midsections with the print facing away from them.)

10–2 THE STRUCTURE AND FUNCTION OF THE URINARY SYSTEM

Part A

Notes:

1. This project, beginning with mechanical digestion, shows how wastes are formed. It presents a unique overview, step by step.
2. This is a self-directed activity.

Teaching Suggestions:

1. Make an overhead transparency of the diagram and use it for demonstration and class discussion.
2. Some students enjoy coming to the front of the class and telling what they have learned. Ask for volunteers to describe the sequence of events using the overhead transparency you have made.
3. Remind the students that they should look for the answers in both the diagram and the statements.

Answers to the Statement Questions:

Level One

1. chicken
2. two
3. hydrochloric acid and pepsin
4. mechanically digested food that has been changed into a liquid
5. two

6. B

7. hepatic portal vein

8. removes harmful bacteria; chemically changes and stores certain nutrients (As you know, the liver also has other functions.)

9. $CH_3-\underset{\underset{O}{\|}}{C}-OOH$ and NH_3

10. ammonia

11. $CH_3-\underset{\underset{O}{\|}}{C}-COOH$

12. can be used by the cell or stored in the liver

13. It is being stored by the liver.

14. Ammonia is highly poisonous; urea is also toxic, but the cells can more easily tolerate it.

15. equation 2

16. $NH_2-\underset{\underset{O}{\|}}{C}-NH_2$

17. C

18. inferior vena cava

19. aorta

20. oxygen, glucose, amino acids (This answer is to be written on the diagram.)

21. urea

22. D

23. no

24. to filter blood and remove urea and other toxic substances

25. renal

26. inferior vena cava

27. Urea and other wastes are collectively called "urine."

28. ureter

29. stores urine until it is expelled from the body

30. directs urine out of the bladder and removes it from the body

31. F

Part B

No questions; students will simply check off the steps in coloring.

–3 VOCABULARY: THE URINARY SYSTEM

Answers to the Puzzle:

Across

3. inferiorvenacava

6. kidney

7. renalartery

Down

1. ureter
2. bladder
4. renalvein
5. aorta

10–4 THE INTERNAL ANATOMY OF THE KIDNEY

Note: This is a self-directed activity.

Teaching Suggestion:

Obtain and dissect a kidney to show the students. Whole pork kidneys may be purchased at many grocery stores.

Answers to the Questions:

Level One

1. capsule
2. pyramids
3. eight
4. medulla
5. ureter
6. about 10 cm
7. about 6.5 cm

10–5 THE ANATOMY OF THE NEPHRON

Answers to the Statement Questions:

Level One

a. no
b. renal artery
d. G
e. four
f. other nephrons
g. Bowman's capsule
h. I
i. five
j. glomeruli
k. water, wastes, and small molecules of other substances
l. two
m. D
n. E
p. They leave the Bowman's capsule and travel to the capillary net.

q. C
r. water, sodium ions, chlorine ions
s. They are needed by the body.
t. to the collecting tubes
u. to the bladder
v. Cleaned blood leaves the kidney through the renal vein and joins the blood in the inferior vena cava.
w. to the heart

10–6 FILTRATION OF BLOOD IN THE BOWMAN'S CAPSULE

Special Precaution: Remind the students that iodine is poisonous if swallowed and that repeated applications can burn sensitive skin. (The activity does not call for application to the skin; you will have to watch only for an adolescent tendency toward imitation tattooing.)

Teaching Suggestion:

Demonstrate all lab procedures.

Answers to the Questions:

Level One

1. filtration process
2. wastes
3. water, glucose, certain dissolved ions
4. They are later returned to the useful fraction of blood.
5. B
6. afferent tubule
7. efferent tubule
8. five
9. Since blood cells are too large to pass through the filter tube, this liquid consists mostly of blood plasma with both useful substances and waste.
10. proximal tubule
11. The iodine made the starch-and-water mixture turn purple.
12. The filtrate was yellow.
13. blood cells

Level Two

14. The filter tubes of the glomerulus allow only certain substances to pass through. The same is true with the filtration apparatus—the water and the yellow food coloring easily pass through the filter, while the starch and iodine remain behind.

Level Three

15. The pressure inside the Bowman's capsule is increased when the plasma exits through a tubule with a smaller diameter than the one through which it entered. An increase in pressure helps the filtration process.

10–7 MAKING AN ACTION CARTOON: REABSORPTION

Note: Most students enjoy this activity.

Teaching Suggestions:

1. Tell the students that the right edges must be even before they staple.
2. Make an overhead transparency of an uncut cartoon. Use this transparency to help you to explain how the nephron works.

Answers to the Questions:

Level One

1. yes
2. They enter the capillary net, mix with the plasma, and then leave the nephron to join the circulatory system as clean blood.
3. They travel to the collecting tube and then to the bladder.

10–8 OBSERVING THE KIDNEY THROUGH THE MICROSCOPE

Note: This is a self-directed activity.

Teaching Suggestion:

Make an overhead transparency of the diagrams and use it to assist the students while they are identifying the structures on their microscope slides.

10–1. EXCRETION

Instructions: (1.) Read the text. (2.) Use the text and the diagram to help you to answer the questions.

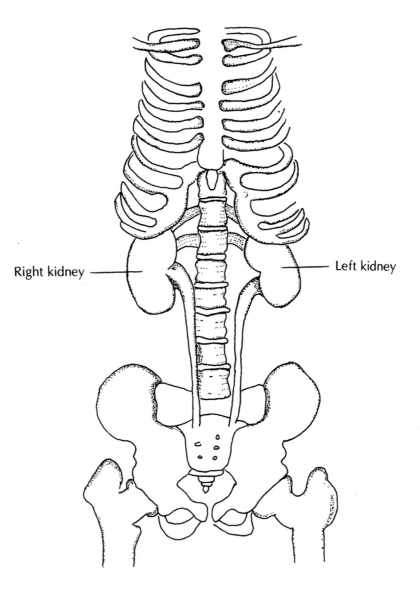

Right kidney ————   ———— Left kidney

During excretion, wastes are removed from the body. The skin, the lungs, and the kidneys all contribute to this process. The lungs remove carbon dioxide, a waste that is produced during cellular oxidation; the kidneys, and to a certain extent the skin, remove wastes that are produced during cellular metabolism. Metabolic wastes such as urea and ammonia are toxic (poisonous).

The primary organs of excretion are the kidneys. These paired organs are located toward the back of the abdomen just below the liver; the diagram shows the location of the kidneys. Because of the way the liver (not shown in the diagram) is situated, one kidney is slightly lower than the other.

Level One Questions:

1. During excretion, wastes are _____ from the body.

2. List three organs that help the body to remove wastes.

   _____

   _____

3. The _____, and to a certain extent the _____,

   remove wastes that are produced during cellular _____.

4. Name two poisonous metabolic wastes.

   _____

   _____

5. What are the primary organs of excretion?

   _____

6. Why is one kidney slightly lower than the other?

   _____

7. Use the diagram to determine which kidney is slightly lower. Is it the left kidney or the right kidney?

   _____

10–2. THE STRUCTURE AND FUNCTION OF THE URINARY SYSTEM

Instructions for Part A: (1.) Read the text. (2.) Use the text and the diagram to help you to answer the questions. (3.) Complete the project that follows. *Note:* You will need map pencils or markers.

Amino acids (the molecular building blocks of protein) are sometimes used by the body for energy. But before they can be used, the NH_2 part of the amino acid molecule (also called the "amine group") must be removed. This removal process is called "deamination."

As deamination occurs, a poisonous molecule is formed. This happens when the NH_2 breaks away from the amino acid and combines with a free hydrogen and NH_3, or ammonia, is produced. Ammonia is poisonous and must be removed from the cell; in the liver, it is quickly changed into urea before it is removed from the body.

While completing this project, you will follow the steps that a piece of fried chicken would follow while being digested and converted into an energy-producing form. (Even though this project focuses on the breakdown of protein, it is important for you to keep in mind that fried chicken contains other nutrients as well.)

Note: For instructional purposes many of the structures on the diagram have been exaggerated.

Statements

a. A good source of protein is meat.

   1. The person in the diagram is eating _____.

b. In the mouth, the chicken is being mechanically digested. The teeth tear, grind, and shred it into pieces small enough to be swallowed. When swallowing occurs, the mechanically digested chicken is forced into the esophagus.

   2. In the diagram, how many pieces of mechanically digested chicken are in the esophagus?

   _____

c. A wave of muscular contractions squeezes swallowed food through the esophagus into the stomach, where two chemical substances, hydrochloric acid and pepsin, change the mechanically digested chicken into a liquid called "chyme."

   3. What two substances change food into chyme?

   _____

   4. What is chyme?

   _____

d. Chyme is released into the small intestine where chemical digestion is completed. Trypsin, a digestive chemical from the pancreas (not shown in the diagram), breaks the protein in the chyme into its building blocks, the amino acids. (One of the amino acids that you are to count is clearly passing into a vein.)

5. How many amino acids are in the small intestines? _____

e. As absorption occurs, amino acids leave the small intestines and join the circulatory system. Arrow A points to the mesenteric blood vessels, and arrow B points to a mesenteric vein that has been greatly enlarged.

6. Which arrow points to a mesenteric vein with an amino acid passing through it?

   _____

f. Normally, veins carry blood directly to the heart. Blood carrying newly digested nutrients, however, is first sent to the liver, where harmful bacteria are removed and where certain nutrients are chemically changed and stored.

7. Name the large vein that carries blood from the mesentery blood vessels to the liver.

   _____

8. Describe two functions of the liver.

   _____

   _____

g. You will recall that if an amino acid is to be used for energy, the amine group (NH_2) must be removed by the liver. Locate the liver in the diagram. Equation one shows two molecules that result after deamination occurs.

9. After deamination (the removal of NH_2 in equation one), two molecules result. Copy the formulae for these molecules. (Helpful reminder: A solid arrow in a chemical equation means "yields"; it is similar to an "equals" sign in mathematics.)

h. NH_3 is ammonia. The other product that results from deamination of this amino acid (equation one) is pyruvic acid. Pyruvic acid can be used by the cell for producing energy, or it can be stored in the liver after it has been chemically changed. The dashed arrow in equation one shows what happens to pyruvic acid in this instance.

10. NH_3 is the formula for _____.

11. Copy the formula for pyruvic acid.

12. What two things can happen to pyruvic acid?

_____

_____

13. In this instance, what happens to pyruvic acid?

_____

i. Because ammonia is highly poisonous, the liver quickly changes it to urea, a less toxic substance. Equation two shows ammonia being changed to urea.

14. Why does the liver change ammonia into urea?

_____

15. Which equation shows ammonia changing to urea? _____

j. In equation two, two molecules of ammonia ($2NH_3$) combine with one molecule of carbon dioxide (CO_2) to yield one molecule of water and one molecule of urea.

16. If H_2O is the formula for water, what is the formula for urea? (Remember that the solid arrow means "yields.")

k. Urea is a waste product; it must be removed from the body.

17. Which arrow points to a molecule of urea that is in a blood vessel, ready to leave the liver? (An arrow will help you to answer this question.)

_____

l. From the liver, blood travels to the heart; from there it is sent to the lungs and returned to the body's tissues.

18. A blood vessel travels from the liver to the heart; it carries urea mixed with the blood. Name this blood vessel. (Use the diagram to help you to answer this question.)

_____

19. Name the blood vessel that sends blood from the heart to the cells.

_____

m. As blood passes through the body's tissues, certain substances such as oxygen, glucose, and amino acids enter the cells. In general, urea does not enter the cells as it travels to the kidneys for removal.

20. On the lines in the cell, write three substances that enter it.

21. What substance does not enter it?

_____

n. As the blood continues its course through the body, it eventually passes the kidneys. Some of this blood passes through the renal artery and enters the kidneys.

22. Which arrow points to a molecule of urea that is about to enter a kidney?

_____

23. Does all of the blood enter the kidney? _____

o. The function of the kidney is to filter blood and to remove urea and other toxic substances. After it is cleaned (filtered), the blood leaves the kidney through the renal vein. (Arrow E points to the renal vein.) The renal vein immediately empties into a larger vein that returns the filtered blood to the heart.

24. Describe the function of the kidneys.

_____

25. Cleaned blood leaves the kidney through the _____ vein.

26. Name the *large* vein that returns filtered blood to the heart.

_____

p. Urea and other wastes—collectively called "urine"—leave the kidney via the ureter, a large tube that directs urine to the bladder; from there it is eventually expelled from the body through a short tube called the "urethra."

27. What is urine?

_____

28. Name the tube that carries urine from the kidney to the bladder.

_____

29. Describe the function of the bladder.

_____

30. Describe the function of the urethra.

_____

31. Which arrow points to the urethra? _____

Instructions for Part B: Use what you have learned in Part A to help you to color-code the following diagram.

☐ Color the descending aorta and the renal arteries red. (The arrows on the diagram will help you to identify these structures.)

☐ Color the inferior vena cava and the renal veins blue.

☐ Color the kidneys brown.

☐ Color the bladder orange.

☐ Color the ureters yellow.

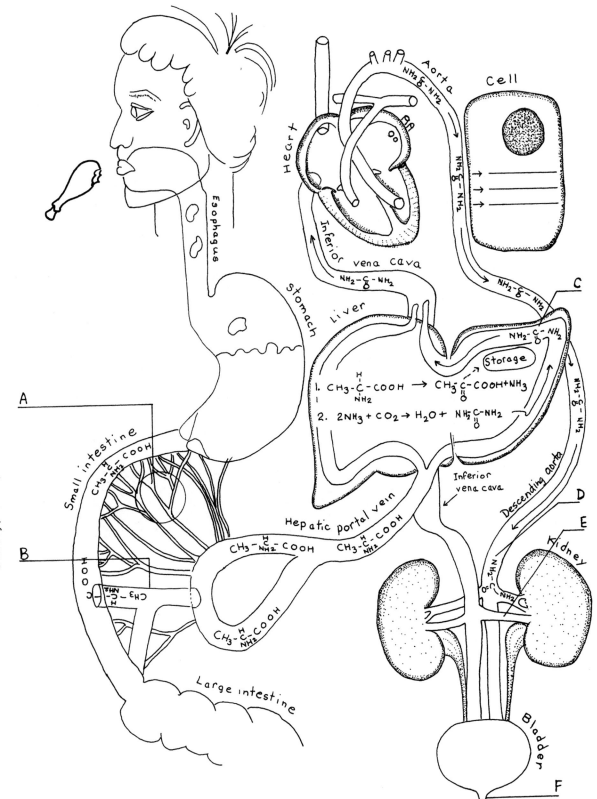

10–3. VOCABULARY: THE URINARY SYSTEM

Part I: Crossword Puzzle

Instructions: Use the last project, "The Structure and Function of the Urinary System," to help you to find the answers to this puzzle. (*Note:* If the answer has two or more words, do not leave spaces between the words.)

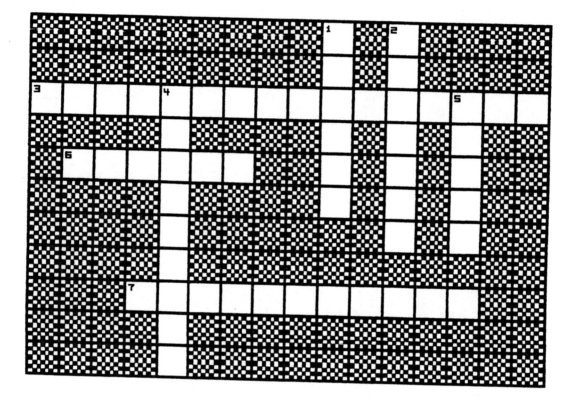

Across

3. the large vein that carries blood from the kidneys and other structures to the heart
6. the organ that filters and cleans blood
7. a short tube that carries blood into the kidney to be filtered

Down

1. the tube that removes urine from the kidney
2. a saclike structure that stores urine before it is removed from the body
4. a short tube that carries blood away from the kidney
5. the large blood vessel carrying blood from the heart to the kidneys and other structures

Part II: Flash Cards

Instructions: (1.) Cut out these cards. (2.) Use the clues from the crossword puzzle to help you to write the definitions on the backs of these cards. (3.) Study these cards until you have learned the terms on them.

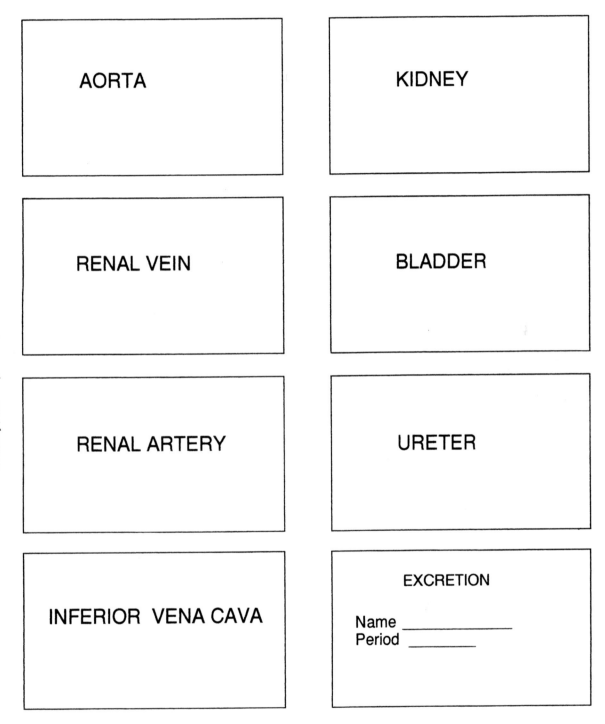

AORTA

KIDNEY

RENAL VEIN

BLADDER

RENAL ARTERY

URETER

INFERIOR VENA CAVA

EXCRETION

Name _____
Period _____

10–4. THE INTERNAL ANATOMY OF THE KIDNEY

Instructions: (1.) Read the text. (2.) Use the text and the diagram to help you to answer the questions. *Note:* You will need a metric ruler.

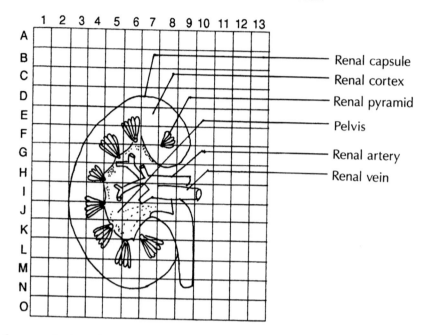

While completing this project, you will sketch a kidney with the same dimensions as a human kidney. You will also learn to identify and name its internal structures. To complete this project—

☐ Use the enlargement grid on the next page to help you to sketch a life-sized kidney. To begin, locate box D6 on the above diagram; sketch what you see there on the corresponding box (D6) on the enlargement grid. Complete the enlargement.

☐ Label the drawing that you have enlarged.

☐ Use a metric ruler to measure the length and width of the enlarged kidney. You will use your measurements to answer questions 6 and 7.

Level One Questions:

1. The outer covering of the kidney is called the renal _____.

2. The triangular structures are called the renal _____.

3. The number of renal pyramids varies from individual to individual. How many renal pyramids are in this kidney? _____

4. The area in which the renal pyramids lie is called the _____.

5. As urine forms, it collects in the pelvis of the kidney before it leaves through a tube called the

_____.

6. The human kidney is about _____ cm. long.

7. The human kidney is about _____ cm. wide.

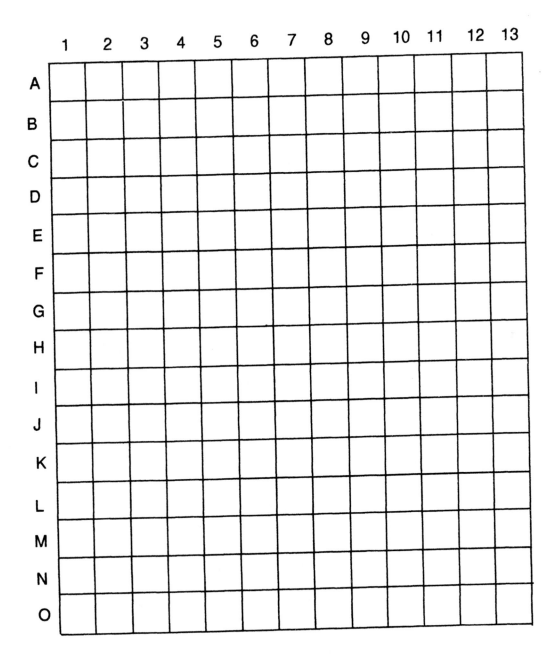

10–5. THE ANATOMY OF THE NEPHRON

Instructions: (1.) Label the diagram. (2.) Answer the questions and follow the special instructions at the end of each statement. *Note:* You will need map pencils or markers.

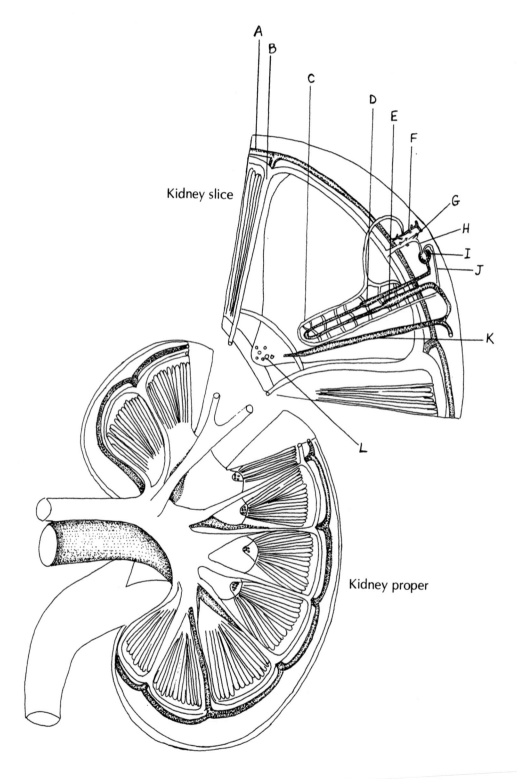

Kidney slice

Kidney proper

Label the following arrows:

A arcuate vein

B arcuate artery

C capillary net

D proximal tubule

E distal tubule

F interlobular vein

G interlobular artery

H afferent arteriole

I Bowman's capsule

J efferent arteriole

K collecting duct

L papilla

Many scientists classify the kidney as a tubular gland, because each kidney contains over one million filter tubes called "nephrons." Usually, these nephrons are lined up in the renal pyramids; this arrangement gives the pyramids their characteristic shape.

The diagram is in two parts. They are labeled "Kidney Proper" and "Kidney Slice." The kidney slice shows an enlargement of a renal pyramid and includes one nephron and its associated structures. It is important for you to realize that these structures are greatly enlarged; they would look much smaller in an actual kidney.

Statements

1. A fraction of the blood that travels down the descending aorta enters the kidney through the renal artery. As the renal artery enters the kidney, it branches to form loops around the renal pyramids. These loops are called "arcuate arteries."

   a. Does all the blood that passes down the aorta enter the renal artery? _____

   b. The loops that direct blood around the renal pyramids are branches of the

   _____ artery.

   c. Use a red pencil to color the renal artery and the arcuate arteries.

2. From the arcuate arteries, blood travels up short tubes called "interlobular arteries."

   d. Which arrow points to an interlobular artery? _____

   e. Notice that the top branch of the interlobular artery attaches to the nephron and that the remaining branches have been cut. How many cut branches do you see on the interlobular artery?

   _____

   f. What do you think the remaining branches of the interlobular artery would attach to if they had not been cut?

   _____

3. Incoming blood travels into the Bowman's capsule through the afferent arteriole. Arrow H points to the afferent arteriole.

g. Where does the afferent arteriole send blood?

_____

h. Which arrow points to the Bowman's capsule? _____

4. Five tightly wrapped tubes lie inside the Bowman's capsule. These tubes are collectively called the "glomerulus." Water, wastes, and small molecules of other substances pass through small pores in these tubes to enter the proximal tubule. Since this is a filtering process, all the substances passing through these pores are called the "glomerular filtrate."

i. How many tubes are in the Bowman's capsule? _____

j. What are these tubes called?

_____

k. List three substances in the glomerular filtrate.

_____

_____

5. The two main sections of the loop of Henle are the proximal tubule and the distal tubule.

l. How many main segments are in the loop of Henle? _____

m. Which arrow points to the proximal tubule? _____

n. Which arrow points to the distal tubule? _____

o. Use a blue pencil to color the loop of Henle.

6. The remaining plasma and blood cells, and any molecules that are too large to pass through the glomerulus, leave the Bowman's capsule through a tube called the "efferent arteriole"; it directs these components into the capillary net.

p. Describe what happens to the remaining plasma and blood cells and to large molecules that do not pass through the pores of the glomerulus.

_____

_____

q. Which arrow points to the capillary net? _____

7. Many essential substances such as water, sodium ions, and chlorine ions pass through the glomerulus as part of the filtrate. Because these substances are needed by the body, they leave the loop of Henle to rejoin the blood cells in the capillary net. This process is called "reabsorption."

r. List three essential substances that pass through the glomerulus along with the filtrate.

_____

_____

s. Why is it important for these substances to leave the loop of Henle?

_____

_____

8. Wastes remaining in the loop of Henle travel through the distal tubule to enter the collecting tube. The collecting tube directs the wastes—now called "urine"—to the base of the pyramid where it drips through small holes into the pelvis of the kidney. These wastes leave the pelvis through the ureters—large tubes that direct urine to the bladder.

t. From the distal tubule, where is blood sent?

_____

u. Where do the ureters take urine?

_____

9. Cleaned blood in the capillary net is sent through the interlobular vein, which eventually leads to the renal vein. Cleaned blood leaves the kidney through the renal vein and joins the blood in the inferior vena cava. The inferior vena cava directs the blood to the heart.

v. Describe how cleaned blood leaves the kidney.

_____

_____

_____

w. Where does the inferior vena cava send this blood?

_____

10–6. FILTRATION OF BLOOD IN THE BOWMAN'S CAPSULE

Instructions: (1.) Read the text. (2.) Use the text and the diagrams to help you to answer the questions.

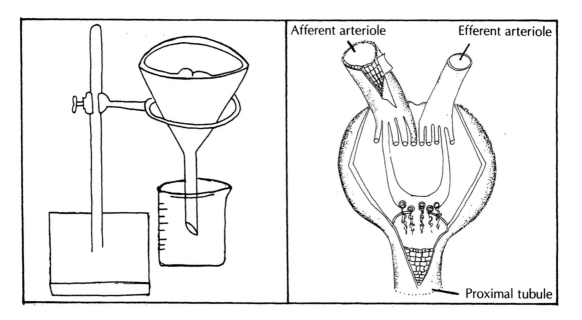

Afferent arteriole   Efferent arteriole

Proximal tubule

Diagram A   Diagram B

The first part of blood cleaning is a filtration process. During this process, most of the useful substances such as the blood cells that are mixed with the blood are separated from the wastes that have accumulated during cellular metabolism. The term "most" is used in this instance because some useful substances such as water, glucose, and certain dissolved ions pass through the minute pores of the natural filter along with the waste. These substances that have slipped into the loop of Henle are later returned to the useful fraction of blood.

Inside the Bowman's capsule the afferent arteriole branches into five coiled tubes collectively called the "glomerulus." On Diagram B, the glomerulus has been simplified for instructional purposes; notice that four of these tubes have been cut. The uncut tube shows the pores where filtration occurs. Scientists are not sure whether specialized pores such as these actually exist; filtration may simply occur through unmodified pores similar to the ones found in the plasma membranes of most other cells.

The filtration lab that you are about to complete has been designed to simulate filtration as it occurs in the Bowman's capsule.

Procedure:

1. Obtain the following materials:
   ☐ ring stand   ☐ ring
   ☐ small funnel   ☐ cornstarch

☐ eyedropper   ☐ spatula or plastic spoon
☐ filter paper   ☐ two 250-ml beakers or small jars
☐ iodine   ☐ yellow food coloring
☐ water

Special Precaution: Iodine is poisonous. Use it with caution and do not allow it to get into your mouth.

2. Set up a filtration apparatus as shown in Diagram A. The following diagrams show instructions for folding the filter paper. After you insert the filter paper into the funnel, wet it by pouring a small amount of water through it. This will help to hold it in the funnel.

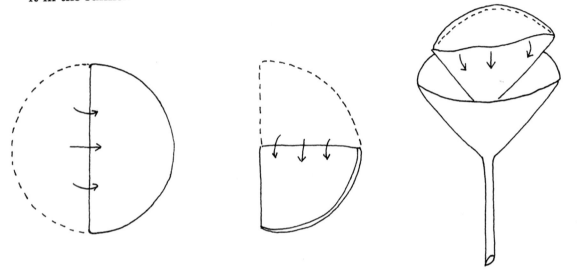

3. Fill the second beaker (the one that was not used as part of the filtering apparatus) about half full of water and then add a spatulaful (spoonful) of starch.
4. Add three drops of iodine to the starch mixture. Then fill the eyedropper with yellow food coloring and add ten drops to the mixture.
5. Using the spoon, stir the mixture and then pour it through the filtering apparatus.

Level One Questions:

1. The first part of blood cleaning is a ————————————— process.

2. During filtration in the Bowman's capsule, most of the useful substances mixed with the blood are separated from the

_____.

3. List three useful substances that pass through the minute pores of the natural filter tubes of the glomerulus.

   a. ————————————————

   b. ————————————————

   c. ————————————————

4. What happens to the useful substances that pass into the loop of Henle?

   _____

5. Which diagram (A or B) shows the Bowman's capsule? _____

6. Notice that there are two tubes on the top surface of the Bowman's capsule. The tube that brings blood into the Bowman's capsule to be filtered has the larger diameter. What is the name of this tube?

   _____

7. The fraction of blood that does not pass through the pores of the filter tubes leaves the Bowman's capsule through the smaller tube on the top surface of the Bowman's capsule. What is the name of this tube?

   _____

8. How many tubes branch from the afferent tubule? _____

9. The diagram shows liquid passing through the pores of one tube of the glomerulus. Describe this liquid and mention some of the substances that are mixed in it.

   _____

   _____

10. What structure is this liquid pouring into? _____

11. Describe what happened when you added the iodine to the starch and water mixture.

    _____

12. The "filtrate" is the substance that passes through a filter. Describe the filtrate that resulted after you poured the starch and water mixture through the filter paper.

    _____

13. If the filtration that you did represents what occurs in the Bowman's capsule, what would the red powder that remained in the filter paper represent?

    _____

Level Two Question:

14. Explain the similarities you find between the functions of the glomerulus and the functions of the filtration apparatus shown in Diagram A.

    _____

    _____

    _____

Level Three Question:

15. Why do you think it is important for the diameter of the afferent arteriole to be greater than the diameter of the efferent arteriole?

    _____

    _____

10–7. MAKING AN ACTION CARTOON: REABSORPTION

Instructions: (1.) Follow the procedures to help you to cut out and assemble the cartoon. (2.) Use the cartoon and the text to help you to answer the questions.

Blood passing into the Bowman's capsule is filled with both wastes and useful substances. Some of the useful substances pass with the wastes through the filtering tubes of the glomerulus and into the loop of Henle; these useful substances must be returned to the clean blood that is waiting in the capillary net. This process of reabsorbing these useful substances can be referred to as "cleaning the blood."

The action cartoon that you are about to make will show you how glucose (represented by a triangle), sodium (represented by a circle), and water (represented by three dots) are reabsorbed. Carefully observe the blood as it enters the Bowman's capsule through the afferent arteriole, passes through the filter tubes of the glomerulus, and enters the proximal tubule of the loop of Henle. Next watch as three useful substances pass out of the proximal tubule to rejoin the clean blood in the capillary net.

Procedure

1. Using scissors, carefully cut out the frames of the cartoon.

2. Stack the frames so that frame number one is on top.

3. Staple this stack twice on its left edge, making sure that the outer edges are even.

4. Riffle through the cartoon booklet from front to back and watch the action.

5. Using your observations and the text, answer the questions that follow.

Notes:

a. The solid dark line represents filtrate;

b. the triangle, circle, and dots represent useful substances mixed with the filtrate.

Level One Questions:

1. Did the useful substances that were mixed with the filtrate leave the loop of Henle?

   _____

2. Describe what ultimately happens to these useful substances.

   _____

   _____

3. After the useful substances leave, wastes remain in the filtrate. What ultimately happens to these wastes?

   _____

   _____

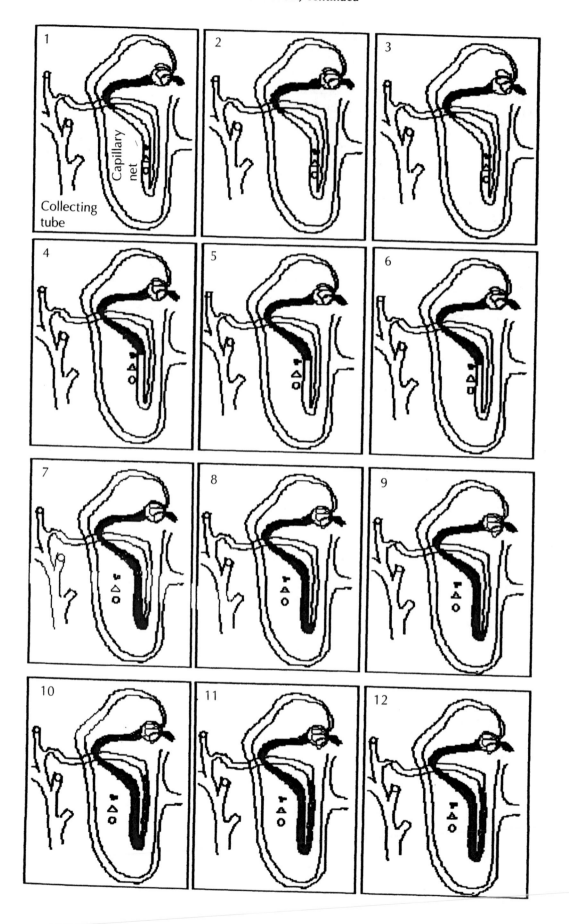

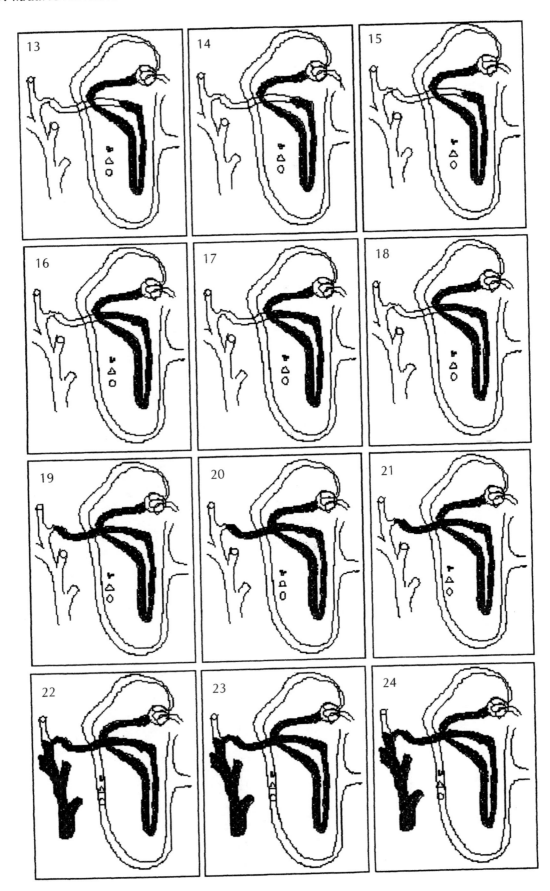

10–8. OBSERVING THE KIDNEY THROUGH THE MICROSCOPE

Instructions: (1.) Read the text. (2.) Use the text and the diagrams to help you to complete a microscope drawing.

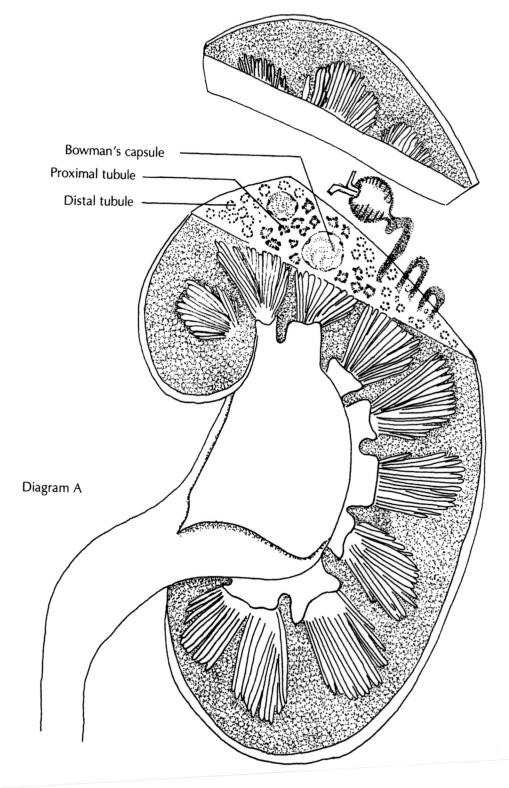

Bowman's capsule

Proximal tubule

Distal tubule

Diagram A

Obtain the following materials:

☐ microscope
☐ prepared microscope slide of a human kidney

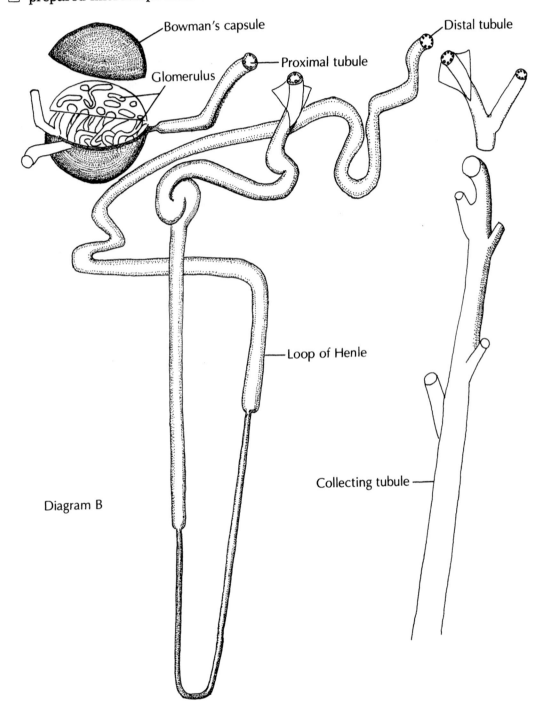

Diagram B

Even though nephrons are about an inch and a half long, a microscope is needed to see them because they are very thin. Unfortunately, many commercially prepared microscope slides show only a cross-section of the kidney's tissue. This means that the kidney has been sliced in such a way that all you can see are the cut ends of the tubular nephrons; naturally, they appear to be nothing more than small holes.

Carefully study Diagram A before you focus your microscope. This diagram shows a kidney with its top sliced off. The small holes are nephrons that have been cut. To help you to understand what you are actually observing, one nephron on the diagram remains uncut. Diagram B will also help you to understand what you are observing through the microscope.

Use the observation notes that follow to help you to interpret these diagrams.

Proximal tubule—The inside and outside diameters of this tubule are approximately the same as those of the distal tubule, but the proximal tubule looks different in one important way. It has a fuzzy lining (also called the "brush border") of microcilia, and this lining makes the tubule's inside diameter look smaller than it really is.

Distal tubule—Because the lining of the distal tubule is much smoother, the tubule's inside diameter looks larger. Another thing that may help you to distinguish the distal tubule from the proximal tubule is that you will probably see only three to four nuclei (black dots) on each section of a proximal tubule; more nuclei can be seen on a distal tubule.

Bowman's capsule—The Bowman's capsule is easy to identify because its diameter is many times larger than the diameters of the proximal and distal tubules. You will see a number of smaller tubules inside it; remember that this is a diagram of a cross section of the Bowman's capsule and that the tubes inside it are also sectioned (sliced).

Procedure

1. Place the slide on the microscope and focus to high power (500X).
2. In the circle, sketch what you observe.

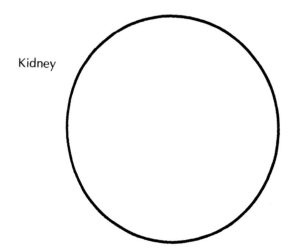

Kidney

3. Use the diagrams to help you to label your sketch.

Unit 11

Reproduction

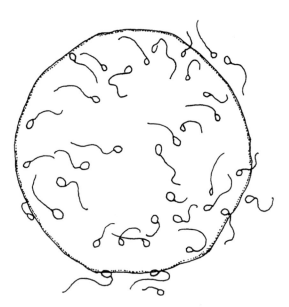

11–1 GAMETES

Teaching Suggestions:

1. Ask students to bring in photographs of family members. If they can find photographs of their parents, grandparents, and siblings that show familial resemblances, consider ways in which you might use them for class discussion.

2. With students' permission, reproduce the pictures (using copy machine or computer scanner) and ask other students to match the families. Discuss things like ear shape, placement of ears, nose shape, color of eyes and hair, shape of face, bone structure, and so forth. *You will, of course, consider your clientele and proceed cautiously until you discover which characteristics your students may be sensitive about. Also remember how many of them may not know (or may not be on good terms with) one or more of their natural parents.*

3. Be sure to protect the original pictures. If students are allowed to handle the originals, consider putting the photographs between clear plastic sheets (maybe overhead projector sheets) with small pieces of tape on all four sides.

Answers to the Questions:

Level One

1. parents
2. genetic material
3. chromosomes
4. gametes
5. 23
6. orange
7. sperm

Level Two

8. The genetic code stores the instructions to construct the body and to start a new life.
9. Answers will vary. Since each gamete—male and female—carries 23 chromosomes, both parents contribute exactly half of the genetic material that produces their offspring.

Level Three

10. Answers will vary, and you may wish to omit this question. In studying the cell, students have probably learned that mitochondria produce energy—in this case, energy needed for the sperm to swim toward the egg.

11–2 THE MALE REPRODUCTIVE SYSTEM

Note: This is a self-directed worksheet.

Answers to the Questions:

Level One

1. testes
2. scrotum
3. 20
4. tube, 12
5. discharge
6. 200

Level Two

7. Body temperature is too hot for the maturation and survival of the sperm.
8. in the epididymis
9. The sperm's head and acrosome change shape, the sperm loses cytoplasm and becomes smaller, the sperm gains the ability to swim.
10. in the vas deferens
11. sperm cells mixed with the liquid substances produced by three glands
12. a. adds a milky substance that may activate the sperm

    b. adds a mucuslike substance containing fructose (a simple sugar)

    c. add a mucuslike substance
13. Cavernous tissue is arranged in three cylindrical structures; it fills with blood and causes the penis to become stiff or erect.

Level Three

14. in this order:

    testes—produce sperm

    epididymis—stores sperm; where the final maturation of sperm takes place

    vas deferens—provides the force that propels the sperm from the body

    urethra—the sperm (along with the other parts of the seminal fluid) leave the body through this tube

11–3 THE FEMALE REPRODUCTIVE SYSTEM

Note: This is a self-directed worksheet.

Answers to the Questions:

Level One

1. vagina, uterus, Fallopian tubes, ovaries
2. vagina
3. 400,000
4. menstrual
5. Graafian

6. primary oocytes
7. secondary follicle
8. Graafian
9. ovary, ruptures

Level Two

10. Answers may vary, but (one hopes) not much.

    vagina—is the opening of the female reproductive tract, provides a receptacle for sperm, widens to serve as birth canal

    ovaries—store ova, where maturation occurs

    Fallopian tubes—receive ova from ovary after stimulation of the follicle; are the site of fertilization; direct ova to the uterus

    uterus—provides lodging place for the fertilized egg and protection and nourishment (through the placenta) for the developing embryo

11. Answers will vary. The corona radiata, which is made of granulosa cells, covers and protects the ovum. Also, scientists think that it nourishes the ovum as it passes through the Fallopian tube.

12. Hyaluronic acid is a liquid substance that fills the empty space within the follicle.

13. Fimbriae are fingerlike structures containing cilia that sweep the ovum into the Fallopian tube.

Level Three

14. Answers will vary. Students may simply visualize a microscopic traffic jam, but some of them will understand about fraternal twins. Some may know about what can happen with fertility drugs.

Quality-points project (optional): You may stimulate so much interest in twinning that some students will want to do a full-blown research paper. Sometimes a teacher in another subject—English, perhaps, or health, or social studies (in connection with population growth)—will cooperate by allowing double credit.

11–4 FERTILIZATION AND THE FORMATION OF THE EMBRYO

Answers to the Questions:

Level One

1. sperm, ovum
2. Fallopian tube, 24
3. seven
4. hyaluronidase
5. corona radiata (outer layer of the egg)
6. twisting
7. 40,000
8. one

Level Two

9. Answers will vary somewhat. During capacitation, chemical substances in the uterus partially dissolve the outer covering of the sperm's head. This is important because it makes hyaluronidase (an enzyme stored in the acrosome) available to dissolve the corona radiata so that the sperm can penetrate and fertilize the egg.

10. inside the ovary

11. just before ovulation, inside the ovary

12. fertilization

13. Answers will vary. Essentially, a polar body contains the half of the genetic material of the primary oocyte that must be discarded so that the remainder will contain the desired number of chromosomes. In other words, unequal cell division (of the primary oocyte) occurs; with a small amount of protoplasm, half of the chromosomes are discarded. Students should understand that this is a sort of trashing operation.

Level Three

14. This is a tough question because there are not many clues; give credit for ingenuity. In general—if the polar body containing 23 chromosomes were not discarded, the ovum would have 46 chromatids; the purpose of this division, of course, is to reduce the number by half so that the mature ovum contributes half of the 46 chromosomes necessary to start the formation of the embryo.

15. Answers may vary somewhat. The second meiotic division results in 46 monads, but half of these are cast out in the polar body. Remember that during the second meiotic division the dyads have separated to become monads or individual chromosomes.

16. There is no telling what you may get on this. Some students may have heard about ectopic pregnancies or may intuitively realize that the Fallopian tube is not designed to accommodate anything larger than an ovum and could require medical intervention if the zygote were to begin to develop there.

11–5 MAKING A PLASTER MODEL OF A HUMAN EMBRYO

Teaching Suggestion:

You will probably want to buy a 10-pound bag of plaster (dry, of course) and a large bag of vermiculite. You may find both at a hardware store, or you may have to go to a nursery to find the vermiculite. Line a large box with a garbage bag and make your own mixture: 3 parts plaster to 1 part of vermiculite. (Dump them in alternately to make the mixing easier.) Keep track of the number of cups as you go, so that you will know whether you have enough for the number of students you have—1½ cups of mixture each, or 15 cups for 10 kids.

Answers to the Questions:

Level One

1. blastocyst, uterus

2. embryo

3. embryonic disc

4. nervous system, skin, nails, tooth enamel

5. epithelial linings of certain organs and glands

6. mesodermic cells

11–1. GAMETES

Instructions: (1.) Read the text and study the diagrams. (2.) Use the text and the diagrams to help you to answer the questions and complete the project. *Note:* You will need map pencils or color markers.

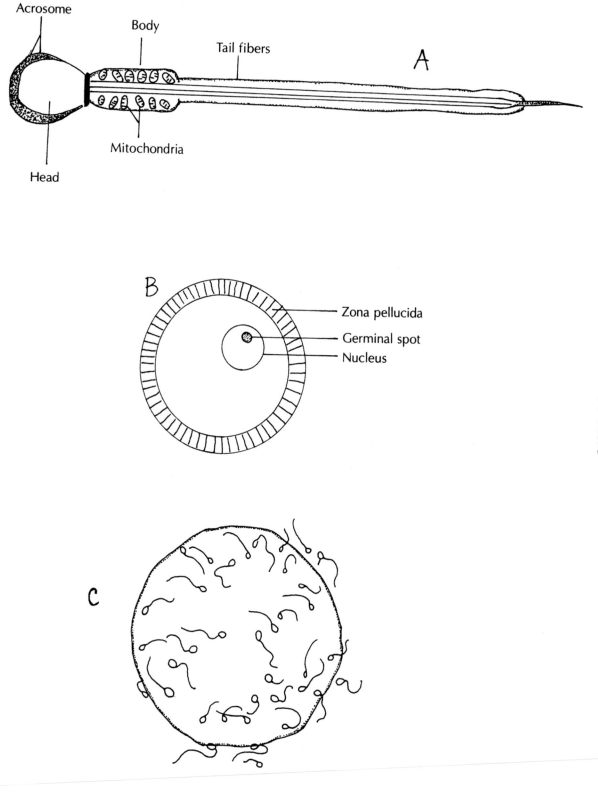

Friends and relatives who visit a newborn baby often say things such as, "He looks just like his father!" or "She certainly has her grandfather's eyes!" Do you have a family photo? If so, look closely at it to see if the members of your family resemble one another.

Each of your parents contributed exactly half of the genetic material that, in many respects, makes you the person you are. Using a molecular code called the "genetic code," this genetic material provided the instructions necessary to construct your body and to start your life. Almost every cell in your body carries your blueprint on 46 rod-shaped structures called "chromosomes."

Only sex cells, also called "gametes," have the ability to pass on traits to a new generation. Each sex cell—the sperm cell (the male gamete) and the ovum or egg cell (the female gamete)—possesses only 23 chromosomes, half as many as the other cells of the body contain. When a sperm and an ovum fuse, each one contributes its 23 chromosomes to make a new cell with 46 chromosomes—the correct number to start the construction of a new life.

The diagrams show both male and female gametes. Diagram A shows a sperm cell, and Diagram B shows an egg cell or ovum. Diagram C shows an ovum being attacked by many sperm cells.

To complete this project—

1. Use markers or map pencils to color the diagrams as follows:

    ☐ On Diagram A, color the acrosome (on the sperm's head) orange.

    ☐ On Diagram A, color the rest of the sperm's head blue.

    ☐ On Diagram A, color the mitochondria red.

    ☐ On Diagram A, color the sperm's tail black.

    ☐ On Diagram B, color the zona pellucida orange.

    ☐ On Diagram B, color the nucleus blue.

    ☐ Diagram C shows sperm cells attacking an ovum. Color these sperm cells red.

2. Using a short line that looks like this ⏀ to represent a chromosome, sketch 23 chromosomes in the head of the sperm cell (Diagram A).

Level One Questions:

1. The way you look is passed on to you by your _____.

2. Each of your parents contributed half the _____ that makes you the person you are.

3. Almost every cell in your body carries 46 rod-shaped structures called _____

    _____.

4. Only special cells called _____ (sex cells) have the ability to pass on traits to a new generation.

5. Each sperm cell and each egg cell carries only _____ chromosomes.

Use the diagrams to help you to answer the remaining Level One questions.

6. What color did you use for the acrosome? _____

7. Which gamete contains mitochondria? _____

Level Two Questions:

8. Explain the importance of the genetic code.

   _____

   _____

9. Why is it important for the sperm and the ovum to carry only 23 chromosomes each?

   _____

   _____

Level Three Question:

10. Why is it important for the sperm cell to possess so many mitochondria?

   _____

   _____

   _____

   _____

   _____

   _____

   _____

   _____

   _____

   _____

   _____

   _____

11–2. THE MALE REPRODUCTIVE SYSTEM

Instructions: (1.) Read the text and the descriptions. (2.) Use the text and the descriptions to help you to answer the questions.

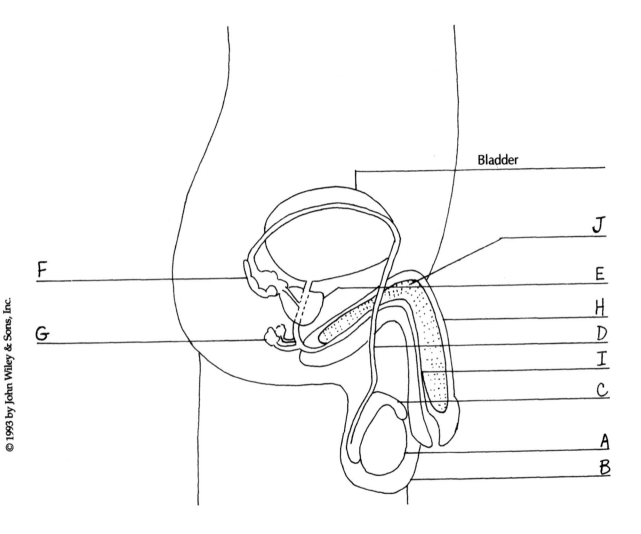

The purpose of the male reproductive system is to produce sperm cells and to transfer them to the female reproductive system. This project will teach you about the structure and function of the male reproductive system.

Statements

1. Sperm are made in two oval structures called "testes." Each testis is about 1½ inches long and about 1 inch wide. Since body temperature (98.6 F) is too hot for the maturation and the survival of sperm cells, the testes are located outside the body cavity in a sac called the "scrotum." Arrow A points to the testes, and arrow B points to the scrotum. Locate these arrows on the diagram and label them.

2. Muscular contractions propel newly formed sperm from the testes to the epididymis, a comma-shaped structure attached to the testis. It contains a coiled tube about 20 feet long. Within this tube, newly formed sperm cells reach maturity; the sperm's head and acrosome change shape slightly, and the sperm loses cytoplasm and becomes somewhat smaller. The sperm also acquires the ability to swim. Arrow C points to the epididymis. Locate arrow C and label it "epididymis."

3. Mature sperm cells leave the epididymis and pass into the vas deferens for storage. The vas deferens is a tube about 12 inches long. Arrow D points to the vas deferens. Locate arrow D and label it "vas deferens."

4. The term *ejaculate* means "to discharge suddenly." When ejaculation occurs during sexual contact, the walls of the vas deferens contract rapidly, propelling the sperm cells from the body. Scientists have estimated that the speed at which sperm leave the body is about 200 feet per second.

Before leaving the body, the sperm cells pass three glands that secrete liquid substances. These substances, when mixed with sperm, are collectively called "semen." The functions of these glands are as follows:

a. The prostate gland, which is about 1½ inches long, lies just below the bladder. During ejaculation, this gland adds a milky fluid to the sperm. Scientists think that this fluid contains substances that somehow activate the sperm and cause them to wave their flagella. Arrow E points to the prostate gland. Locate arrow E and label it "prostate gland."

b. Attached to the back wall of the bladder are two seminal vesicles about 2½ inches long. Through a tube called the "ejaculatory duct," the seminal vesicles add a mucuslike fluid to the sperm. This fluid contains the monosaccharide (simple sugar) fructose. Arrow F points to the seminal vesicles. Locate arrow F and label it "seminal vesicles."

c. Two pea-sized glands called "Cowper's glands" release a mucuslike lubricant substance. Arrow G points to the Cowper's glands. Locate arrow G and label it "Cowper's glands."

5. After the sperm have combined with the seminal fluid, they leave the body through a tube called the "urethra." The urethra passes through the penis. The function of the penis is to transfer seminal fluid to the female reproductive system. Arrow H points to the penis, and arrow I points to the urethra. Locate these arrows and label them.

6. The penis contains three cylindrical structures made of a spongy tissue called "cavernous tissue." When cavernous tissue fills with blood, it makes the penis stiff. This stiffness, which is called an "erection," makes it possible for the penis to enter the female reproductive system. Arrow J points to the cavernous tissue. Locate arrow J and label it "cavernous tissue."

Level One Questions:

1. Sperm are made in two oval structures called _____.

2. The testes are located in a saclike structure called the _____.

3. The epididymis is a coiled tube about _____ feet long.

4. The vas deferens is a _____ about _____ inches long.

5. The term *ejaculate* means to _____ suddenly.

6. Sperm leave the body at a speed of about _____ feet per second.

Level Two Questions:

7. Why are the testes located outside the body cavity?

   _____

8. Where does final maturation of a sperm cell occur?

   _____

9. What three things occur during final maturation?

   _____

   _____

   _____

10. Where are sperm stored after they leave the epididymis?

    _____

11. What is semen?

    _____

12. Describe the function of each of the following:

    a. prostate gland _____

       _____

    b. seminal vesicles _____

       _____

    c. Cowper's glands _____

       _____

13. Describe the structure and function of cavernous tissue.

    _____

    _____

    _____

Level Three Question:

14. Arrange the following terms in the order in which semen travels as it leaves the testes to be ejaculated from the body. Next to each term in your list, describe its function.

    vas deferens   urethra   testes   epididymis

    _____

    _____

    _____

    _____

11–3. THE FEMALE REPRODUCTIVE SYSTEM

Instructions: (1.) Read the text and the descriptions. (2.) Use the text and the descriptions to help you to answer the questions.

The main structures of the female reproductive system are the vagina, the uterus, the Fallopian tubes, and the ovaries. These organs are responsible for the maturation of ova (eggs), for facilitating fertilization, and for providing a suitable environment for the growth and development of the embryo.

This project will help you to learn about the structures and functions of the female reproductive system.

Statements

1. The vagina is a muscular tube that begins at the opening of the female reproductive tract. It extends upward and behind the bladder where it is connected to the uterus. Male gametes (sperm) are introduced into the female reproductive system through this tube. During childbirth, this flexible tube widens and serves as the birth canal. Arrow A points to the vagina. Locate arrow A and label it "vagina."

2. The ovaries are two almond-shaped structures about 1½ inches in length (about 3.5 centimeters). When she is born, a female has about 400,000 primary oocytes (immature eggs) stored in her ovaries. Arrow B points to the left ovary. Locate arrow B and label it "ovary."

3. The primary oocytes remain relatively dormant until the female reaches puberty (sexual maturity) and the menstrual cycle begins. During the monthly menstrual cycle, changes occur within the female reproductive system. These changes provide mature ova (eggs) and prepare the uterus for pregnancy.

   At the beginning of each menstrual cycle, several primary follicles containing immature ova or eggs are stimulated, but usually only one ovum reaches maturity. This ripened ovum is contained in a transparent vesicle called a "Graafian follicle."

   Beginning with the primary follicle, the following steps describe the formation of the Graafian follicle. Arrow C points to a cross-section of the ovary. This ovary has been lowered and slightly enlarged to show the developing follicles inside. Identify and sketch the structures as they are described here.

   Step one: Before every female is born, her primary follicles are already formed. Each primary follicle contains an oocyte surrounded by a ring of granulosa cells. Arrow D points to a primary follicle. Locate this arrow and use it to help you to sketch (in the space here) a primary follicle.

Step two: The secondary follicle forms as the oocyte enlarges and the granulosa cells surrounding it increase in number. Some of these granulosa cells grow over and cover the oocyte, while others form a stalk or pedicle to support the oocyte. Also during this stage of development, the empty space within the follicle begins to fill with a liquid called "hyaluronic acid." Arrow E points to a secondary follicle. Locate this arrow and use it to help you to sketch (in the space here) a secondary follicle.

Step three: The secondary follicle—but not the oocyte—continues to grow until it is about 1 centimeter in diameter. At this stage of development, the secondary follicle becomes a Graafian follicle and the oocyte within it is now the ovum. The pedicle becomes more defined. Another change occurs during this stage: The granulosa cells covering the ovum elongate, forming a protective cover called the "corona radiata." Scientists think that the corona radiata nourishes the ovum as it travels through the Fallopian tube. Arrow F points to a Graafian follicle. Locate this arrow and use it to help you to sketch (in the space here) a Graafian follicle.

4. Ovulation occurs when a Graafian follicle approaches the inner wall of the ovary and ruptures. When this occurs, the mature ovum or egg bursts out of the Graafian follicle, leaves the ovary, and is swept into the Fallopian tube. Arrow G points to the right Fallopian tube. Locate this arrow and label it "Fallopian tube."

5. The open end of a Fallopian tube (the end nearest the ovary) is wide and funnel-shaped. Attached to this structure are fingerlike structures called "fimbriae." Lining the inner surface of the fimbriae are hairlike cilia. The beating action of these cilia helps to sweep the ovum into the Fallopian tube. Arrow L points to the fimbriae. Locate this arrow and label it "fimbriae."

6. Cilia are also located on the inner membrane of the Fallopian tube. Their beating action helps to direct the sperm to the uterus. The uterus is a muscular organ; a fertilized egg attaches to its walls while it develops into a baby. Arrow H points to the uterus. Locate this arrow and label it "uterus."

Level One Questions:

1. List the main structures of the female reproductive system.

_____

_____

_____

_____

2. The _____ is a muscular tube that begins at the opening of the female reproductive tract.

3. At birth, about how many primary oocytes are stored in the ovaries? _____

4. The _____ cycle is a monthly cycle, during which certain changes occur within the female reproductive system.

5. A ripened ovum is contained in a transparent vesicle called a _____ follicle.

6. The _____ _____ remains relatively dormant until the female reaches puberty.

7. The _____ _____ forms as the oocyte enlarges and the granulosa cells surrounding it increase in number.

8. After the secondary follicle reaches about 1 centimeter in diameter, it becomes a

_____ follicle.

9. Ovulation occurs when a Graafian follicle approaches the inner wall of the

_____ and _____.

© 1993 by John Wiley & Sons, Inc.

Level Two Questions:

10. Describe the functions of each of the following structures:

    a. vagina _____

    _____

    _____

    b. ovary _____

    _____

    _____

    c. Fallopian tube _____

    _____

    _____

    d. uterus _____

    _____

    _____

11. What is the corona radiata? How does it benefit the ovum?

    _____

    _____

    _____

12. What is hyaluronic acid?

    _____

13. What are fimbriae? What is the function of these structures?

    _____

    _____

Level Three Question:

14. What could happen if two ova were to reach maturity at the same time, reach a Fallopian tube successfully, and find a sufficient supply of sperm awaiting them?

    _____

    _____

Bonus Points—

You may find the subject of twinning fascinating. If you do, your teacher may encourage you to investigate the events that lead to fraternal twins, identical twins, mirror twins, conjoined ("Siamese") twins, and other multiple births.

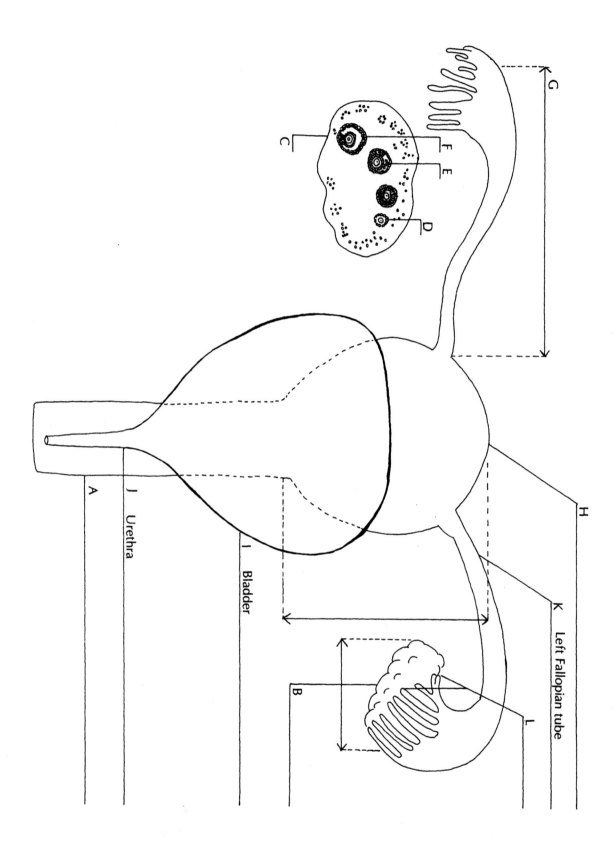

11–4. FERTILIZATION AND THE FORMATION OF THE EMBRYO

Instructions: (1.) Read the text and study the diagrams. (2.) Use the text and the diagrams to help you to answer the questions and complete the project.

Fertilization (the penetration of an ovum by a sperm cell) generally occurs shortly after the egg leaves the ovary and is swept into the Fallopian tube. If fertilization does not occur within about 24 hours, a kind of enzymatic action called "autolysis" begins and the ovum will degenerate.

Before a sperm cell can fertilize an egg, it must undergo capacitation. That is, it must remain in the female reproductive system until chemical substances in the uterus partially dissolve the outer covering of the sperm's head. This process, which takes about seven hours, frees the hyaluronidase, an enzyme that is stored in a small compartment within the sperm's head; this enzyme will weaken the corona radiata, the outer layer of the egg.

Hyaluronidase works by dissolving hyaluronic acid, the chemical substance that helps to hold the cells of the corona radiata together. This enzyme, aided by the twisting action of the sperm as it attaches to the egg, makes it possible for the sperm to enter the egg and fertilize it. As this happens, a new life begins.

To complete this project—

☐ 1. Along the dashed lines, cut out the circles that are below the diagram.

☐ 2. As you are instructed to do so, glue them to the numbered circles.

Descriptions

1. During sexual intercourse, the male's penis fills with blood, causing it to become erect so that it can enter the female's vagina and release sperm. For fertilization to be reasonably certain, at least 40,000 sperm must be released. Locate the vagina on the diagram. If each sperm pictured there represents 10,000 sperm, are there enough sperm to make fertilization probable?

2. Of the 40,000 or more sperm that are released into the vagina, only a few hundred actually reach the site of fertilization. And only one of the sperm that reach an ovum may enter and fertilize it, because the outer layer of the ovum changes quickly so that no other sperm cells may enter. Fertilization generally occurs in the upper third (nearest the ovary) of the Fallopian tube. On the diagram, circle one indicates where fertilization normally occurs. One circle that you have cut out shows fertilization; find it and glue it onto circle one.

3. Just before ovulation, the ovum replicates (doubles) its chromosomes and then divides (first meiotic division). Half of these chromosome pairs, with a small amount of cytoplasm (cell fluids), are discarded as a "polar body." The remaining part still has 23 chromosome dyads (pairs). Then another meiotic division begins, but this time the chromosomes are not replicated. This second meiotic division is not completed until fertilization has occurred. After fertilization, the second division resumes. The ovum still has 23 dyads, which separate to form 46 monads or single-thread chromosomes. Half of these are cast out in a second polar body. The

remaining 23 monads (which are now really 23 full-fledged chromosomes) in the ovum are now ready to combine with the 23 chromosomes that the sperm will contribute to begin the formation of an embryo.

The polar bodies look like two small circles. Identify the cut-out circle that represents this stage and glue it to circle two.

4. The chromosomes in the ovum's nucleus, which is now called the "female pronucleus" because it contains only 23 chromosomes, will fuse with the 23 chromosomes found within the sperm or the male pronucleus. This occurrence stimulates a special kind of cellular division called "cleavage." During cleavage, the cells increase in number; but the developing ovum, which is now called the "zygote," does not increase in size. After the first cleavage, the zygote has only two cells, and it is called the "two-cell stage." Identify the cut-out circle representing this stage and glue it to circle three.

5. Cleavage continues as the zygote continues its four- to five-day journey through the Fallopian tube. The two-cell stage divides to form the four-cell stage; these cells become eight, then sixteen, and so forth. A compact ball of cells called a "morula" is eventually formed. Identify the cut-out circle representing the morula stage and glue it to circle four.

6. Once formed, the morula fills with fluid, which somehow causes an inner cavity called a "blastocoele" to form; the ball of cells, now hollow, is called a "blastocyst." The blastocyst leaves the Fallopian tube and enters the uterus, where it remains unattached for about four days before it becomes implanted in the uterine lining. An active mass of cells within the implanted blastocyst forms the human embryo. Identify the circle representing the blastocyst stage and glue it to circle five.

Level One Questions:

1. Fertilization occurs when a _____ cell penetrates an _____.

2. Fertilization occurs shortly after the ovum leaves the ovary and is swept into the

   _____, and about _____ hours after the sperm have been deposited in the vagina.

3. About how many hours are required for capacitation to take place? _____

4. During capacitation, what enzyme is released from the sperm's head?

   _____

5. This enzyme weakens the _____, the outer covering of the egg.

6. Another thing that helps the sperm to penetrate the ovum is its _____ action.

7. About how many sperm must be released before fertilization is likely? _____

8. How many sperm can fertilize a single egg? _____

Level Two Questions:

9. What is capacitation, and why is it important?

_____

_____

10. Where does the first meiosis occur?

_____

11. When and where does the second meiosis begin?

_____

12. What must happen before the second meiosis continues?

_____

13. What is a polar body?

_____

Level Three Questions:

14. Why is it necessary for the polar bodies to be separated from the cell and discarded?

_____

_____

_____

15. The first meiosis results in 23 dyads. How is this result different from the result of the second meiotic division?

_____

_____

_____

16. Occasionally a fertilized egg remains in the Fallopian tube after fertilization instead of moving into the uterus. What resulting problems can you visualize?

_____

_____

_____

_____

_____

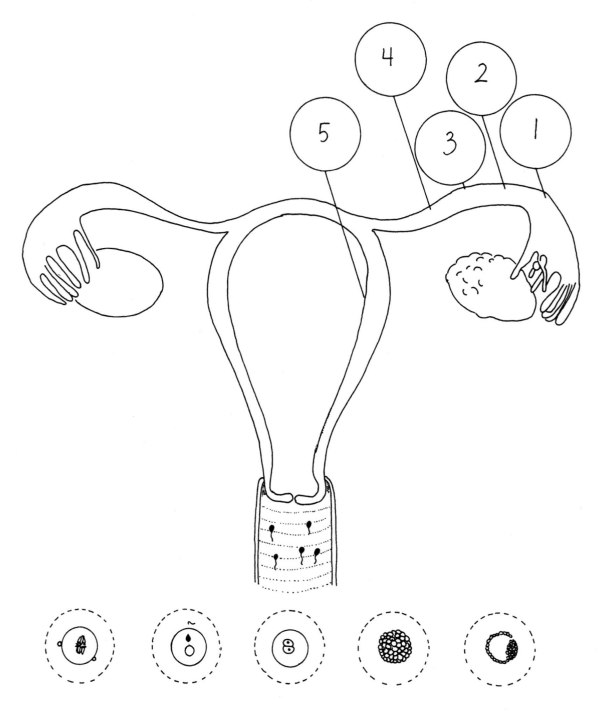

11–5. MAKING A PLASTER MODEL OF A HUMAN EMBRYO

Instructions: (1.) Read the text and study the diagrams. (2.) Use the text and the diagrams to help you to answer the questions and complete the project.

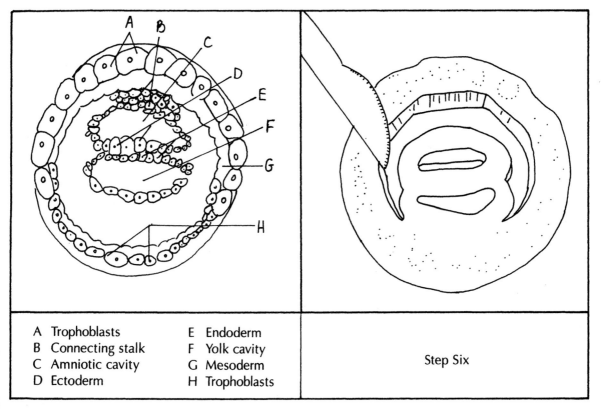

A	Trophoblasts	E	Endoderm
B	Connecting stalk	F	Yolk cavity
C	Amniotic cavity	G	Mesoderm
D	Ectoderm	H	Trophoblasts

Step Six

The human embryo begins to form after a rapidly dividing ball of cells called the "blastocyst" becomes implanted in the lining of the uterus. The blastocyst is hollow, and attached to its inner wall is a mass of cells called the "inner cell mass," part of which will form the embryo. After about three to four days following implantation, the blastocyst has undergone the following changes:

1. Some of the cells of the inner cell mass atrophy (degenerate) and two hollow spaces (cavities) are formed. The upper cavity eventually becomes the amniotic sac in which the developing embryo floats, and the lower cavity becomes the yolk sac which, in humans, plays only a minor role.

2. Between the amniotic sac and the yolk sac a double layer of cells (called the "embryonic disc") forms. The top layer of cells (called the "ectoderm") eventually forms the nervous system, skin, nails, tooth enamel, and the lining of the pharynx. The lower layer (called the "endoderm") forms the epithelium (outer linings) of certain organs and glands.

3. Later, a layer of mesodermic cells invades the space between the top (ectodermic) and the lower (endodermic) layers. The mesodermic cells eventually form organs and other structures such as the muscles and skeleton.

Template

Decals

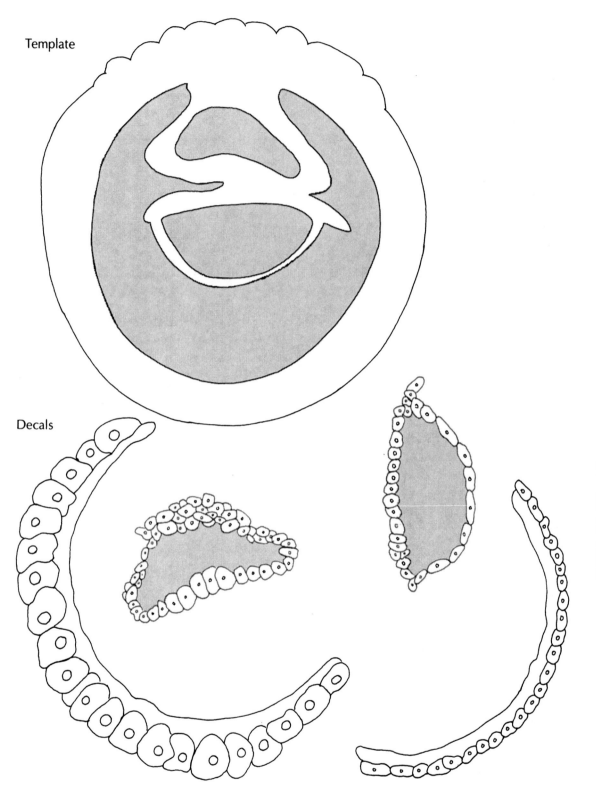

To complete this project—

1. Obtain the following materials:
   - ☐ scissors
   - ☐ plastic knife and spoon
   - ☐ map pencils
   - ☐ 1½ cups of plaster and vermiculite mix (three parts plaster to one part vermiculite)
   - ☐ about ½ cup of water (this amount will vary)
   - ☐ medium-sized freezer bag or a bowl for mixing the plaster and vermiculite

2. Color the diagram and the decals as follows:
   - ☐ Color the trophoblasts (outer ring of cells) blue.
   - ☐ Color the ectoderm yellow.
   - ☐ Color the endoderm red.

3. Cut out the decals and template. Cutting out the template will be easier if you first remove the shaded centers of the amniotic sac and the yolk sac and then the shaded area between them and the cell wall. Be sure to leave the rings around the sacs intact and joined.

4. Put the plaster mix into the freezer bag or mixing bowl. Add a little less than ½ cup of water and stir quickly. Your mixture needs to be pourable but thick—like smooth, thick oatmeal. Add more water if you need to, but be careful not to use too much.

5. After the plaster mix has been stirred thoroughly, pour it onto a sheet of paper (any kind) so that it forms a "cookie" slightly larger than the template. **Caution**—the plaster starts to harden as soon as it is mixed; mix and pour it quickly.

6. Place the template on top of the plaster. Use the knife to outline and dig out the hollow spaces around the amniotic sac and yolk sac.

7. Use the diagram as your guide to press the decals gently into the plaster. If your plaster has completely hardened, you may have to use glue to attach the decals.

Level One Questions:

1. The human embryo begins to form after a rapidly dividing ball of cells called the

   _____ becomes embedded in the lining of the _____.

2. The inner cell mass of the blastocyst will form the _____.

3. Between the amniotic sac and the yolk sac, a double layer of cells called the _____

   _____ forms.

4. What does the ectoderm eventually form? _____

5. What does the endoderm form? _____

6. What eventually forms the organs, muscles, and skeleton?

   _____

CPSIA information can be obtained at www.ICGtesting.com
Printed in the USA
2 659 20BV00002B/1/P